Welcome to the *EVERYTHING*® series:

These handy, accessible books give you all you need to tackle a difficult project, gain a new hobby, comprehend a fascinating topic, prepare for an exam, or even brush up on something you learned back in school but have since forgotten.

You can read an *EVERYTHING*® book from cover-to-cover or just pick out the information you want from our four useful boxes: e-facts, e-ssentials, e-alerts, and e-questions. We literally give you everything you need to know on the subject, but throw in a lot of fun stuff along the way, too.

We now have well over 100 *EVERYTHING*® books in print, spanning such wide-ranging topics as weddings, pregnancy, wine, learning guitar, one-pot cooking, managing people, and so much more. When you're done reading them all, you can finally say you know *EVERYTHING*®!

FACTS

Important sound bytes
of information

ESSENTIALS

Quick handy tips

ALERT

Urgent warnings

QUESTIONS?

Solutions to
common problems

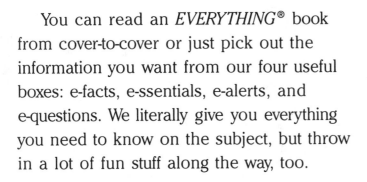

THE
EVERYTHING®
Series

Dear Fellow Collector:

When I was six years old, a neighbor of mine handed me a red and white "Nixon's The One" campaign button, which I promptly secured to my little person. No, I wasn't a child prodigy making a political statement, just a boy fascinated with a shiny pin-back button. Nevertheless, I knew, right then and there, that I wanted to collect buttons—and I did.

Soon after, I started collecting baseball cards, admittedly a more common collectible for a kid. And through the years, I've collected many different things, from old advertising signs to autographs to postcards.

What I've learned is that in collecting, knowledge is power. There's a lot that you should know when navigating the sometimes-choppy collectible seas. My aim in this book is to enhance your overall collecting experience by providing you with helpful buying and selling tips, as well as proven techniques in caring for some of the most popular collectible items around—from stamps to comic books to glassware. I also strive to impart valuable information on the collectibles marketplace as a whole, including the significance of the Internet.

So, I hope you'll use this book to further your collectibles education. The more you know, the more fun you'll have. And that's what collecting is all about!

Happy collecting!

Nicholas Nigro

THE
EVERYTHING
COLLECTIBLES
BOOK

How to buy and sell your favorite treasures—
from fabulous flea market
finds to incredible online deals

Nicholas Nigro

Adams Media Corporation
Avon, Massachusetts

EDITORIAL
Publishing Director: Gary M. Krebs
Managing Editor: Kate McBride
Copy Chief: Laura MacLaughlin
Acquisitions Editor: Bethany Brown
Development Editor: Lesley Bolton

PRODUCTION
Production Director: Susan Beale
Production Manager: Michelle Roy Kelly
Series Designer: Daria Perreault
Layout and Graphics: Arlene Apone,
Paul Beatrice, Brooke Camfield,
Colleen Cunningham, Daria Perreault,
Frank Rivera

An Everything® Series Book.
Everything® is a registered trademark of Adams Media Corporation.

Published by Adams Media Corporation
57 Littlefield Street, Avon, MA 02322 U.S.A.
www.adamsmedia.com

ISBN: 1-58062-645-9
Printed in the United States of America.

J I H G F E D C B A

Library of Congress Cataloging-in-Publication Data
Nigro, Nicholas J.
The everything collectibles book : buy and sell your favorite treasures
from fabulous flea market finds to incredible online deals / Nick Nigro.
p.   cm.
Includes index.
ISBN 1-58062-645-9
1. Collectors and collecting–United States–Handbooks, manuals, etc.
2. Collectibles–United States–Marketing–Handbooks, manuals, etc. I. Title.
NK1125 .N54   2002
745.1'068'8–dc21   2001053950

Many of the designations used by manufacturers and sellers to distinguish their products are claimed as trademarks. Where those designations appear in this book and Adams Media was aware of a trademark claim, the designations have been printed in initial capital letters.

This publication is designed to provide accurate and authoritative information with regard to the subject matter covered. It is sold with the understanding that the publisher is not engaged in rendering legal, accounting, or other professional advice. If legal advice or other expert assistance is required, the services of a competent professional person should be sought.
—From a *Declaration of Principles* jointly adopted by a Committee of the American Bar Association and a Committee of Publishers and Associations

Illustrations by Barry Littmann.

This book is available at quantity discounts for bulk purchases.
For information, call 1-800-872-5627.

Visit the entire Everything® series at everything.com

Contents

Introduction

Prior to the twentieth century, collectors and collections were the province of persons of means. Wealthy jet-setters—even before the invention of jet planes—collected things of quality, rarity, and awe-inspiring beauty (translation: things that cost a lot of money). The affluent, influential folks in society adorned their stately mansions with fine art, exquisite musical instruments, ancient coins, uncommon books, and porcelain pots and vases from faraway dynasties with funny names. There were no Pokémon cards in John D. Rockefeller's desk drawers; no comic books resting on Andrew Carnegie's laundry hamper; and no Dreamsicles collector plates hanging in Cornelius Vanderbilt's study.

Our forebears, the Common Man and Woman collector, arrived on the scene sometime in the early twentieth century, the children of the Industrial Revolution and its cumbersome new machinery. Put quite simply: Mass production of lots and lots of things placed lots and lots of things in the hands of lots and lots of people. With more and more stuff winding its way through assembly lines, more and more commercial promotions were targeted at the lower classes, offering items at prices they could afford. The end result: Collecting things beyond butterflies, rocks, and autumn leaves, were possible for everyone, regardless of net worth.

The breadth of the collectible realm is massive. Within each collectible field, there are, of course, prized items in great demand that are trading in the big-money stratosphere. A movie poster from the 1934 film *Three Little Pigskins,* starring the *Three Stooges* and Lucille Ball (in her first movie billing), fetched $96,000 in a recent Sotheby's auction. A movie poster from the 1998 film *Meet Joe Black,* starring Brad Pitt, on the other hand, is pulling in less than the cost of a movie ticket. Yes, it's true: The vast majority of collectibles and memorabilia, beyond the considerable sentimental value they offer for their respective owners, are not commanding mega-dollars in the marketplace.

It's a collector's world out there. In many ways, it always has been. Oh sure, the world has changed a wee bit over time—or hadn't you noticed? There were no Bubonic Plague series collector cards for kids to swap in the fourteenth century. George Washington's wooden dentures didn't find themselves on the auction block of an early American equivalent of Sotheby's. Still, don't be surprised to learn someday, courtesy of an archeological dig, that the Cro-Magnon man collected artifacts of his primitive predecessor, the Neanderthal man, and proudly mounted them on the wall of the humble cave he called home.

It's the nature of the beast. The human animal was born to collect things. We just can't help ourselves. It's as instinctual as finding our next meal or coming in out of the rain. In reality, we are not far removed from the pack rat on the evolutionary scale, accumulating with abandon everything from empty grocery bags to bakery box string to burned out Christmas light bulbs. Rummage through Grandma's desk drawer sometime, or look in Uncle Joe's hall closet—with their permission, of course. You might very well be dumbfounded at the spectacle of what they've collected through the years—and I'm not talking about their cash stash (that's for another book).

Fortunately though, millions of us collect things of greater value—esthetically, sentimentally, and yes, monetarily—than the aforementioned fragments of everyday living. It's for these varied souls—be they collectors of baseball cards, stamps, coins, autographs, dolls, figurines, political buttons, comic books, beer steins, bobbing heads, postcards, books, records, ceramics, jewelry, or a thousand other things—that this book was written.

As a user-friendly primer, the book will introduce you to the brave new world of collecting and collectibles. It will assist you, whether you are a new or seasoned collector, in getting the most out of your collecting experience.

To maximize the pleasures of collecting something—anything—you need to achieve a higher education in your collector field, while fully understanding the ins and outs of the overall collectibles environment. You need to become aware of the unpredictable flights of fancy of the always-fickle collectible marketplace. After all, you deserve to get the most bang for your buck while you're pursuing your hobby, whether it be in the sheer pleasure of adding an item to your collection or in watching it appreciate in value.

Yogi Berra once said, "When you come to a fork in the road, take it." There are plenty of forks in the collectible world's roads. The more you know, the more right and proper turns you'll make. And the happier you'll be.

CHAPTER 1
Don't Throw It All Away

It's become the stuff of legend: one person's trash becoming another person's Caribbean vacation. From the unearthing of valuables in dusty attics and malodorous trashcans, to penny purchases at flea markets, collectible gems are like pearls in an oyster: You never know when you'll discover one.

The popular PBS program *Antiques Roadshow* regularly refinishes the legend with highly entertaining and fascinating examples and anecdotes of collectibles and antiques of great value being found in the strangest places. It's even spawned a competitor called *The Incurable Collector* on cable television's A&E network.

These TV shows underscore the monetary rewards of collecting, but they tend to gloss over the more soulful pleasures of collecting. It's the money angle that brings in the ratings—all part of the lottery mentality that pervades present-day society.

Antiques Roadshow Primer: The Introductory Guide to Antiques and Collectibles from the Most Watched Series on PBS by Carol Pisant, provides plenty of helpful hints on how you can determine whether that family heirloom of yours is worth a pretty penny or is just a sentimental trip down Memory Lane.

Learning a Lesson from Mom

In recent years, Baby Boomer mothers have been getting a lot of flak for being dream busters. They have been charged with tossing out their sons' baseball card collections when Junior wasn't looking, or when the young boy's fancy turned from baseball to love, or when he left home. Said mothers stand accused of dispatching to the "ash heap of history" the very cards that are today termed *vintage* (worth a nice piece of change). The verdict in the court of public opinion: guilty as charged.

There's no getting around it. Mothers (and some fathers, too) have, in effect, thrown thousands and thousands of dollars worth of cards into the trash along with decomposing banana peels and coffee grinds. They may just as well have set ablaze a stack of government T-bills and maturing municipal bonds.

The proof is in the pudding . . . or landfills and incinerators, in these inauspicious instances. To further illustrate this point, I need you to traverse the time barrier and travel back with me to a very good year: 1958. (I promise that you'll be home in time for supper.) World War II hero Dwight "Ike" Eisenhower is the President of the United States; the most popular program on television is *Gunsmoke;* a first-class postage stamp costs four cents; and Friskies is marketing the first-of-its-kind dry

1969 Topps Deckle Edge Roberto Clemente baseball card

cat food. The perennial World's Champions New York Yankees are managed by a non-sequitur-spouting senior citizen named Casey Stengel. The American pastime is baseball, when it truly is a game—unsullied by artificial turf, domed stadiums, mega-million-dollar player contracts, sky-high ticket prices, and eardrum-piercing rock music blasting between innings at the old ballpark.

Kids collect baseball cards, relishing the mystique of the game most of all. Topps cards are the tops, and they aren't competing with a mob of card companies for a share of the collector's market. The ten-year-old wide-eyed boy of 1958 opens his packs of cards containing such star players as:

- Ted Williams (valued today, in near-mint condition, at $500)
- Willie Mays (valued today, in near-mint condition, at $225)
- Mickey Mantle (valued today, in near-mint condition, at $800)
- Hank Aaron (valued today, in near-mint condition, at $200)
- Roger Maris (valued today, in near-mint condition, at $400)
- Roberto Clemente (valued today, in near-mint condition, at $300)

We're back. It's the twenty-first century again. Now it's time to do a little math. In this teeny-tiny sampling of six cards, many parents tossed away $2,425 in today's dollars. And in mint condition, the same cards are worth a whole lot more.

In his fifties now, Junior is getting a little long in the tooth, contemplating his own retirement. With all his money tied up in the whims of the volatile stock market, he watches as those discarded cards of his continue to appreciate in value. It'll haunt him to his dying day.

True, this little case study ignores a couple of meaningful variables. Namely, the cards that were kept in a kid's not-so-gentle care aren't likely

George Washington commemorative hanging plaque (1930s)

to be in pristine condition these many years later, even without short-sighted mothers. And, had every kid held on to his cards, there would be a whole lot more of them in today's marketplace. The law of supply and demand teaches us that the cards would be much *less* valuable had parents left the cards to rest comfortably in their shoeboxes for a *Rip Van Winkle* siesta. It's called *dilution*, and it happens when too much of a particular item is available. The law of supply and demand applies to every collectible imaginable.

Seeing How Kids Have Changed

Enough mom bashing for the time being. The truth is that kids, prior to the late 1980s or early 1990s, focused on collecting things for the sheer allure of collecting. It was fun. Their eyes weren't fixed on the future worth of their baseball cards, comic books, and Barbie dolls.

Young boys flipped their cards on concrete city sidewalks and fired them against brick walls. They attached them with clothespins to the spokes of their bicycles, generating breezy, whirring sounds only a kid could love. These sorts of normal juvenile behaviors scratched, scuffed, creased, and chipped their cards. Some youngsters even marked them with crayons and pens. Ouch! Kiss that future value goodbye!

A 1969 collector of baseball cards, for instance, could not possibly have foreseen that Topps card #260, of a then unknown rookie player named Reggie Jackson, would be worth over $5,000 in mint condition three decades later. Nor did he much care. From a penny to $5,000.

Pay Toilet
metal sign
(early 1970s)

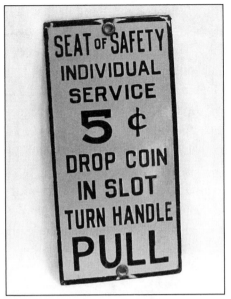

That's a 500,000 percent return on investment—a little better than even the vaunted Kaufmann Fund's thirty-year average return.

Meanwhile, little girls of that same year played with their Barbie dolls, twisting thousands of arms and legs in the process, doing to their doll set-ups what the boys were doing to their baseball cards. Countless Ken and Barbie dolls met the same fate as did Tom Seaver and Nolan Ryan baseball cards. And today there's a considerable Barbie doll collector's market, with many highly coveted vintage dolls (1959–1966), as well as some of the contemporary, limited editions, doing a brisk trade.

FACTS

Since her birth as a teenager in 1959, Barbie has worn a billion pairs of shoes and had over 500 professional makeovers. Barbie has also been dating Ken for over forty years with no marriage plans in the offing. And, believe it or not, Barbie has been a very controversial figure during her lifetime, offending everyone from women's groups to peace groups to child psychologists. Dr. James Dobson has dubbed Barbie a "role model for anorexia."

Being a kid nowadays really is difficult—and a lot less fun. Boys and girls are inundated with mixed messages on television, in the movies, and on the Internet. Childhood itself has been considerably shortened. Collecting things for pleasure as an innocent, non-jaded kid is harder to do. The passion of youth is worth a whole lot more than any inflated dollar figure put on their Pokémon cards and pogs. Yet, many of today's young kids are acutely aware of the money value of things that they're collecting, and they're more than happy to discourse on the subject.

George and Martha Washington salt and pepper shakers

True, a little financial savvy goes a long way. Little Scotty and Melissa should be taught the meaning of a dollar. (It's worth about 35 cents in 1974 dollars, by the way.) However, eight-year-olds talking about Ken Griffey Jr. being a great baseball player is one thing; deliberating on the latest market price of their Ken Griffey Jr. baseball cards is quite another kettle of fish—and not a positive development.

If you're a PEZ collector, visit *www.pezcollectorsnews.com* and find out what PEZ Heads are up to, when and where their conventions are held, and even where there's a PEZ museum.

Knowing What to Keep

Throwing things away, especially in this day and age, is as much a human necessity as collecting is a compulsion. Cereal boxes, chewing gum wrappers, expired calendars, repair manuals, magazine ads, vegetable crates, TV sets, merchandise catalogues, coffee pots, beer cans, and books from days gone by are now sought after pieces of memorabilia. Are moms alone responsible for tossing all this stuff away? Not very likely.

President John Adams often collected memorabilia from his trips overseas. While visiting Shakespeare's birthplace, Adams sliced a sliver of wood from one of the Bard's chairs. A great addition to his collection, no doubt, but a crime. As you add to your collection, don't use Adams as a role model.

Here's a random sampling of some of yesterday's throwaways trading as desired collectibles in today's marketplace:

- An aluminum lid off of a "Big Top Smooth Peanut Butter" jar
- A celluloid bookmark and company giveaway featuring the ringmistress from Miller High Life beer
- A 1950s model 14T011 art deco, black-and-white General Electric TV set with its original antenna
- A Sen-Sen chewing gum box
- A book about the breeding of poultry entitled "The Call of the Hen" by Walter Hogan, copyright 1913
- An old, empty Vaseline jar with its original label
- A 1950s glossy yellow metal breadbox strewn with flower decals
- A Burger Chef mesh worker hat
- A 1939 Budweiser beer can
- A 1940s aluminum electric coffee pot

FACTS

It's probably not politically correct to collect these items in this day and age. But these collectors blow smoke rings around most others. They're collectors of smoking-related items, and the hobby is labeled *tobacciana*. If you collect ashtrays, cigars, cigarette boxes, lighters, or pipes, then this is where you belong, and you're in good company: President Andrew Jackson collected tobacciana. He amassed a sizeable collection of pipes from all over the world.

And while I'm on the subject of stuff from the past put out to the curbside: What ever happened to all those toys and games we played with as kids? They vanished into thin air when our childhood ended, just as surely as did those trading cards. The toy soldiers, mini-cars, pull toys, and board games that were once so dear to us are also valuable pieces of memorabilia in today's collectible marketplace. Collectors are buying and selling past childhood gems like these:

- A Matchbox Studebaker Wagonaire, with those unmatched thin wheels
- A Playskool milk truck with a pull string
- A 1965 Milton Bradley Trouble board game with wooden dice
- A 1970s Campbell Kids picture puzzle
- A 1960s Fisher Price Tiny Teddy pull toy
- A Tonka toy dump truck
- A 1954 Parker Brothers Hickety Pickety game
- A 1974 Milton Bradley "The Waltons" game
- A Cootie board game
- A 1968 Hot Wheels Custom Firebird Convertible

These vintage items were tossed away by not only moms, but also dads, and—dare we say it—by you, too. You've sentenced your parents to eternity in purgatory for tossing away so many priceless things from your past. But are you behaving any differently? Are you saving every catalogue you receive in the mail? Are you preserving for posterity every one of your children's toys and games? Are you rinsing out each finished jar of Smuckers grape jelly and tucking them away in boxes in the attic, with the hopes of unwrapping them in thirty or forty years to sell on eBay? No, of course you're not.

Vintage telephone company metal sign

This is not a clarion call for you to start saving everything, either. However, just remember: That empty box of Hungry Jack mashed potatoes, that empty bottle of Liquid Plumber, and even your obsolete VCR and Dell computer, are the memorabilia of tomorrow. So, if you've got the space, why not hold on to a few of these things? Food for thought. Food for collectibles.

FACTS

The Milton Bradley Company, founded in 1860, is one of the world's oldest manufacturers of board games. No company has produced more popular, bestselling board games. Paradoxically, Milton Bradley games are not generally at the top of game collectors' most wanted lists.

Among some of the more popular items in this collector field are TV sitcom board games and Hanna-Barbera cartoon board games. For more information, check out the Association of Game and Puzzle Collectors at *www.agca.com.*

Understanding the Terminology of Collecting

What the devil makes a collectible a "collectible?" Try the dictionary and you'll find a definition similar to this: "an object that is collected by fanciers, especially one other than traditionally collected items as art, stamps, coins, and antiques." Bet you never thought of yourself as a "fancier."

This is a dictionary compiler's attempt to make chicken soup from chicken feathers. A *collectible* is a rather broad, all-encompassing word. There is a very real distinction between what are *collectibles* and what is *memorabilia*, although the words are often used interchangeably and will be throughout this book. Precisely, the term *memorabilia* refers to items that once functioned in utilitarian roles, or had some pleasing attributes that subsequently generated a popular, nostalgic interest. A glass Coca-Cola bottle from the 1950s, for example, manufactured solely as a repository for a refreshing and tasty carbonated beverage, is presently a piece of memorabilia. A 1933 *King Kong* movie poster, produced to advertise the movie, is today an object of movie memorabilia. A 1964 "In Your Heart, You Know He's

Right" Goldwater-for-President button, distributed at campaign rallies to promote a presidential candidacy, is an item of memorabilia in many political pin collections.

Collectibles, in the strictest sense of the word, are things marketed as collector items, with no practical use other than as decorative pieces.

Porcelain Stitzel Weller Distillery commemorative decanter (1969)

Hamilton collector plates and Enesco figurines are examples of collectibles manufactured as collectibles—period. You're not supposed to eat off of a collector plate—you'd destroy its colorful finish and poison yourself in the process. And the *Austin Powers* bobbing head doll on your mantel isn't going to help you dust the coffee table or clean out the garage. Then again, certain sources define collectibles as "something worth collecting."

And what about antiques? According to the U.S. Customs Office, an *antique* is any item more than 100 years old. Most collectors and dealers of antiques, however, are more liberal in their interpretations and use fifty to seventy-five years as the cut-off point for delineating *antique* from *modern.*

Antiquities, not to be confused with those run-of-the-mill antiques, are artifacts and items fashioned prior to the start of the Dark Ages/Fall of the Roman Empire (A.D. 477), give or take a few centuries. Ancient Times, as they are known on the historical timeline, produced a plethora of coins and statues, many of which are still around today in collections and museums all over the world.

A *vintage collectible* is a collectible from the past—usually a secondary-market item. Generously interpreted, *vintage* means "from a past year." But at least ten years should pass before applying the "vintage" tag to an item. In the baseball card trade, the "vintage" moniker is reserved for pre-1970 cards. A *contemporary collectible* is an item from the immediate past—something from last year, for instance. A recent phenomenon is the production of items hyped as collectibles with a great future value. It remains to be seen how many of these "collectibles" will be worth big bucks down the road.

QUESTIONS?

What is a secondary-market item?
In the collectible domain, a *secondary-market item* is an object sold or traded after its initial sale or distribution. In other words, somebody already purchased the item, or used it, and now he or she wants to pass it on to another somebody.

The word *ephemera* pops up in the collectible sphere all the time, and refers to things that were produced without an eye on longevity. Movie tickets, menus, greeting cards, matchbooks, postcards, pay stubs, ration cards, letters, bumper stickers, catalogues, calendars, lottery tickets, brochures, and so on, are examples of ephemera.

Early twentieth-century circus ephemera

Ephemera comprise a legion of paper items. After all, if manufacturers of dinner menus and theater tickets were thinking about their condition a century later, they'd have had them printed on something other than cheap paper, like stone.

Paper doesn't mean ephemera, even though most ephemera are paper products. Political buttons, for one, are considered ephemera—they were manufactured for the moment of a campaign and not for tomorrow's collectors.

1861 Civil War recruitment poster with foxing along the bottom (Union/ Pennsylvania)

While I'm on the subject of paper, there is another term spotted often in the collectible realm that you should be made aware of. It's called *foxing,* and it has nothing to do with putting on tight equestrian outfits and setting the dogs on cute little orange animals. *Foxing* refers to those ubiquitous brown spots that form on paper items. It's the scourge of rare books. Celluloid pin-back buttons have also known the ravages of foxing.

Why does foxing occur? Too much bleach used in the manufacturing of the paper reacts chemically with dampness. The solution to the problem: Protect your items from the dampness and you'll keep foxing at bay.

CHAPTER 2

Shopping for Collectibles

There are no better places to find collectible bargains and other treasures than at flea markets and garage, yard, and porch sales. You may have to wade through a heap of junk to find items of interest to you, but there's always the potential of reeling in a big fish at these unique sales.

Finding Fortune at Flea Markets

For many people, the term *flea market* conjures up the image of an outdoor hodgepodge of sellers of secondhand articles and old stuff, including antiques. To these folks, a flea market is America's version of a Middle Eastern street bazaar. The flea-market tradition functions just as effectively indoors as it does in the great outdoors. To be sure, there's nothing quite like the ambience of an open-air flea market held in a sprawling, weed-strewn, dusty field and former home of a drive-in movie theater.

ESSENTIALS

The *U.S. Flea Market Directory: A Guide to the Best Flea Markets in All 50 States* by Albert Lafarge is a great resource on flea markets. *Flea Market Trader: Thousands of Items with Current Values* by Bob and Sharon Huxford contains over 10,000 items and their present market values.

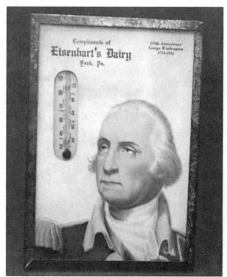

Eisenhart's Dairy promotional plaque/thermometer commemorating George Washington's 200th birthday (1932)

Of course, Mother Nature doesn't always respect and appreciate our weather preferences, so indoor trading is perfectly acceptable to buyers and sellers alike. As a matter of fact, it's preferred in wintertime, on hot and humid summer days, and, yes, when the rain clouds gather, as they often do on flea market day. Indoor flea markets can be found in a wide variety of locations: school auditoriums, legion halls, and church basements, to name just a few of the popular spots. Some big-time flea markets take place in convention centers. There are also combination indoor and outdoor flea markets. Don't be surprised to see sellers peddling their wares on the ball field of the junior high and in the school lunchroom, too.

FACTS

Older parents, whose kids have long since flown the coop, often set up shop in flea markets and host yard sales and garage sales. Left behind by their kids, and a mystery to these parental peddlers, are many prized items to memorabilia collectors. Nostalgic browsers have scooped up the likes of old Hula Hoops, Mighty Mikes, and Klik-Klaks (also known as Knockers or Clackers), at these mom-and-pop sales.

Aside from location, there are two main types of flea markets, which are covered in the following sections.

Level One: The Informal Flea Market

The level one flea market is a rather informal affair, featuring a preponderance of first-time sellers, many of whom just cleaned out their

A flea market find! Heavy metal horse and wagon (early twentieth century)

basements and attics, and want to make a few bucks selling things they haven't used in years and have no intention of ever using again. Other sellers have just performed the task of emptying out a dearly departed relation's lifetime of accumulation. And they, too, want to make a dollar or two before summoning the Salvation Army to cart off the deceased's remaining earthly possessions.

ESSENTIALS

A general rule of thumb to follow at flea markets is this: If the item for sale is patently old, in decent condition, and cheaply priced, buy it! Of course, it's up to you to determine what "cheap" means to you. If you're sinking this month's electric bill into the acquisition, you might want to reconsider.

In these more casual flea markets—usually held in small auditoriums, or maybe out in the church parking lot—there are generous amounts of junk and bric-a-brac up for sale. But it is at these flea markets where many hidden gems lurk as well. Amid granny's old silk stockings and dad's leisure suit jacket are sometimes valuable antiques and coveted collectibles. With so many amateur sellers peddling their stuff, bargains await you. They want to get rid of what they're selling, and this often means getting anything they can for it.

ALERT

Just as you shouldn't sleep late on flea market day, or risk letting your collector competition beat you to the punch, don't forget to return for a second helping later in the day. Many sellers lower their prices as the day goes on.

These sellers aren't ordinarily well informed about the business of collectibles and antiques. For this reason, as a potential buyer, it is wise to get to these flea markets as early as possible. Although the sellers may

"T.V. Bank" appliance store giveaway (1950s)

not have schooled themselves on the collectible marketplace, there are many buyers who have, and who are steeped in separating the antique jewelry from the worthless baubles. And bear in mind, *early* means getting there before the scheduled opening time. Flea market doors usually open well before the starting time to give vendors ample time to unpack their wares. What does this mean? Early bird buyers can roam around, too, while the sellers load up their tables. The best and most sought-after merchandise is more times than not snatched up immediately by the collectible-informed, who are also early risers. Meanwhile, the collectible-challenged sellers are as pleased as punch to make early sales. It inspires them to go on.

A trek to *www.fleamarket.com* will give you information on currently scheduled flea markets in the United States and Canada. Searching for a flea market in your area is made simple. The listings contain such fundamental facts as their frequency, times, directions, variety of merchandise sold, and cost to rent a space.

Level Two: More Organization, More People

Level two is the larger, more organized, regularly held, and better-attended flea market. These affairs showcase many professional and business sellers, who are also more experienced flea market vendors. The cost for a spot at these flea markets is higher than at level one events, but usually worth the price of admission because of the greater customer traffic. There is a tremendous variety to choose from, with plenty of great buys to be found, but also some higher-priced, upscale items. The emphasis at level two flea markets is not on household trinkets and old clothes, although you'll likely find plenty.

There are wholesale businesses who specialize in selling to flea market vendors. If you're interested in selling porcelain dolls, sports collectibles, collectors' knives, figurines, jewelry, and more, visit the Bargain Mall *(www.bargain-mall.com),* which offers a lengthy list of wholesalers catering to flea market vendors.

Getting What You Want at Garage Sales

Garage/yard/porch sales are basically flea markets with one seller, and treasure hunters know that these types of sales are potential collectible and antique bonanzas. Why? Because most garage and yard sales are

1950s
barbershop
poster

organized by the sellers to get rid of stuff, come hell or high water. The prices are usually right and sometimes—yes, sometimes—an antique chair or rare piece of memorabilia can be picked up for a song and a dance.

For this reason, on garage and yard sale days prospective customers have been known to camp out in front of the homes running the sales, sometimes hours before their advertised scheduled start. They want to be the first to fix their eyes on the pickings, lest someone beat them to that rare first edition book or porcelain bowl priced at $5 but worth more than $500 to an experienced collector.

ALERT

If you haven't ventured into the land of garage and yard sales yet, be prepared for a few surprises along the way. Although many of these sales are worth the trip, some are memorable only for what you *don't* come home with.

Hosting a Garage Sale

When you host a garage or yard sale, the first rule is to advertise. This means posting fliers—lots of them—all around town, and in the next town, too. Nowadays, courtesy of the computer, you can produce a nifty-looking flier with minimal effort. On the flier, summarize the kinds of items that

Framed "Lincoln at Home" taken from newspaper of the time, 1861 (foxing visible on left)

you'll have up for sale. Don't forget the date, time, and location—you wouldn't want to leave these out. And make sure potential customers know how to find you. This might entail that you include on the flier some directions and a basic map—a few key street names and accompanying arrows pointing the way.

ESSENTIALS

Like just about everything else, the flea market has entered cyberspace. At *www.qflea.com,* a virtual flea market experience has taken shape with crafters, soap makers, candle makers, and quilt makers setting up shop on the Internet.

Make the fliers bold and readable, and use a catchy ink and paper color combination. It has been scientifically determined that black ink on yellow paper is the most eye-catching, readable mix. Blue ink on yellow also scored high on the readable chart. Black ink on old-fashioned white paper will also do just fine. Avoid fuchsia-on-pale-green paper combos.

ESSENTIALS

Garage sale mavens look no further than *Once upon a Garage Sale: From Fairy Tale to Reality: How to Make More Money, Get Rid of More Stuff, and Otherwise Succeed at Your Garage Sale* by Lisa Rogovin Payne. This is an A to Z guide to prospective garage- and yard-sale sellers.

In addition to posting fliers, be sure to advertise in the local newspapers. And, spread the word the traditional way. A wagging tongue or two is worth a heap of fliers posted on telephone polls and in barbershop windows.

ESSENTIALS

A Web site that's recommended for garage and yard sale enthusiasts is *www.garagesale.nearu.com.* This site will let you in on the whereabouts of garage and yard sales all across the fruited plain.

After you've taken care of advertising, it's time to prepare your items for the crowds that'll surely be heading your way. First things first: Price everything. Some people won't consider buying an item if it's not priced. They are either very shy and won't ask you the price, or they are leery of being taken advantage of. "Different prices for different folks" is not proper business etiquette.

Make sure you have some cash and coins at the beginning of the sale. If you don't, you can count on your first customer of the day asking you to change a $100 bill.

Get bags of some kind. Asking customers to put their purchases in their pockets is bad form. And, if you're selling anything breakable—like glassware—have some wrapping material available. Yesterday's news will fill the bill.

A positive attitude, a few smiles, and you're set.

A L E R T

Before posting fliers advertising your garage or yard sale, educate yourself on your city or town's ordinances, to see if you need a permit, or if you are required to adhere to certain guidelines in conducting your sale.

Going Through the Garbage for Gold

Maybe you've seen something in somebody else's garbage that captured your fancy. There are people who, as a matter of course, drive around town and check out what's been put out at the curbside. It is an honored American tradition. We Americans are the wealthiest people on earth. We buy more things than anybody else on the planet does—by far. It stands to reason then that we also discard more stuff than anyone else does, too. And some of our refuse doesn't exactly meet the dictionary definition of garbage.

There are people who have completely furnished their homes with other people's garbage. Lots of goodies, including antiques and prized collectibles, are discovered in trash-cans and in plastic garbage bags every day. Stuff regularly turning up in the trash includes furniture, books, lamps, jewelry, children's games, and paintings.

Lincoln Bust aftershave bottle

There's a new wrinkle in the more traditional garbage hunt of cruising around for hours looking for sights for sore eyes amidst mounds of trash. It's got a designation all its own. It's called *dumpster diving*—an active quest for beneficial stuff that's been thrown away, not only by individual families, but by businesses and apartment complexes that utilize dumpsters to dispense with their garbage. Unlike street trash in cans and bags, dumpster diving entails getting down and dirty by literally climbing into garbage dumpsters. Dumpster diving can be as rewarding as the flea market and the garage and yard sale. But you've got to be in it to win it. It's a dirty job.

Here are some helpful dumpster diving tips from the skilled practitioners themselves:

- This kind of work is for adults only.
- Be careful that the Dumpster lid doesn't slam shut on you.
- Watch out for sharp materials, such as broken glass and metals.
- Food discarded in dumpsters is often purposely contaminated with bleach to discourage the scavenging around in dumpsters, so don't eat anything you find.
- Leave the dumpster exactly like you found it or, better yet, in neater order.

Although there's usually no law against taking things from garbage cans and dumpsters, authorities often frown upon crawling inside dumpsters. The best advice from successful dumpster divers is to tell anyone who asks what you're doing that you're looking for empty boxes—a white lie, perhaps, but harmless.

FACTS

The Supreme Court has actually ruled on dumpster diving in *California v. Greenwood.* Police found incriminating evidence in Billy Greenwood's garbage and attained a search warrant for his home. Greenwood was found guilty and sentenced to prison. In his appeal, Greenwood claimed that the search of his garbage was illegal. The Court decreed that trash was open to inspection by "animals, children, scavengers, snoops, and other members of the public." A landmark victory for garbage pickers and dumpster divers everywhere.

CHAPTER 3
Sports Cards

The foremost collectible hobby on the American landscape—measured in notoriety, if not in dollars—is sports memorabilia. People routinely shell out big money for vintage sports cards, the topic of this chapter (turn to the next chapter for all other sports memorabilia).

Seeing How Sports Cards Got Their Start

The truest collectors are those who know the history of their collectibles inside and out, who know all about the life and times from which they originate. The baseball card and its past reveals so much about not only the cards themselves, but about life in America in a fast-changing, tempestuous century.

FACTS

Some say the first card ever issued for a professional sport was a hockey card, manufactured in 1879, though there is room for debate. Hockey cards, both vintage and modern, are the most popular collector cards in Canada; whereas in the United States, collecting hockey memorabilia takes a backseat in the penalty box to baseball, basketball, and football.

The original baseball card—produced in a series at least—was born in 1887, the progeny of Allen & Ginter, a tobacco company that issued a set of "World Champions" cards that year. These tobacco premium cards included baseball players, but also boxers, wrestlers, oarsmen, sharpshooters, and pool players. Captain Jack Glasscock and Charles Comiskey, recognized players of the late nineteenth century, were featured in this set, which also included Annie Oakley and Buffalo Bill Cody. To say the least, the Allen & Ginter's set was a very eclectic and attractive assortment of cards. The ten baseball cards in the series proved the most popular with the public.

A year later, New York's Goodwin & Co. issued a series of eight baseball cards as part of their "Champions" set, which featured bicyclists, marksmen, boxers, wrestlers, college football stars, and weightlifters. The cards were inserted in packs of their Old Judge and Gypsy Queen cigarettes. Featuring numbered backs and sepia-toned photographs of familiar star baseball players like Cap Anson and King Kelly, the cards came to be known as the Old Judge brand series and are very popular in today's card marketplace.

Baseball cards rapidly caught on as people found they had more leisure time and the opportunity to at last collect something. They also smoked like chimneys in those bygone days, with an estimated 90 percent of the adult male population partaking in the poisonous pleasure. After a lull in the first decade of the twentieth century, the baseball card returned with a vengeance in 1909, and collecting cards became widespread, with nearly seventy-five different baseball series issued by competing cigarette companies.

The American Tobacco Co.'s famous T206 and T205 card sets are the most visible and sought-after in today's collector market. The T206 contained 524 cards and is known as the "white-bordered set." Included in this set is the renowned Honus Wagner card. Honus "the Flying Dutchman" Wagner, the grizzled Pittsburgh Pirates star shortstop of the time, complained that his face was being used on a tobacco card without his consent. He disapproved of the use of his likeness to—as the story goes—promote cigarettes, which he felt invited kids to descend down the slippery slope of a lifetime smoking habit. This was at least how the Wagner versus Big Tobacco affair was reported in a 1912 issue of *The Sporting News*. Other more reliable sources say that Wagner, a tobacco-chewing devotee himself, who had appeared in tobacco advertising through the years, wasn't an anti-smoking trailblazer at all, but rather a modern athlete frontiersman holding out for a piece of the money pie.

Whether the Flying Dutchman's motives were as pure as the driven snow, or as green as the Almighty Dollar, is a moot point as far as today's collectors are concerned. American Tobacco pulled the card from its distribution at Wagner's request, resulting in very few T206 Wagner cards making it into circulation, and even fewer existing almost a century later (estimated by some experts at fewer than thirty cards). The payoff is that the T206 Honus Wagner card is today valued at over $1 million in mint condition.

The T205 set is commonly referred to as the "gold-bordered set." The cards were both $1\frac{7}{16}$ inches in width and $2\frac{5}{8}$ inches in height and printed on quality paper, making them quite handsome and more durable than many of the other tobacco cards from that day (which aren't around anymore). The backs of the cards contained ads for one of sixteen brands of cigarettes. Early-twentieth-century collectors adored them; twenty-first century collectors desire them, too, particularly since only a modest number survive in tiptop condition. There are, nevertheless, plenty of these cards available at affordable prices. They are great cards to collect, and hark back to an epoch far removed from the present.

As time passed, World War I brought great changes and shifts to the tobacco industry. Tobacco companies began merging with one another. The fierce competition in the industry diminished accordingly. With fewer rival companies in the marketplace, the need to offer baseball cards to attract customers dropped, too. Goodbye tobacco cards, hello *Sporting Life* and *The Sporting News,* creating cards to help them sell subscriptions to their publications. Cracker Jack—of "buy me some peanuts and Cracker Jack" fame—also jumped into the baseball card fray.

PSA-graded cards, Clemens/ Ripken/ Jordan

Finally, in the Roaring Twenties, baseball cards were manufactured to sell solely as baseball cards, and not as any advertising gimmick for cigarettes, magazines, or candy. The W514 Strip card of 1928 was one of the earliest baseball cards sold individually as a baseball card, promoting nothing but itself. Unfortunately, the good times of the 1920s came to an abrupt end—but not for the baseball card.

Who better to enter the baseball card picture during a Great Depression than a bubble gum maker? In 1933, the Goudey Gum Company produced a set of 239 baseball cards, introducing the "bubble gum card" into American life. The cards were well received. Major

League Baseball loomed increasingly larger in the public consciousness during those downcast economic years. Baseball stars like Lou Gehrig, Rogers Hornsby, Mel Ott, Frankie Frisch, Napoleon Lajoie, and the Sultan of Swat himself, the Great Bambino Babe Ruth, were demigods in a country hungry for diversions from the hardscrabble reality of life during the Depression.

The 1933 Goudey set of colorful portraits, containing two cards of Gehrig and four of Ruth, is enormously popular with collectors today. There are over fifty Hall of Fame players in the set! What are they trading for? Babe Ruth cards and the Napoleon Lajoie card in near mint and

1934 baseball card

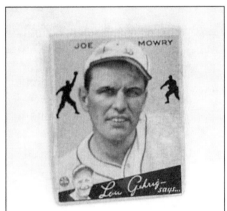

better condition command thousands of dollars. Not all the cards from this series are as valuable, but this set rates as one of the finest ever made. If you can acquire a card or two from it, you will have acquired a rare slice of American history.

Goudey continued generating baseball cards until 1941. Other companies like Diamond Star, Batter Up, and Play Ball manufactured cards at various times through the 1930s and into the early 1940s. Then World War II came to America's shores, and baseball was put on the backburner. Attendance dropped dramatically in ballparks all over the country. Baseball card production also went by the wayside due to wartime paper rationing and diminished interest. There were more pressing things on Americans' minds than baseball, and many of the game's greats joined the service and went off to fight in places far away from Wrigley Field, Shibe Park, and Tiger Stadium.

It was only after the war that baseball resumed its rightful place as America's game; only a matter of time, too, before baseball cards made their comeback. In 1948, a company called Bowman began cranking out cards from the sports worlds of baseball, basketball, and football. The Leaf Company simultaneously produced the first post-war set of full-color baseball cards.

Four years later, in 1952, Sy Berger, a war veteran and huge baseball fan, perfected what is generally considered the first "modern baseball card," replete with a player image, career statistics, and team logo. A couple of years prior to the Berger innovation, Topps Gum company had jumped into the trading card arena, believing it could sell more chewing gum by inserting cards into packs of their products. This set the stage for the marriage of the century. The Berger concept and a company by the name of Topps locked arms. The result: the 1952 Topps set of 407 cards (the largest set to date), ushering in the baseball card size and pattern that most of us came to know and love as kid collectors.

The popularity of the 1952 series and subsequent ones put Topps on top of the heap in the trading-card business. Topps bought out Bowman, its prime competitor, in 1956, and more or less reigned supreme in the baseball card business for over thirty years.

Fleer, another bubble-gum-company-turned-card-manufacturer, issued baseball card series from 1959 to 1963, and then resumed production in 1981. Donruss, one more card company in the mix, produced its first baseball card series in 1981.

FACTS

In some of the earliest baseball cards, ballplayers are shown on the field without baseball gloves on their hands. There's a good reason for that. They didn't use gloves in those rough-and-tumble days. Men were men in the late 1800s and used their own mitts—their bare hands—to catch batted and thrown balls. Catchers even caught barehanded and didn't wear masks to protect them from foul tips. Runners were called out when hit by a thrown ball.

The prodigious change in the baseball card market occurred in 1989, when the Upper Deck Company went public with the first baseball card series printed on a high gloss, quality stock with eye-catching holograms. This initiated all sorts of glitzy offshoots like SP, SPX, SP Authentic, UD3, and Collector's Choice. The card competition soon became so stiff that even the czar of sports cards, Topps, got into the act of issuing specialty sets like Topps Chrome, Tiffany, and Stadium Club, in addition to its longstanding regular series. Topps resurrected the Bowman name, too, in 1989. Times have changed in the baseball card marketplace, and there is no turning back. The bucolic card collecting days are a thing of the past.

Starting a Sports Card Collection

If you want to start collecting baseball cards, or other related memorabilia, it is wise to forge a plan and stick by it. The baseball card market is too sprawling today to haphazardly buy this and buy that and expect to fashion an impressive collection. The Topps series of cards isn't all you can collect anymore. Numerous card companies are pumping out regular series and special series on top of those. The average collector just can't keep track of, let alone afford, every baseball card that comes down the pike.

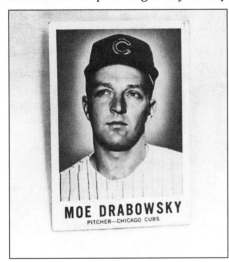

Moe Drabowsky baseball card (1960)

MOE DRABOWSKY
PITCHER—CHICAGO CUBS

If you have finite resources—and limited time—here are some helpful hints on collecting baseball cards and building a collection that you can be proud of, and that you can maintain with the least amount of wear and tear on your mental and spiritual health. You could concentrate your dollars and hobby education on the following:

- Collecting a series from a specific year—the year of your birth, the year you saw your first Major League game
- Collecting one or more players from the exclusive clubs of baseball—players who have reached the 500 homerun plateau, players who have accumulated 3,000 hits, or pitchers who have reached 300 wins
- Collecting your favorite player (or players) throughout their entire careers
- Collecting award winners from such prestigious categories as MVP, Cy Young, Rookie of the Year, or the Triple Crown

- Collecting Hall of Fame players—generally speaking, the most valuable cards in the hobby
- Collecting rookie cards of current stars and possible future Hall of Famers—which can be very lucrative down the road, since rookie cards are ordinarily the most cherished cards of Hall of Famers, as well as the stars of today
- Collecting select vintage cards from some of the classic series of all time (1887 Allen & Ginter, 1911 T205, 1915 Cracker Jack, 1933 Goudey, 1952 Topps)

The truth is that it's a necessity when buying and trading for cards to set some kind of parameters in building a collection. Otherwise, you'll end up with a unwieldy, out-of-control assortment that your significant other might one day ask you to part with. So, plan your work, work your plan, and most of all—have fun in the process.

QUESTIONS?

What is the obverse of a sports card?
The front of a sports card is often referred to as its *obverse*. The back of a card is deemed its *reverse*. This terminology is also commonplace in other collectible hobbies. Coin collectors, for instance, refer to the head of a coin as its obverse.

Knowing How Much Your Cards Are Worth

Ah, the value of the baseball card. It's taken on a life of its own and transcends both the sport of baseball and the card-collecting hobby. Thousands and thousands of dollars' worth of baseball cards have been thrown away over the years. But today, even non-sports fans are aware of the baseball card and its presumed value—and no one would dare throw them out.

Beckett's Price Guides

It was in 1979 that a man named James Beckett published the first comprehensive book of its kind: a baseball card price guide. Perhaps no book since the Bible has quite revolutionized the sports collector's world like *The Beckett Baseball Card Price Guide.* Prior to 1979, Dr. Beckett had produced some small pamphlets containing estimated card values, which he distributed free of charge to interested parties in the hobby. A comprehensive, full-length book, updated annually established a valuable precedent.

The buying and selling of baseball cards represent the heart and soul of the sports memorabilia market. Beckett's card pricing guide is credited with (or blamed for, depending on your perspective) turning the pedestrian baseball card into the most coveted bit of paper product in human history; for turning a drowsy hobby into a big business. From the moment the Beckett price guide saw the light of day, the average collector has had ready access to a publication with up-to-date values of his or her baseball cards. With its publication, being an educated collector became possible for everyone who collected—or would collect—cards. The card collector circle has enlarged dramatically, courtesy of Beckett identifying card values and putting them on collectors' radar screens.

The Beckett Baseball Card Price Guide remains, over two decades since its first publication, one of the most important sources in the marketplace for discerning card values. The Beckett name is trusted and respected. It's become synonymous with "price guide."

In addition to the annual publication, there is also *The Beckett Baseball Card Monthly,* a subscription magazine that provides monthly updates in card pricing. Some card prices are dynamic and change in a flash. An unforeseen event such as the 1998 Sammy Sosa–Mark McGwire home run race, for instance, created fast upward pressures on both Sosa and McGwire card prices. *Baseball Card Monthly* keeps collectors informed on the latest market trends and publishes listings of the upcoming card shows throughout the country. Helpful articles on relevant topics aimed at enhancing your collecting experience regularly appear in the magazine. Useful advice is continually dispensed on how to maintain your cards in the best possible condition, which, you should always remember, is the key to their value.

Although *The Beckett Baseball Card Price Guide* is the most popular, there are a series of books published by Beckett and House of

Collectibles. *The Beckett Basketball Card Price Guide, The Beckett Football Card Price Guide,* and *The Beckett Hockey Card Price Guide* are popular with collectors in these sports. In fact, basketball card collecting has become very hot. Collecting Michael Jordan cards and memorabilia is an industry in and of itself.

Other useful Beckett publications include *The Beckett Official Price Guide to Baseball Cards,* which is published each year with the current year's cards only. Then there's *The Beckett Baseball Card Alphabetical Checklist,* with players listed alphabetically for easy reference. Just keep in mind when purchasing any Beckett publication, or other price guide, to make certain that you've got the most updated edition. This is essential in the world of prices. A 1987 price list won't do you much good today.

You can also check out *www.beckett.com* for Beckett online. This Web site will furnish you with up-to-the-minute happenings in the world of card collecting. A "Daily Hot List" and "Card of the Day" are just a couple of the features that you'll find here.

Ironically, even old Beckett pricing guides are collectors' items; particularly those with star players on their covers, like Nolan Ryan and Ken Griffey Jr. So, don't recycle those old price guides—hang on to them.

FACTS

Originally, card manufacturers issued their cards in series. In early springtime, the first series hit the stores, followed in a few weeks by the second series, the third series, and so on. As the summer wound down, interest in card collecting did, too. The card companies—aware of the law of supply and demand—printed smaller runs of their later series. Because there are less of them in existence, high numbered cards are more valuable today.

Standard Catalogs

No, it's not the Federal Budget. It's the Sports Collectors Digest *Standard Catalog of BASEBALL CARDS.* This annual publication takes the Beckett price guide more than a few steps further. You might need help carrying this book home—it's that thick. The *Standard Catalog* is over 1,500 pages, lists more cards than any other source, and provides current market prices and a variety of photos. The most unique feature of the book is the wealth of historical references and descriptions that precede each of the card listings.

The *Standard Catalog of BASKETBALL CARDS* is available for basketball fans; the *Standard Catalog of FOOTBALL CARDS*, for football fans. Again, make sure you pick up the most recent edition of any of these books, they are updated annually.

Visit *www.krause.com* for more information on Sports Collectors Digest books and their highly regarded magazine, *Sports Collectors Digest,* the largest publication in the hobby. Known affectionately in the industry as *SCD,* this magazine has it all. Whether you're looking to buy, or looking to sell, look here. Can't surf there, then call 800-258-0929 for a free copy of the *Sports Collectors Digest* catalog.

Where does the *book price* or *book value* come from? From price guides like Beckett and others, which base their prices on what's happening in the marketplace. When selling a card, however, don't expect to get the full book value for it.

And You Thought You Were Done with Grades

One of the most intriguing developments in the sports card boom of the 1990s was the introduction of card grading services. The foremost card grader in the world of sports is Professional Sports Authenticator (PSA). PSA was founded in 1991 and is now regarded as the giant in the card-grading industry.

Understanding What Card Grading Is

PSA-graded cards command the highest prices in the trade because the cards' conditions are accepted by buyers as having been vetted by a group of independent experts, whose business is the meticulous inspections of cards. In a nutshell, the PSA card submission process works like this: You mail your card (or cards) directly to PSA. The experienced PSA staff closely examines your card and determines its precise condition. A grade is then issued, anywhere from 1/Poor to Fair up to 10/Gem-Mint. Each grade conferred on a card corresponds to a very specific criterion established by PSA, which takes into account the card's corners, centering, surface and edge wear, creases, loss of original gloss, and other factors. PSA will grade just about every card submitted to its service, unless the card exhibits evidence of having been tampered with (trimming, recoloring, restoration) or is of dubious authenticity.

You may think your card is in mint condition, and describe it as such. But, upon closer inspection, you notice a very slight fraying at a corner or two. This might render the card a 7/Near Mint on the PSA grading scale. And the difference in what collectors of PSA cards will pay for a 9/Mint versus a 7/Near Mint is dramatic. It's not unusual to see anywhere from a fourfold to as much as a tenfold price difference.

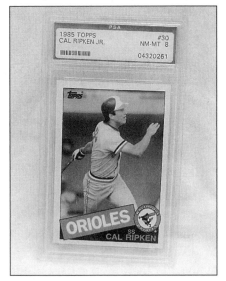

PSA-graded card, Cal Ripken Jr.

A 1973 Topps Nolan Ryan with a PSA 7/Near Mint grade is selling for $60; the same card with a PSA 9/Mint grade is pulling in $415. A 1975 Topps George Brett rookie card with a PSA 7/Near Mint grade is seeing $95 in the marketplace; a PSA 9/Mint, $450. To the casual card collector, the differences in the card's appearance and appeal might be insignificant, but in current climate of today's marketplace, it is very significant.

A PSA-graded card is placed in an attractive-looking, protective, clear plastic case. The card's year and manufacturer (1959 Topps, 1991 Upper Deck, and so on), a PSA serial number, and—most important— its grade are printed on a paper insert and placed atop the card in the casing. PSA grades cards from all sports: baseball, basketball, football, hockey, boxing, and even golf. They also grade Minor League cards.

There are a growing number of dealers in sports cards who will only buy PSA-graded items.

Visit PSA at *www.psacard.com* or contact them at 800-325-1121. You'll receive all the details on how to go about getting your cards graded. Many collectors choose to become members of PSA and receive the *Sportscard Market Report,* a monthly publication that lists the latest marketplace prices of PSA-graded cards, from the turn-of-the-twentieth-century tobacco cards to the most popular of present-day issues. There are also feature articles in this thorough publication, which are of special relevance to PSA card buyers and sellers. In the *Sportscard Market Report,* you also get access to the names of PSA-authorized dealers of PSA-graded cards, as well as other buyers and sellers who specialize in these highly sought-after cards.

PSA-graded cards are also perfect for display, because they are in protective cases that are pleasing to the eye. You can now have your most precious cards out in the open for all to see, instead of tucked away in binders, boxes, and drawers.

It's important to note that PSA is not alone in the card-grading arena. Our old friend Beckett also offers grading services. The Beckett Grading Service operates on a similar 1 to 10 scale, just like PSA. What differentiates them from PSA is that they use half points (7.5, 8.5, and so on) and issue Report Card style grades, leaving no confusion in why a card gets the final grade that it does. Beckett grades each card in four categories—centering, corners, edges, and surface—and then assigns an overall composite grade. A Beckett-graded card is then placed in a secure plastic case—similar to PSA's—with all the pertinent details on how the grade was determined inserted inside. The final grade appears on the front; the category grades on the back. Still another card grading service—and increasingly popular in the sports card market—is Sportscard Guaranty, known as SGC. SGC uses a 1 to 100 grading scale (just like high school). SGC grades Pokémon cards, too, and can be found at *www.sgccard.com.* Both Beckett and SGC card grading services are more cost-conscious than is PSA, and their turnaround time is routinely much faster.

Deciding Whether to Have Your Cards Graded

Card grading, as you probably suspected, isn't free. In fact, as more and more card collectors utilize this service, the cost for grading has gone up, and the turnaround time on the grading process (the amount of time it'll take before you get your card back) has gotten longer and longer.

Nevertheless, if you have vintage cards on the high end of the condition scale, grading them will greatly enhance their values in today's marketplace. Buyers will know exactly what they are getting when you say you have a 1953 Topps Ralph Kiner, PSA 7/Near Mint. If you described the same card, without a professional grading, as being in near mint condition, it would not attract many buyers willing to pay anywhere near the book price. Buyers are often leery of accepting at face value a seller's description of his or her card.

Generally speaking, except for vintage cards, grading is reserved for star players or rare issues. Often, if your cards are on the bottom of the condition charts, it's not worth making the $15 to $20 per card investment, or sometimes more, necessary to get them graded.

Investing in sports cards is quite commonplace these days. And if you can't get enough of the Dow Jones and NASDAQ, visit *www.thepit.com,* the first Sports Card Stock Market, with a running ticker and up-to-the-minute notice on "advancers" and "decliners."

Assessing Your Card's Condition Yourself

Your sports card's condition will determine its value—in both dollars and in attractiveness. This is the reason why card grading has blossomed into a business in its own right. If you'd rather not fork over the money to have your cards professionally graded, you can try to pinpoint for yourself their exact conditions. In the following sections, I cover several areas that greatly impact a card's grade and, hence, its value.

Corners

A card's grade rests largely on the condition of its corners. For if the card's corners are razor sharp, it's more than likely that the rest of the card will be in similar, unsullied shape. A mint card does not exhibit any signs of fraying at its corners. A near mint card may show miniscule fraying on some of its corners, but not any graduated fraying. *Graduated fraying* is considered a more advanced form of this particular card malady, when the fraying becomes multi-layered. Ultimately, extensive corner wear leads to rounding at the edges. When this occurs, the card's grade drops considerably.

Ding

Ding is a word used to describe damage on the corner of a card, when the evolution of corner wear is substantial.

Crease

A bend or fold in the card is a *crease*. Extensive handling of a card will sometimes result in a crease (or two or three). And all creases are not created equal. Some are quite visible; some are only visible in reflected light. Some are long; some are short. It's better to have a card without any creases. No card can be considered mint or near mint if it is in any way creased.

Centering

A card's centering is central to its value. Well-versed collectors measure the distance between the card's photo and its four borders. And if a card measures 50/50 top to bottom and 65/35 left to right, it is considered perfectly centered on its top and bottom borders, and shifted to the left with 65 percent of the border to the left of the photo and 35 percent to the right. This may sound confusing, even bizarre, but this centering lingo is used quite frequently in the card trade.

Perfectly centered cards are the most sought after cards by collectors. Cards that have lost a border due to a production miscut, for instance, are the orphans of the card world. Nobody wants them.

Gloss

Gloss refers to the shine on the surface of a card. As time passes, some cards lose their initial gloss. Older cards with their original gloss intact are prized.

Chipping

Chipping is a word often seen in card descriptions and refers to a card's edges, as opposed to its corners. Edges sometimes start chipping in a piecemeal way, just as the descriptive word suggests. This phenomenon is more prevalent in some series than in others.

Notching

The term *notching* is applied to edge wear indentations on a card caused, for example, by rubber bands pressuring its sides. Additional factors that come into play when evaluating a card's condition are wax stains from the card's initial packaging, picture focus, printing defects, scuffing, scratching, and marks made by the human hand, such as ink, crayon, and pencil notations.

Keeping Your Cards Safe

Sports cards should be placed in protective holders—in a plastic sleeve and then in a top-loader plastic card sheet. More valuable cards can be placed in solid plastic card frames, or, at the very least, firm card savers, which permit cards to be comfortably slipped into them and prevent any bending.

There are many sellers of protective materials for cards. In *Sports Collectors Digest* and other hobby magazines, you'll find many sources of protective sheets, card frames, and storage boxes to preserve your cards. BCW is a supplier of everything from protective pages to albums to cardholders to bat and ball holders. They are online at *www.bcwsupplies.com.* For the actual displaying, there are frames made specifically for cards that fit anywhere from one to nine cards. There are swivel stands for these card displays, too.

CHAPTER 4

Sports Memorabilia

The sports collectibles hobby embodies the good, the bad, and the ugly of the collectible realm. There are far-ranging buying and selling avenues in sports memorabilia, significant returns on some investments, and an abundance of counterfeits to contend with. Sports memorabilia span a wealth of items—the expanse is massive.

Recognizing the Pitfalls

When San Diego Padres star outfielder Tony Gwynn noticed "Tony Gwynn" autographed memorabilia in the team's gift shop, it upset him.

Brooklyn Dodgers "Brooklyn Bum" latex squeeze toy (1950s)

Why? Because Gwynn knew the autographed materials, reputedly signed by him, were forgeries—and in the team gift shop! Gwynn took his discovery to the FBI, which was already investigating fraud throughout the entire memorabilia marketplace. What the FBI found was stunning in scope. Sports-related autographs on photos, plaques, bats, balls, basketballs, footballs, hockey sticks, and so on, were found to be suspect all around. The FBI estimated that 99 percent of Mark McGwire autographs in the marketplace were phonies!

How the Fraud Is Perpetrated

How is this fraudulent activity perpetrated on such a large scale? It's easy. When the skyrocketing demand for sports memorabilia runs up against a limited supply of such items, the counterfeiters move in to make up the difference. Modern technology makes forgeries a cinch in the hands of unscrupulous, but crafty, individuals. There are numerous players in this industry scam, but the FBI determined that the majority of bogus memorabilia distributed throughout the country can be traced to just a handful of accomplished counterfeiters, who are responsible for supplying the lion's share of phony items to the marketplace.

How does it work? The counterfeit operation sells its high-quality, fraudulent autographed memorabilia, and other items like uniforms, to large-scale distributors. These distributors then supply the fakes to major retail outlets and smaller distributors in the chain. When the counterfeit items worm their way into the world of legitimate commerce, the fakes and frauds find themselves in Internet auctions, mail-order catalogs, retail stores, franchise outlets in malls, home-shopping channels, and memorabilia shows—all places where buyers should have every reason to believe that the merchandise being sold is legitimate.

A recent FBI investigation concluded that as much as 90 percent of sports autographs for sale are fakes, but that hasn't dampened the spirits of sports memorabilia enthusiasts. When purchasing items ready-made for fraud—like autographs, player uniforms and equipment, and game-used equipment—be sure you know what you're getting.

Which Fakes Are Legal

When you were a kid, did you send a baseball card to your favorite player, care of the ballpark, and request that it be autographed? Did you write to your favorite team and ask for a signed picture of your hero? Many fans did—and still do—these very things. Today's youngsters are enjoying the same thrill their parents did. They're getting their baseball cards returned with a signature scribbled across.

There is a term bandied about in the sports memorabilia marketplace called the *clubhouse signature.* It is applied to athlete signatures made—not by them—but by batboys, equipment personnel, and miscellaneous clubhouse workers. Star athletes, in particular, who receive lots of mail, utilize these ballpark employees to sign items for them, such as cards, balls, and pictures. The reality is that often what you get returned to you has the mark of Billy the batboy on it, and not Mike Piazza, the home run–hitting catcher. No FBI investigation needed here. Just be aware of the phenomenon of the clubhouse signature.

But keep in mind that if you think an autograph is real, it is—to you, at least. Who's to contest an autograph's authenticity while it's tucked away in a folder somewhere, or hanging on your bedroom wall behind a glass picture frame? A problem arises only when you decide to sell or swap your autograph in the marketplace.

Don't tell the kids just yet. Let them believe that the signature on their sports cards, or on that glossy 5 × 7 picture, is the genuine article, even though it may not be. Sometimes just believing is enough.

ESSENTIALS Before Jackie Robinson signed a contract with the Brooklyn Dodgers in 1947, the Negro Leagues were the only places that black ballplayers could showcase their talents. Today, baseball's Negro Leagues hold an important place in sports history. To learn more and get links to Negro Leagues memorabilia, visit *www.blackbaseball.com.*

What You Can Do to Steer Clear of Fraud

In the world of collecting, as in life itself, real guarantees are hard to come by. What you need to do in your everyday life, as well as in all your collecting endeavors, is take the necessary precautions to avoid getting ripped off by a scam artist.

To avoid being defrauded, demand a Certificate of Authenticity (COA) on any item that you purchase. But keep in mind that a COA is not worth the paper it's printed on if the seller is a charlatan. (For more on COAs,

"Official League" Cincinnati Reds baseball clock (turn of the twentieth century)

turn to Chapter 8.) Limit your buying of memorabilia to reputable sources. There are plenty of honest sellers in the marketplace, even, believe it or not, in the sports collectible world. True, the hobby has taken a public relations' bath lately with all the real evidence of chicanery out there. Nevertheless, there are many sellers of sports memorabilia who have been around for a long time and have well-deserved reputations of selling genuine and quality materials. COAs from these businesses are the closest things to a guarantee you can get in life.

If a price seems too good to be true, whether in an auction, at a card show, or in a collector magazine ad, then the odds are that it *is* too good to be true. Walk away from it. No, on second thought, run!

The sports collectibles realm is huge. Take your time in navigating it, do your homework, and never dive into a purchase that you might one day regret. The red flags are all over the place, but this doesn't mean that you can't avoid them and come out smelling like a rose.

ESSENTIALS

For a thorough book on die-cast collectibles from the sport of racing, check out *Racing Die-Cast Collectibles: The Industry's Most Comprehensive Pricing and Checklists of Die-Cast Cars and Accessories* by Mark Zeske. This book is loaded with color photos and checklists for all scales of die-cast racing cars.

Protecting Your Sports Memorabilia

In the world of collecting, we keep talking about the monetary value of collectibles, particularly in sports memorabilia. Then we rue the very fact that

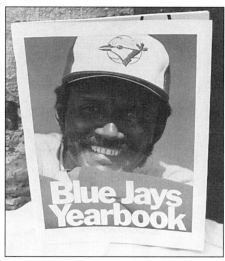

1979 Toronto Blue Jays yearbook

we talk about it so much. The sensible center in this collectible world dilemma meets right here. Every collector wants to maintain his or her collection in the best possible condition. A collection is more impressive when it's properly tended to—and it's also worth more in dollars.

For your memorabilia out on display, be sure to keep it away from direct sunlight. Memorabilia aren't houseplants—they don't need light and water. In a very short period of time, the sun can destroy anything from a card to an autograph. Window films are available to filter the sun's damaging rays. If you can't keep

Mother Nature at bay any other way, look into these films. You'll be glad you did.

The sun isn't the only memorabilia destroyer. There's old-fashioned dust to do battle with. When dust gets into hats and jerseys, for instance, there's no amount of dust busting that can do away with it without doing away with the piece being dusted. Let a display case bear the brunt of the dust mites.

If you have anything in your collection that means something to you, it is wise to encase it somehow, and to display it. What's the point of having an impressive item or collection tucked away in a box in the basement? If you want to showcase your ticket stubs, you can find frames designed specifically for this purpose. There are cases made specifically for basketballs, for footballs, and for hockey pucks. And there are displays designed with the sports jersey in mind—even ones that hats and caps fit comfortably into.

Look through the hobby newspapers and magazines for dealers in these displays and frames. There are plenty of them. Attend shows and you'll find display merchandise for sale. Surf the Internet. Check out *www.creativesportsent.com* for a variety of display cases for sale.

FACTS

The memorabilia marketplace is not a very sentimental environment. The death of a star, past or present, means one thing: It's time to sell. The popular-selling Dale Earnhardt memorabilia, in stores at the time of his death, sold out in less than twenty-four hours, leaving a great unmet demand. The day after Earnhardt's accident, the *Daytona Beach News-Journal* needed to print an extra 90,000 copies to satisfy public demand. That same day, copies of the newspaper were selling on eBay.

Insuring Your Memorabilia

Your sports memorabilia collection obviously means something to you. Once you've invested serious money in your collectibles, it's time to give thoughtful consideration to insuring them.

If you already have a homeowner's or renter's insurance policy, it is possible to acquire an addendum to cover your collectibles. A phone call to your insurance agent will let you know if it can be done and at what additional cost. Sometimes, though, this insurance rider costs more than what you've invested in your entire collection. If this is the case, it would be wise to insure only specific items in your collection—the most valuable pieces. In any event, save receipts from all your collectible forays. Take pictures of everything, too, and keep an updated inventory of your entire collection.

"Original Mets" scorecard (1962)

The odds are on your side that you'll never have to collect any insurance. But if you happen to be one of the unlucky ones who loses his or her home and valuables to fire, flood, or theft, you'll be glad you took out the extra insurance. Cherished collectibles cannot be replaced, but recovering their monetary value might at least provide some solace. It's better to be safe than sorry.

FACTS

In 1998, twenty-one collectible savants devised the Universal Rarity Scale, which locates rare items within various collectible fields and make this information available to both collectors and dealers. The Universal Rarity Scale features ten points. The least-rare collectibles—designated "UR1" and deemed "readily available"—are those items in circulation that number 10,000 or greater. The rarest items—designated "UR10" and classified as "unique"—are those for which only one example is known to exist. Everything else falls in between.

CHAPTER 5
Stamps

Stamp collecting has been called "the hobby of kings" and "the king of hobbies." Stamp collections reach across the world. There are more international collectors of stamps than any other collectible piece. The hobby does not generate the publicity of sports memorabilia, but it's a vibrant pastime rooted in a long tradition.

Knowing the History of the Stamp

The first postage stamp was a British innovation. Prior to 1840, in the United Kingdom—and just about everywhere else—postal charges were collected upon delivery of the mail. If you mailed a letter to Aunt Agnes, she had two choices: She could foot the mailing bill, or she could refuse delivery. You can see the dilemma that the post office faced. A good portion of its delivered mail was, in fact, refused, resulting in lost revenue.

Miscellaneous
U.S. 5-cent
stamps
(1963–1967
issues)

Fortunately for Her Majesty's subjects, and for the rest of the planet, along came a former schoolteacher and citizen reformer named Rowland Hill. He proposed revamping the entire British postal system. His inspired idea revolved around the prepayment of postage at the point of mailing—a novel approach in the middle of the nineteenth century. One uniform rate for mailing letters, regardless of distance, was the heart and soul of Hill's plan. Higher mailing rates based on weight were also included in his scheme.

The Hill scheme was not only lauded by the politicians, but quickly implemented, revolutionizing post offices and mailing practices throughout the British Isles, and soon after, the world. This new-fashioned postal system ushered in the first of its kind adhesive stamp for mailing letters. The very first stamps were sold on May 6, 1840, and are known in today's trade as the *penny black*. Featuring an image of Queen Victoria on a black background, the stamps were cancelled using a red ink. This red cancel, it turned out, was so easily removable that some of the citizenry were reusing their penny blacks. This prompted the government to switch over to the *penny red* stamp, cancelled with a more permanent black ink.

The postage stamp caught on with the public-at-large immediately, and with fledgling stamp collectors, too. There are reports of stamp collecting occurring almost immediately after the stamp's inception. India was the first Asian country to issue postage stamps. The first American stamps saw the light of day in 1847, sporting the likeness of first Postmaster General Ben Franklin on a five-cent stamp and the image of the first president, George Washington, on a ten-cent stamp.

Philately is the term applied to stamp collecting or the study of stamps. If you collect stamps, you are a *philatelist*. The term was coined by a nineteenth-century French stamp collector named M. G. Herpin. The origins of the word are Greek. *Philo* means "lover of." *Atelia,* literally defined, is "free of payment of tax." There are millions of philatelists in the world—and millions of people who wish they were free of tax payments, too.

If you want to get a jump on history as a philatelist, keep in mind that in the coming years, the following stamps will be flooding the market. Based on total U.S. Post Office sales figures, these are the most popular American stamps ever issued:

- Elvis Presley (1993): 124 million
- Wildflowers (1992): 76.2 million
- Rock & Roll/Rhythm & Blues (1993): 75.8 million
- Civil War (1995): 46.6 million
- Legends of the West (1994): 46.5 million
- Marilyn Monroe (1995): 46.3 million
- Bugs Bunny (1997): 44 million
- Summer Olympics Games (1992): 39.6 million
- The World of Dinosaurs (1997): 38.5 million
- Centennial Olympic Games (1996): 38.1 million

Planning Your Stamp Collection

The stamp collector has the world at his or her feet. Stamps personify every aspect of the society and the time that we live in. Stamps celebrate great works of art, cultural events and institutions, important people, holidays, sports, noteworthy moments in history, geographical wonders, botanical marvels, technological innovations, scientific discoveries, great feats of architecture, popular culture, economics, and almost everything else.

SSENTIALS

The American Philatelic Society Web site at *www.stamps.org* is loaded with information and history, has a store and a library to rummage through, and provides resource links and an almanac. You can also write to them at 100 Oakwood Avenue, P.O. Box 8000, State College, PA 16803, for more information.

And since societies and cultures differ so mightily, so do the stamps that come out of them. This has been the case since the introduction of the postage stamp. Authoritarian Tsarist Russia's stamps showcased far different things than did the burgeoning, open society across the ocean called America. And it's no different today. Free societies that recognize free expression and free thinking have a wide variety of stamps in circulation. Closed, repressive societies do not.

In addition to the historical scope that stamp collecting affords its collectors, it is also affordable. Stamp collecting is one of the least expensive hobbies to pursue. You don't need a lot of money to be a stamp collector. But plotting a strategy is a necessity. Beginning stamp collectors often collect, literally, all over the map, because stamps are truly a worldly collectible. And why not? Stamps on letters in the mailbox are varied and unique. It's a great way to feel your way around the hobby, and to learn the basics, including how to remove stamps from their envelopes without damaging them. It's good form to first practice this technique on common, everyday stamps before moving up the philatelist ladder.

As time passes, and you become more experienced, however, you might want to consider taking the path that many of the more seasoned stamp collectors venture down. These collectors put all their stamps in one basket—or one album, as it were. If you are interested in starting a stamp collection with a design in mind, or getting an existing one under control, contemplate collecting within one of the popular parameters listed in the following sections.

> Stamps issued to raise funds for a charity or nonprofit organization are referred to as *semi-postals.* The United States has only issued one semi-postal stamp, and that was for breast cancer research. It was a regular first-class stamp, but it cost 40 cents, with the premium on the price going to support breast cancer research. Semi-postal stamps are very popular among the Kiwis in New Zealand.

Collect Commemoratives

You will have to narrow this category down even further—to a specific country, for starters. The United States Postal Service, for example, issues commemorative stamps in all categories. From U.S. presidents to military heroes to historical events to famous movie monsters, they've all been honored by the Postal Service. This is fertile territory for stamp collecting.

The most popular stamp collector magazine is *Stamp Collector.* This biweekly journal is written by collectors for collectors, keeping hobbyists informed on all the latest happenings in the world of stamp collecting. Subscribe at *www.krause.com/stamps,* or pick up a copy at any bookstore or retailer that carries magazines.

Collect Thematically

Collecting stamps of a particular motif is the most widespread form of stamp collecting. Collectors select stamp subjects that coincide with their own interests and lifestyles. Some hobbyists collect stamps that feature great patriots, civil rights pioneers, prominent political leaders, pets and animals, states, flowers, architecture, weapons, locomotives, ships, space exploration, comely women, environmental treasures, favorite vacation spots, and on and on. The scope of theme stamp collecting is limitless.

Collect First-Day Covers (FDCs)

You've no doubt seen envelopes with a stamp and cancellation on them indicating the first day of issue. Variations of first-day covers include first-flight covers and special-event covers. These catchy-looking covers sport an imprint (for whomever or whatever is being honored) to the left of the cancellation. This imprint is called a *cachet*. Covers, by the way, refer to the envelopes or postcards to which stamps are attached.

FACTS

The Citizen's Stamp Advisory Committee (CSAC) was created to give people a voice in selecting stamp honorees. If you think a certain person or event merits placement on a stamp, send your idea to the CSAC, U.S. Postal Service, 475 L'Enfant Plaza, SW, Room 4474E, Washington, DC 20260-2437. Keep in mind that a person needs to be dead for at least ten years before being commemorated, unless it's a U.S. president, who only has to be dead for one year.

Collect Error, Freak, and Oddity Stamps (EFOs)

Some collectors just relish collecting the mistakes of life. On the stamp scene, they seek out stamps born with deformities, the result of printing or perforation blunders somewhere in the production process.

SSENTIALS

The Collectibles Insurance Agency at *www.collectinsure.com* is the insurer of the American Association of Philatelic Exhibitors. Online quotes are available. Beyond stamp collections, they insure autographs, books and manuscripts, ceramics, comics, dolls, records, postcards, trains, toys, and guns and firearms. For a quote by phone, call them at 888-837-9537.

Collect Complete Covers

These are the entire mailing pieces, replete with their original stamps and postal markings. Letters dropped in the mail become, in effect, globetrotters. They zip across the country in a matter of days, and sometimes travel abroad. Many people live vicariously through these letters. Some collectors are fascinated with the life stories of pieces of mail, and they relish finding unique machine and town postmarks on envelopes and postcards.

A great Web site to visit is *www.the-stamp-collector.com*. Here you'll get links to dealers, auctioneers, magazines, exhibitions, societies, and literature. Want to join the Chess on Stamps Study Unit? How about the Cats on Stamps Study Unit? Or the Maritime Postmark Society? You'll find them all here.

Collect Christmas Seals, Easter Seals, or Other Non-Postage Stamps

In the world of stamp collecting, non-postage stamps, issued by non-government enterprises, are known as *Cinderellas*. Often, they originate from charity organizations.

Knowing What Condition Your Stamps Are In

Like in every other collectible bailiwick, a stamp's condition is key to its value. There's more leeway given in condition, of course, to the rare birds of stamps. Generally speaking, though, stamps without defects are preferred. Scuffs, tears, lost pieces, holes, creases, *thins* (parts of the stamp that are thinner in certain spots), diminished colors, and dog-ears detract from a stamp's attractiveness and appeal to collectors.

Skilled restorers sometimes mask these defects. This practice is okay if the sellers of restored stamps identify them as having undergone a facelift. Needless to say, they don't always do that. Just be aware of this practice when making a purchase that involves a substantial sum of money. Knowing from whom you are buying always helps.

The following sections cover several important factors that you should know about that will impact on a stamp's condition and its overall desirability.

Coloring

A stamp with its original color, looking exactly as it did upon its issuance, is at the head of the class. One that has faded will be worth less.

Centering

A uniformly centered stamp is what a collector most desires. The evenness between the stamp's *vignette* (image) and its borders is what to look for. Be aware, though, that many older and rarer stamps come from a time when impeccable centering wasn't a printer's top priority.

Gum

Gum is the sticky stuff on the back of the stamp. At some point in all of our lives, we've gagged upon licking the back of a stamp. In the stamp-collecting realm, the adhesive on the backs of stamps greatly impacts on their conditions. The glue applied to a stamp's back has been known to crack with time and damage the stamp's paper. Sometimes, a noticeable stain is left on the stamp when the gum has gone bad. You will encounter such acronyms in the hobby as NG (for "no gum"), which means the gum has been removed from the stamp. Good news: The self-adhesive stamp, the greatest invention since sliced bread, is now commonplace.

Hinges

Hinge sticking is as much a part of a stamp collector's life as Don Ho is a part of Hawaiian nightlife. And it refers to the process of mounting stamps on album pages. While most contemporary hinges are peelable, the hinges of yesteryear were not. They were predominantly slender, translucent slips of paper gummed on one side to facilitate the affixing of stamps to album pages. Predictably, these hinges left their marks on stamps in more ways than one. *NH,* in stamp collecting lingo, means "never hinged." If the hinge has impacted the gum of the stamp proper, it is described sometimes as *VLH* ("very lightly hinged") or, depending on the severity, *HH* ("heavily hinged"). If a section of the hinge is attached to the stamp, it is classified *HR,* for "hinge remnant."

Cancellation

Cancellation is a key component in a stamp's overall appeal to collectors. A stamp is deemed *fresh* when it's hot off the press and resting comfortably in the post office awaiting sale to the public. When it's performing its duty as payment for mailing a letter, it gets cancelled by a postal clerk, or, more likely these days, by a machine. There are many forms of cancellations. A *fully cancelled* stamp is covered entirely. These are less attractive to collectors for obvious reasons. A *partially cancelled* stamp is marked only on a corner, leaving the majority of the stamp's image free from any marking. Sometimes post offices use what are called *fancy cancels,* which are pictorial in nature with stars or some other shapes. These can enhance the stamp's value, provided that they are not oversized. Obliterating postmarks of any type are unwelcome sights on the stamp-collecting playing field.

The *Official Blackbook Price Guide to United States Postage Stamps* by Marc and Tom Hudgeons is teeming with full-color pictures and advice on buying, selling, and caring for your stamps.

Determining Your Stamp's Grade

Knowing the basics of stamp grading will greatly assist you in all your collecting machinations, whether you're looking to buy or to sell stamps. In the twenty-first century that we now call home, it's become increasingly commonplace for collectors to purchase stamps via online auctions or Web sites, rather than in person from dealers, where they can see the stamps up close and personal.

If you're planning to participate in any of these virtual reality transactions, it's essential that you be given a thorough description and grading of the stamp before you consider making a purchase. Make certain that you know what you're buying! If you are a cyberspace seller, it is equally important that you describe your stamp's condition as accurately as possible. You owe it to your prospective buyers.

In the following sections, I cover some basic grading classifications that are regularly used in describing a stamp's overall condition. (You'll find more advanced and thorough condition descriptions as you venture deeper and deeper into the hobby. They all, nevertheless, revolve around these rudimentary grades.)

Superb

The stamp is perfect all around. Nobody's perfect and not many stamps are. Keep this in mind.

Extra-Fine

The stamp is well centered; margins are even; cancellations are light and orderly; colors are undiminished; perforations are perfectly intact; and no faults (scuffs, tears, thins, and so on) are evident. *Imperforates* (stamps without perforations) have wide margins.

QUESTIONS?

What does the word *imperforate* mean?
Early stamp issues, before 1860, had no perforations (or *rouletting*) between the individual stamps on a printed sheet. They were imperforate by design and had to be cut apart, making for some imperfect snippets of stamps.

Very Fine

The stamp is well centered. The margins are adequate but don't have to be perfectly even. Cancellations are light and orderly. The colors are undiminished, the perforations are perfectly intact, and no faults are evident. Imperforates have normal-sized margins on three sides.

Fine/Very Fine

The stamp's image may be slightly off-center, but not close to the perforations. Cancellations don't obscure the image. Colors are undiminished. No faults are evident. Imperforates have normal sized margins on two sides with the image untouched.

FACTS

An 1856 one-cent (black on magenta) British Guyana issue is considered one-of-a-kind. The stamp's history goes something like this: A young boy found it in 1873 and sold it to a collector for a whopping six cents. Two years later, it sold for $122. In 1922, somebody paid $7,343 for it; in 1940, $45,000. By 1970, the stamp brought in $280,000; two years later in that inflationary time, it sold for $850,000. It recently changed hands for $935,000.

Fine

The stamp's image is markedly off-center, both horizontally and vertically, and close to the perforations, though they do not impact on the image. Cancellations may be heavier than usual, concealing some of the image, but no faults are evident. Imperforates reveal slender margins.

Good/Average

The stamp's image is off-center and perforations cut into it. Cancellation is heavy and conceals the image, but no tears or thin spots are evident.

Poor

The stamp's image is off-center and the perforations cut a swath far into it. Cancellation is thick, dark, smeared, or blurred. Poor stamps are generally considered unfit for a collection. But, if you want them, by all means collect them.

Separating a Stamp from an Envelope

Many of the world's best stamp collections contain stamps that have—at some point in time—been removed from covers, i.e. envelopes and

U.S. Mail lunchbox (1950s)

postcards. The removal process is not always a clean and easy task. Nevertheless, you can almost every time affect a separation of a stamp from its cover. But in what condition do the two part company? That's the $64,000 question.

Look upon the stamp and its cover as a married couple. Sometimes the stamp has been attached to it for a long, long time. It stands to reason, then, that the parting isn't always going to go smoothly. Stamp collectors everywhere do it, however. They haven't yet come up with a better way. Philatelists all over the world soak their stamps in bowls of water to weaken the glue's hold on a stamp and separate it from its cover. One thing to consider before giving a stamp a bath is whether or not it is more prized—and preferred to collectors—attached to its original cover. Some stamps are. Once you've answered this question to your satisfaction, let the soaking process begin.

FACTS

There is only one nation on the planet that's got the imprimatur to issue stamps without identifying themselves by name. Every stamp issued in the United States, for instance, is clearly marked "USA." Not in the United Kingdom, though. The British, having issued the very first postage stamp, are exempt from printing "UK" on their stamps if they see fit not to. Instead of their name, they are permitted to include an image of the ruling monarch.

Your first move requires that you trim the cover around the stamp. You don't want or need to dump the entire envelope into a bowl of water. Make certain that you don't touch the stamp in the trimming process. Just use common sense, leave ample room, and you'll be fine. Then place the stamp-cover combo in a bowl of water at room temperature, and about one-half inch deep.

Some stamps will separate very easily, almost immediately after touching the water, while others will take considerably longer. Patience is a virtue. Once the separation occurs, a second bowl of room-temperature water needs to spring into action. The newly freed stamp should be given a second bath in the second bowl to remove any adhesive residue or envelope dye that may still be clinging to it.

A popular stamp-soaking tool is a pair of spade-tip stamp tongs. The tongs can be used to lightly dunk the floating stamp into its first soaking, and they can also be used to remove it from the water. A versatile tool all around.

Today's self-adhesive stamps are more difficult to separate from their covers than the traditional gummed stamps. They do, however, come apart. Just give them a little more time.

Do not ever attempt to peel off a wet stamp from its cover before it is ready to do so in its own right. A stamp can be an obstinate old bugger when it wants to. This is a sure-fire way to destroy it.

Postmarking It

I've mentioned the vital role that the postmark plays in stamp collecting—the impact that it has on the condition and ultimate grade of stamps. A stamp's overall desirability rests in large part on the postmark. Too much of a postmark on a stamp is not a good thing. Unless, of course, you belong to a body of collectors in the world of philately who elevate the postmark to idol status. For this group of men and women, the postmark trumps the stamp every time. Postal history collectors, or postmark collectors, first and foremost check out the postmarks on their letters and packages. Postmarked envelopes at stamp shows are what catch their eyes. Stamps are incidental to them.

A *postmark* is a rather broad term that is applied to the markings acquired by pieces of mail as they pass from point A to point B through the postal system. Getting branded for this reason and that reason is a story every letter or package in the mail has to tell. Those unsightly lines canceling stamps—so that you can't ever use them again—are postmarks. But so are the countless other markings made by postal employees and their mechanized arms. A "Postage Due" or "Special Delivery" ink stamp is a postmark, too. Some of the particular things that postal history collectors look for are covered in the following sections.

FACTS

President Franklin Delano Roosevelt was a philatelist. Upon his inauguration in 1933, he had already amassed a collection of over 25,000 stamps from all over the world. While president, FDR received the first sheet of each new commemorative stamp issued by the Post Office. He even made suggestions on the designs of commemorative stamps.

Date Stamps

These are the most common postmarks that incorporate the date, city, and state information. This indicates where the piece of mail received its baptism. The most common date stamp is circular in shape, and is known, appropriately, as a *circular date stamp* (CDS).

SSENTIALS

The Scott Standard Postage Stamp Catalogue: United States and Affiliated Territories, United Nations, Countries of the World by James Kloetzel comes in alphabetized editions, covering stamps from all over the world. Go to *www.scottonline.com* to get details about the Scott series and purchasing stamp-collecting supplies.

Cancellations

I've previously indicated how these postmarks are often the bane of a stamp collector's existence, shrouding once-attractive stamps behind veils of heavy black ink. Cancellations are the portions of postmarks that postal services around the world use to keep themselves in business. That is, they mark stamps so that they can never again be used for mailing purposes. There are a variety of cancels for postmark collectors to feast their eyes on. *Killers* are those wavy-lined cancels that leave no doubt that a cancellation has occurred. Fancy designs on cancellations are dubbed *obliterators.* *Slogan cancels* are sometimes pressed into service by post offices to celebrate anniversaries and other occasions, be they national, state, or local. Add one more type of cancel to this list: the one made by the human hand. Have you ever received a letter with a stamp on it, seemingly uncanceled, but with a pen mark through it? Well, that stamp's been legally canceled. A handmade slash by a postal employee is justified in some instances.

In the United States, you can use any unused stamp, no matter how old. But you may want to find out what it's worth before you use it!

Canceled-to-Order (CTO)

CTOs are mint issued stamps with the cancellation already on them. These stamps have never been in the mail, and they won't ever be. The cancels are applied to intact sheets of stamps during the printing process and are sold directly to dealers in the stamp trade.

Canceled-by-Favor (CFO)

If a collector, in any fashion, asks that a piece of his or her mail be canceled in a special manner, instead of letting nature run its course through the normal postal pilgrimage, this is called a CFO postmark. It is, in fact, a letter's trek that epitomizes the entire hobby of stamp collecting. You can't help but appreciate the fascinating breadth of stamp collecting and its many intriguing offshoots.

CHAPTER 6
Coins

*N*umismatics is the study of coins, paper money, tokens, and medals. If you are a coin collector, you are a *numismatist*. Broadly speaking, numismatics covers a wealth of items related to the world of finance. Stock certificates, checks, and other financial notes gather under the numismatic umbrella.

The History of Coins

Coins tell a story—an epic story in some cases. The coins minted throughout time mirror the vast and varied societies that have dotted planet Earth since the seventh century B.C. For it was in 650 B.C. that the coin was welcomed with open pockets into society.

The coin's origin can be traced to Lydia and Ionia in Asia Minor—today's Turkey. It was there that coins first appeared on the streets as instruments of monetary exchange, supplementing the *barter system* (in which one commodity was traded for another), which had existed since the day the human species learned to grunt. Gold, silver, and bronze coins were thereafter plentiful throughout antiquity. And it wasn't long after these coins started circulating in the marketplace that the word *money* was uttered for the first time. The world's never been quite the same since. Derived from the Latin *moneo,* which means "to warn," money talk became quite popular among the toga-wearing set.

The word *currency* also entered the vernacular at about the same time. From the Latin *currens,* which means "to run or flow," it shows us that some things never change, like money "flowing" from one person to another—from you to all your creditors.

FACTS

The first official U.S. coin ever issued was authorized by the Continental Congress in 1787. Typically referred to as the *fugio cent,* its design was influenced by Benjamin Franklin (and so it is often referred to as the *Franklin cent).* The word *fugio* (Latin for "I fly") is emblazoned on the coin's obverse.

Paper money didn't rear its pulpy head for another millennium, appearing first in China during the T'ang Dynasty in A.D. 650. And, believe or not, it took more than another millennium before paper money became the rage. It started popping up in the eighteenth century, then more so in the nineteenth century, and finally became the most accepted form of currency in the twentieth century, when it became evident to the moneymakers that it was cheaper to produce paper than coins. (Wood pulp and tree bark are slightly less costly than gold and silver.)

Planning Your Coin Collection

Coin collecting offers collectors many options. Some of the realms of coin collecting are covered in the following sections.

Historical Period

There are coins going far back in time. Collectors have opportunities to own pieces from Ancient History—the "ancients"—to the present, and that covers a whole lot of years.

FACTS

Many coins from ancient times are affordable to the average collector. This makes coin collecting somewhat unique in the hobby world. Think about it: A silver drachma issued during the reign of Alexander the Great (356–323 B.C.) could effortlessly be added to your collection tomorrow. For more information on ancient coins, check out *The Handbook of Ancient Greek and Roman Coins* by Zander H. Klawans.

Country of Origin

A specific country's issued coins is a popular mode of coin collecting. Collectors often narrow down their collections to coins from a particular time period in that country's history.

Series

Collecting coins issued in series—over a period of years—is another avenue coin collectors go down. An example is the U.S. Standing Liberty Quarter, produced from 1916 to 1930.

Type of Set

Some collectors concentrate their collecting efforts and resources on specific types of coins in date or group order. For example, they may focus on the Lincoln penny for their collection.

Commemoratives

Commemoratives are favorites in so many collectors' fields, and they're very appealing to coin collectors, who have a wide selection to choose from. Commemorative coin sets are regularly issued to honor outstanding individuals and momentous historical events.

Errors

Coins are no different from other collectibles, whether produced by man or by machine. Errors in the manufacturing process happen. Some collectors just love these errors.

Die Varieties

Some collectors base their collections on die varieties. For example, they may focus on certain coin impressions, sizes, and shapes.

Paper Money

Numismatics encompasses not only collecting coins, but paper money, too. Certain collectors chase paper currency—and there's plenty for them to chase.

ESSENTIALS At *www.coinclubs.com* you'll get access to community coin clubs and numismatic organizations, shows, and auctions nationwide. A visit to *www.coinlink.com* will link you up with even more coin-related sites, including associations, classified ads, facts and information, supplies, and grading services.

Evaluating a Coin's Condition

Some novice coin collectors labor under the false impression that a coin's overall condition is less important in their hobby than, say, a stamp's condition is in the world of philately. These misinformed individuals believe that a coin is a coin, so what are a few scratches and abrasions between friends? Nothing could be farther from the truth. A coin's condition is key to both its attractiveness and its value. The following sections cover some of the things to look for in evaluating a coin's condition.

**SSENTIALS**

Fingerprints alone can impact a coin's condition and grade. Excessive handling of coins leads to wear and spotting. Pick up your coins by their edges. Keep them away from your mouth and don't ever blow on them. Even a little moisture can damage a coin, particularly an older one.

Hairlines

Hairlines are the light scratches on a coin's *field* (the flat open area of the coin). They are caused by continual handling, inattentive cleaning, or contact with other objects.

Luster

Originally minted coins shine with a brilliance that diminishes with time and handling. The strength of the light reflected from the coin's surface tells a whole lot.

Tarnish

Tarnish is the natural aging process of a coin that often results in changes in its colors. A coin is not immune to the ravages of time.

Understanding the Grading System

If you plan on buying or selling coins in the marketplace, get to know the various grading tags that are attached to them and what the labels mean. The coin's grade, along with its scarcity and demand, is a key determinant in its value:

- Proof: Although the term *proof* refers to a method of manufacture, the term does double duty in describing a coin in its impeccable mint state.
- Mint state: A coin in mint state shows no trace of wear.
- Uncirculated: An uncirculated coin is nearly perfect, exhibiting no trace of wear, except perhaps some contact marks, surface spots, and diminished luster.
- Extra fine: an extra fine coin has sharp features overall, but the design of the coin is lightly worn with diminished luster.
- Very fine: The features of very fine coins are still sharp and well detailed, but the coins have moderate wear on the high points of the design, as well as diminished luster.
- Fine: The features of fine coins are still sharp and well detailed, but there is moderate to considerable wear throughout the coin's design, as well as diminished luster.
- Very good: The features of very good coins are still clear, but the coins are well worn and look flat.
- Good: The features of good coins are still visible, but they are faint in spots, and many of the coins' details are flat.
- Fair: A fair coin has very heavy wear, with portions of the coin's design worn smooth and parts of coin possibly even unreadable.

Some coin collectors utilize a brush or buffing wheel in an attempt to restore a coin's original luster. Sometimes this process, called *whizzing*, is performed to remove surface marks or scratches. It is frowned upon by most collectors, so steer clear of the practice.

Understanding Coin Terminology

Certain terms and phrases are quite unique to coin collectors. It's wise to familiarize yourself with them, because you'll come upon them frequently in the coin-collecting arena. In the following sections are some of the commonly used terms that are bandied about in the numismatic hobby.

 **SSENTIALS**

Scott Travers is a coin connoisseur who is dedicated to making certain that you, the collector, are not taken advantage of in the marketplace. His book, *The Insider's Guide to U.S. Coin Values*, provides a thorough listing of coin values, trends in the hobby, and an explanation of coin grades.

Alloy

An alloy is a combination of two or more metals.

ANA

ANA stands for the American Numismatic Association. They can be found online at *www.money.org*.

Bag Marks

Bag marks is a generic term that applies to scratch marks or minor abrasions on coins caused by contact with one another. The term is derived from the history of newly minted coins getting such boo-boos in their transport bags, as they made their way into circulation. However, coins can have bag marks on them without ever having spent a moment in a bag.

Base Metal

If it isn't gold, silver, or platinum, it's considered a base metal.

Bourse

Bourse refers to a gathering of dealers peddling their wares on tables at conventions and collector shows. You'll see this term used in relation to all kinds of collecting fields, not just coins.

Bronze

Since antiquity, many coins have been composed of predominantly copper, with small amounts of tin and zinc in the mixture. This alloy is known as *bronze*.

Bullion

Bullion is the word that identifies a metal that has yet to be made into coinage. It is also commonplace to see the term *bullion content* used to describe the total amount of gold and silver in a minted coin.

Bust

The *bust* is the portrait on a coin's *obverse* (front side). A bust, more specifically, means the head and upper portion of the shoulders. No full body images are called busts.

Casting

Casting is an alternative method to manufacturing coins. Casting does not involve the more widely used striking process. Instead, molten hot metal is poured into dies bearing a coin's intended design. The liquefied metal fills up the crevices of the die. When the metal cools and hardens, the finished coin is removed from its mold or cast.

Cracked Skull

Defective dies on occasion lead to visible lines on the coin's portrait or image's head. These defects are referred to as *cracked skulls*.

Cull

The word *cull* covers a lot of ground. It is applied to coins with serious damage, wear, or corrosion.

Device

Symbols of consequence that are used repeatedly on the reverse side of a coin—and often in association with a motto—are called *devices.* The American eagle, for example, is a device.

In a maneuver known as *sweating,* people put a bunch of coins in a sack and shake them in order to knock off bits from individual coins. The coins are then introduced back into circulation at face value. And the *sweaters* gather the bits of metals and turn a profit.

Die

In the numismatic world, a *die* is the metallic disc, which is engraved with the image, lettering, and dating that will transform a planchet into a coin. The planchet, or blank—in the position of meat in a sandwich—is simultaneously struck by two dies (one for the obverse side of the coin, and another for the reverse), resulting in the images being transferred onto it. The blank is then blank no more, but a coin.

Planchet

The *planchet,* also called a *blank,* is a flat metal disk, the size and weight of a finished coin. The planchet gets struck with die-cast imprints of a coin's overall image, lettering, and dating.

Toning

Toning refers to the color of a coin. There are various hues and patterns visible on most coins. Tonal changes are inevitable over time.

And so many variables affect a coin's coloring, from where it has been stored, to how it has been handled, to its exposure to the elements.

Starting and Adding to Your Collection

There are many places to find coins to start or add to your collection. Coin shops are obvious places to begin the search. Then there are coin shows, which offer plenty of choices, and often some very good bargains. Unlike a local shop, which sometimes operates like a mini-monopoly, dealers at shows are in competition with one another. A little competition is good for coin collectors.

The hobby magazines are rife with mail-order opportunities. Do your homework before ordering through the mail. Overgrading of coins is a common practice. Know the return policy—and it better be 100 percent satisfaction guaranteed—before ordering anything from a mail dealer. This goes for Web sites and Internet auctions, too. The scam artists, though in the minority, are intermingled with the legitimate businesses, so beware.

Coins magazine covers market trends, buying tips, and historical perspectives on coins. Subscription information is available at *www.krause.com/coins/cm*. *World Coin News*, the leading authority on the coins of the world, reports regularly on worldwide shows, providing in-depth historical backgrounds of many of its featured coins. Check out *www.krause.com/coins/wc* for information.

No matter where you are in your collection, joining a coin collecting society can be a benefit. You'll meet fellow collectors, trade with them, learn the ins and outs of the marketplace, and be less likely to take any wooden nickels. And you might make a friend, too.

CHAPTER 7
Autographs

We live in a culture in which movie and television stars, athletes, musicians, news anchors, millionaires, and political figures are like royalty. Autographs play an important part in the collector's world. There's nothing quite like getting an autograph from a notable. But this field is filled with frauds, and you need to know how to avoid them.

Knowing How Fakes Are Made

Autographs can be faked in numerous ways, which means that whenever you buy an autograph, you need to be especially sure that it's legitimate. In the following sections, I cover some key ways that autographs are faked, so you can know what to watch out for.

ESSENTIALS Autograph collectors should stop by *www.autographworld.com,* a UACC-registered dealer that runs autograph auctions, sells unsigned photographs, and has an amazingly comprehensive authentication guide. Just type in a famous person's name on its search engine, and you're more than likely to see what his or her signature looks like.

The Autopen

With the continuous and dramatic advances in technology over the past decades, it shouldn't come as any shock to you that a machine has been invented that can mechanically duplicate your exact signature. It's called the Autopen. The Autopen is an automated device that is programmed to simulate a precise signature. Anybody's John Hancock will do—any style; any length. A caveman's very unique "X" could be duplicated with cybernetic simplicity.

The Autopen, when called into action, can have any printing device inserted into its mechanical arm. From a ballpoint pen to a Sharpie marker, the Autopen works with the same tools that all of us use when writing letters and signing our names. An Autopenned photograph, or other piece of paper, looks as real as real can be. The best Autopens perform a job strikingly similar to the human hand.

The Autopen immediately positions a few hurdles for autograph collectors to leap over. Fortunately, though, there are often telltale signs of the fruit of an Autopen's labor. An Autopen has the propensity to appear shaky, much more so than the generally steady signature of flesh-and-blood men and women. The armature on the device vibrates when making a signature, and this creates subtle differences that usually can be detected.

If you are purchasing a celebrity's signature from a dealer, or have received one in the mail directly from the celebrity's address, check out some authentic autographs from the same person and compare yours with these. Autopens are consistent across the board. That's the thing about machines. A hundred Autopen autographs will all be alike. Sign your own name 100 times and see what happens. Not one of them will be exactly the same.

Other things to look for with Autopens are lines of identical thickness. Look again at those 100 signatures that you made. Actually, one will do. You'll notice that the lines in your signature vary. There aren't even the slightest variations from most Autopens.

Finally, look for signatures that begin and end with a dot of ink, where the mechanized arm lowers and raises—a sure sign of an Autopen. We the people are notorious for leaving "lift" marks when we come to the end of our signatures. The last letter, in fact, sometimes trails off into the sunset.

You can also check out magazines—such as the *Autograph Collector*—that keep collectors apprised of Autopen patterns. These magazines often print comparisons of real celebrity signatures alongside their evil twins.

FACTS

Politicians' autographs are easily attainable, even though many are the work of Autopens. Write to your senator in care of the U.S. Senate, Washington, DC 20510; your congressman in care of the U.S. House of Representatives, Washington, DC 20515; and the president in care of the White House, 1600 Pennsylvania Avenue NW, Washington, DC 20500.

Secretaries and Assistants

Some of the rich and famous walking among the common folks employ their trusty secretaries to sign their names on autograph picture requests. In fact, some secretaries are so devoted and loyal to their bosses that they seem, almost by osmosis, to be able to precisely replicate their signatures.

Perry Mason wouldn't have asked Della Street to sign his name, because he'd no doubt have seen the ethical problem there. Fooling an admirer just wasn't his style. Not everyone is of Mason's moral character, however. Secretary signatures are commonplace, with no machine marks as a giveaway. Sometimes called *ghost signatures,* these autographs have been known, on occasion, to be really good forgeries—so good that they've fooled even foremost autograph experts.

Most of these imitations, though, can be detected as not being the genuine article. For even when someone masters another's signature, he or she tends to be more deliberate when putting the pen to paper. If you've ever forged a signature in your time, you know how it feels. You're concentrating so much on getting the pattern right that you move with great deliberation. The end result is often a noticeable tick in the final product caused by the slower-than-normal motion. Once again, it's important to have real comparative signatures to look over.

QUESTIONS?

Which celebrities have their secretaries sign their autographs for them?
If you send away for autographs from celebrities such as Kevin Costner, Robert DeNiro, Al Pacino, Robert Redford, Barbra Streisand, and John Travolta, among others, you're likely to get one written by their assistants instead. Consider yourself warned.

Rubber Stamps

Before the invention of the Autopen, a common imitation autograph technique was accomplished with the venerable and reliable rubber stamp. Banks permit businesspersons to use signature rubber stamps when endorsing checks, and celebrities have been known to stamp photographs and postcards with them—or actually celebrities' hired hands have been known to do it.

Rubber-stamped signatures are the most easily detectable. There's a great deal of uneven ink distribution throughout them. If you've ever used a rubber stamp, for any reason at all, you've seen this. It can be quite messy—smudging all over the place. No directional strokes are seen in rubber-stamped signatures. When writing, the normal method of the human hand is to move from left to right. A rubber stamp descends from the air and meets its intended target in one fell swoop. You shouldn't have any problems identifying these signatures as rubber-stamped imitations.

ESSENTIALS

The Official Autograph Collector Price Guide by Kevin Martin shows a whole host of autographs along with their current market values. Also by Martin is *The Autograph Collector Celebrity Autograph Authentication Guide,* a book that offers many samples for you to compare your collected autographs with to verify their authenticity.

Preprints

Yet another machination that sometimes confuses autograph hunters is called the *preprint.* A preprint is simply a reproduction of an original signed photograph or letter. The signature on a preprint is flat. If there's any doubt in your mind as to whether or not a preprint is the real thing, hold the article in question up to a light. A genuine autograph will have been placed atop the photograph or letter. A preprinted autograph will be part of it. This will clearly show—one way or another—in reflected light.

Example of a "preprint" autograph— collectible, but not an actual autograph

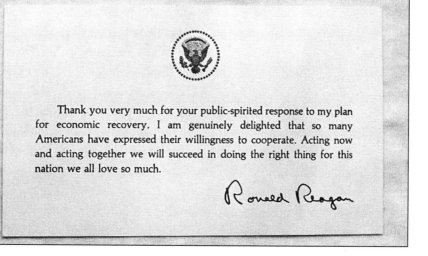

Thank you very much for your public-spirited response to my plan for economic recovery. I am genuinely delighted that so many Americans have expressed their willingness to cooperate. Acting now and acting together we will succeed in doing the right thing for this nation we all love so much.

Ronald Reagan

Getting a Certificate of Authentication and a Guarantee

These days, Certificates of Authenticity (COAs) flow like water through the collectible marketplace. They are most often offered by sellers—and requested by buyers—for items like autographs, where the authenticity may be in question. After all, who's to say that the autograph you are thinking about buying is real or a fake? How do you know that the seller is not one of those scam artists that you've heard so much about? You can never be 100 percent certain of an autograph's authenticity, unless, of course, you witness the signing in person. The best you can do is deal with honest, reliable sellers who back up everything they sell with a long track record of satisfied customers, and a no-strings-attached lifetime guarantee in the event that you discover that you purchased an imitation.

COAs are worth having from reputable sellers in the autograph business. On the other hand, a COA from the den of thieves is more flimsy than a roll of bargain paper towels. The FBI uncovered COA companies waist-deep in the sewer water, issuing fraudulent certificates on a litany of autographed items. Many of the companies involved in the scamming were prominent names in the COA business, too. This perfidy only adds to the collector's already weighty burden. Worrying about fakes and frauds is bad enough, but when known players in the industry are in on it, it creates a blanket of suspicion that can sometimes smother the joys of collecting.

Again, common sense and patience need to be practiced when shopping around for autographs, just like with everything else. Seeing a "handwritten letter by Abraham Lincoln" on eBay, with a COA from "Historical Authenticators, Ent." should immediately send up a few red flares:

- Complete letters written in the hand of Abraham Lincoln are hard to come by—to put it mildly.
- To be sure, there are valuable historical documents on eBay all the time, but it's items precisely like this that need to be thoroughly investigated.
- History Authenticators may not be a legitimate outfit, and at best needs to be researched.

Ethical dealers of autographs offer lifetime guarantees. Nothing short of this is acceptable in the autograph environs. Why isn't a thirty-day money-back guarantee sufficient? Because many counterfeit autographs are discovered years after their purchases. Often, it's an honest mistake by an honest dealer. Worthy dealers will refund your money at any point in time, provided you are still breathing and you satisfactorily prove to them that the autograph they sold to you is a forgery. That's just what the good guys and gals do.

 **SSENTIALS**

Some of the tried-and-true COAs in the autograph business come from PSA/DNA, Upper Deck Authenticated (UDA), Tri Star, Green Diamond, Steiner, and Superstar Sports. At PSA/DNA, three experts review every autograph they receive. When the autograph is certified authentic, it's marked with an invisible, synthetic, DNA-laced ink and tamper-evident label.

Understanding the Terminology

The autograph marketplace is loaded with acronyms and initials to describe various autographed items. If you're looking through autograph magazines, or combing the Internet auction sites looking for autographs, you will come upon these abbreviations:

- ALS: Autograph letter signed
- LS: Letter signed
- TLS: Typed letter signed
- DS: Document signed
- SP: Signed photograph
- B/W: Black and white
- CSP: Color signed photograph
- ANS: Autographed note signed
- ADS: Autographed document signed
- I: Inscribed (personalized)
- ISP: Inscribed signed photo

- CISP: Color inscribed signed photo
- AQS: Autographed quotation signed
- TTM: Through the mail
- UACC: Universal Autograph Collector's Club
- PP: Preprint

FACTS

Autograph collectors seek out celebrities. But do celebrities ever collect autographs? They are certainly in the best position to get in-person signatures—and there's no need for a Certificate of Authenticity. Jennifer Love Hewitt, a television and film star, is one celebrity who collects autographs of her fellow actors. And who can blame her? When you've worked in films with people like Sigourney Weaver and Gene Hackman, why not?

Deciding Which Autographs to Collect

Autograph collectors, like collectors in so many other hobbies, often collect autographed materials in precise categories. A fan of a particular celebrity might concentrate solely on collecting that star's autographs. Many collectors expand the field a bit and collect, for instance, classic TV stars only, from Lucille Ball to George Burns to Richard Boone. Other collectors refuse to buy an autograph and gather autographs of living beings only—and only through mail requests or in-person encounters.

Other collector themes range far and wide. Some devote their collector energies in seeking autographs exclusively from young female movie stars, aging male comedians, astronauts, politicians currently in office, 1969 World's Champions New York Mets players, jazz musicians, and so on. There's a bounty of autographs out there for collectors to gather, and a variety of ways to acquire them. In many instances, you don't have to pay for autographs. Other autographs can only be secured by parting with a few dollars. It's your call.

In any event, autographs are a stimulating collectible field. Collecting autographs is also one of the best hobbies around to get your children involved in. Have them write fan letters to their favorite TV characters or athletes. Letter writing will improve their communication skills. And for kids, really, there's no greater thrill than getting mail of their own, particularly pictures, perhaps even autographed, for them and them alone.

FACTS

Many collectors—young women, in particular—are after Leonardo DiCaprio's autograph, which sells in the range of $50 to $100. Microsoft founder Bill Gates recently paid $30.8 million for a handwritten notebook, once the property of another guy named Leonardo. Gates was more impressed with da Vinci.

Requesting Autographs from Your Favorite Celebrities

For the average autograph collector, the best method for acquiring an autograph is through the mail. In-person signings are the ultimate in autograph satisfaction. You know for certain what you're getting, and there's

Newsman David Brinkley's autographed photo

the added thrill that you experience in seeing your favorite celebrity in the flesh. These chance encounters, however, or even scheduled autograph signings, are quite rare.

Athletes now and then sign autographs at card shows. And some celebrities who write books—or more likely have them ghost-written—appear at bookstores to tout their titles. Neither of these two options offer fans and admirers much of an opportunity to shake hands or make small talk with their idols. Card shows and book signings, in general, are coldly impersonal cattle shows, where fans pay top dollar for an autograph, wait in a long line, and are paraded along like herds of cattle heading off to slaughter.

This sober reality leaves fans with only one viable alternative to get an autograph of their favorite star. The old-fashioned letter, dropped in the snail mailbox, is still the best route to take, short of purchasing an autograph. This is one area where e-mail won't ever do as a substitute. Autopens and secretarial signatures are commonplace, however, not to mention the most deflating response of them all—no response.

ESSENTIALS

The Standard Guide to Collecting Autographs: A Reference & Value Guide by Mark Allen Baker is the best at bringing together the fundamental elements of the autograph hobby. Facsimile signatures, a "most sought-after" section, and the values of autographs are some of the topics covered in the book.

That said, a mail request is still the cheapest and easiest way to get a real autograph from a star. Believe it or not, many people have gotten the genuine article back from their screen idol, favorite politician, astronaut, or sports hero. It's worth making the effort, because it's not really a big effort at all. On the contrary, it is at once fun and exciting. So what if you get an Autopenned item back from time to time, or a preprint, or nothing at all? If at first you don't succeed, try, try again. In the following sections, I offer some tips for requesting autographs from your favorite stars.

Address Your Letter Properly

Always begin a letter with the proper salutation, and if the person you are writing to has a title, use it. A letter to Henry Kissinger, for example, should be addressed to "Dr. Kissinger." In a letter to comedian Jim Carrey, "Jim" will do.

FACTS

George Burns and Jimmy Stewart both signed many autographs for many fans. The result is that their autographs are plentiful and relatively cheap. On the other hand, Marilyn Monroe's autograph is a hard find—and an expensive one at that. And if you're looking for something really unusual, search for an autograph from Apache Chief Geronimo, who was at the 1904 World's Fair, signing his name on small cards for attendees. These hard-to-come-by Geronimo autographs sell for over $5,000 today.

Write a Personal Letter

Say something in the letter to let the celebrity know that you are a big fan. Give it a unique, personal twist. Mention an oddball piece of trivia or observation that'll let the recipient know that you are more than just a garden-variety admirer, but a fan to the core. Of course, don't go overboard in this department. You don't want to come across as a fruitcake and potential stalker. Conclude the letter and request for the autograph with a *please* and *thank you* and a few words about how much you appreciate your favorite star taking the time to answer you.

Don't Mention That You Collect Autographs

Collect is a commendable word in this book. But it's a four-letter word in many celebrities' eyes, who associate it with dealers looking for their signatures to sell, or they view the request as just a collector's pursuit of another autograph—one of many. The reality is that there are a lot of autograph sellers who do exactly what you are being instructed to do. And they all have dollar signs in their eyes.

FACTS

The Universal Autograph Collectors Club (UACC) at *www.uacc.org* is the preeminent club in the hobby. UACC keeps collectors abreast of autograph news and has its own constitution and code of ethics; those who break the rules are inducted into the UACC Hall of Shame. UACC also publishes an autograph show schedule. One of its best features is its Registered Dealer Program. Sellers of autographs who meet their criteria are accredited, which helps autograph seekers in finding aboveboard sellers.

Keep It Short

Don't write a letter that's longer than one page. Celebrities get an awful lot of mail and are more apt to read short letters. There's no need to write a novella of a letter, because it probably won't be read. As Shakespeare wrote, "Brevity is the soul of wit."

Here's a sample fan letter requesting an autograph, for you to mimic if you so desire. This is a letter sent to the king of insult humor, comedian Don Rickles.

Dear Mr. Rickles:

I have been a fan of yours for many years. You've made me laugh like no other comedian. I've also enjoyed your work as an actor in both television and the movies. From your hilarious appearances on *F Troop* as Bald Eagle, to your both amusing and moving performance in *Kelly's Heroes,* you've entertained me for over three decades. I thought your own TV show, *CPO Sharkey,* was one of the funniest of all time. I've also had the good fortune of seeing your hilarious stage act. Today's current crop of comedians can't shine your shoes—in my humble opinion.

If at all possible, could you please send me an autographed photo of yourself? I'd greatly appreciate it. Thank you for this consideration and for all your work through the years. Please, don't ever retire! Entertainers of your caliber come by once in a lifetime.

Sincerely,
Andy Superfan

The letter is short, courteous, and touches all the necessary bases. Andy Superfan succinctly exhibits his impressive knowledge of Don Rickles's career by citing his guest appearances on the 1960s sitcom *F Troop*. Only a true fan would remember and note this in a letter. The fan is complimentary, but not overly sycophantic.

Include a Self-Addressed Stamped Envelope

Including a self-addressed stamped envelope (SASE) with your letter will dramatically increase your chances of getting a return response! Provide a 9 × 12-inch envelope with a first class stamp plus at least one additional ounce stamp or two just to be safe. This will cover the cost of a photograph and even a piece of cardboard to keep the picture from bending.

Include a Specific Item to Be Signed

If you want, you can include your own celebrity picture or another item to be signed. Don't include more than one item per request. What you insert is up to you. Just factor in the possibility that you might not get a response back, so you could lose the item you sent along with the letter. It also costs a little more in postage to both send your own celebrity photograph and to have it returned with your SASE. And if you get no response, you lose both the insert and the cost of the return postage.

Keep Track of Your Requests

Keep a thorough list of all your autograph requests. Make note of what, if anything, you sent to be autographed, what came back, and how long it took to be returned. Ultimately, your autograph requests will fall into one of these three categories:

- No response or wrong address
- A response, but no autograph
- A response with an autograph

If you get what you are hoping for, you need to figure out whether or not it's the real thing or an imitation. If you're just planning on hanging it on your wall or putting it in your autograph album, assume it's real and enjoy it. If you'll sell it someday, verifying its authenticity is more important.

FACTS

Some actors refuse to sign autographs, or rarely sign them. Marlon Brando, throughout his entire acting life, has signed few autographs. So his John Hancock is considered a tough find—and it costs more than a few pennies when it's located. Brando autographs are regularly seen in online auctions. Seeing is disbelieving in this case. If you spot a Brando autograph for sale, it's most likely a phony.

To track down the addresses of your favorite celebrities, a comprehensive free site for addresses of celebrities in all fields can be found at *www.stararchive.com.* This site is an autograph hunter's heaven. Other sources include address lists for sale from *www.old-pete.com* and *www.celebritylocators.com,* which offer various lists, including specifically targeted addresses of sex symbols and TV celebrities. There are many sources of celebrity addresses on the Internet. Search around. You'll find many that are freebies, and some with sellers charging for complete address lists.

Always keep in mind that with these address lists—even the best ones—a portion of the specific addresses will be outdated. We live in a very mobile society. And nobody moves more often than the wealthy and the famous. Don't get discouraged. Sometimes celebrity autographs take many months, even years, to get returned to you. A collector's mail request for actor Harrison Ford's autograph took five years, but he got it—and it was genuine. Don't write off a request as a "no response" too quickly.

Caring For and Displaying Your Autographs

Caring for your autographs is essential. Actually, caring for your autographs is even more essential because of the unique nature of this collectible. Autographs are in essence ink marks—or, in some cases, pencil marks—made by human beings on an endless parade of paper, photographs, and other items. These marks are made with the assistance of various writing instruments dispensing ink. If you have used a pen or magic marker at some point in your life, then you know that ink—in a variety of ways—does not always treat its target in the kindest ways. Sometimes it smears, and often it fades with time. Indeed, a lot can happen to a signature, so it behooves you, the collector, to do everything humanly possible to protect your autographs from the slings and arrows that have been known to ravage them.

Direct sunlight and your autographs are not the marrying kind. Even minimal exposure to the sunlight's rays can fade a signature on a photograph or destroy a handwritten document—and shockingly fast! Fluorescent lighting even damages autographs!

Never apply glue to the back of an autographed item of any kind. Lots of collectors build autograph scrapbook albums, and some paste their signed photographs into them—a bad idea. Over time, glue is an autograph's assassin, because it destroys the paper and ultimately the writing on it—your autograph. And if someday you wanted to remove it from the album, it wouldn't be possible.

FACTS

Sometimes autograph frauds are laughable. One such eBay "autograph" on auction featured a "Ronald Reagan" signature on a preprint card that read "Nancy and I appreciate very much your support of me and the conservative cause." The president's initials, "R.R.," ended the note. A supposed "genuine" signature was then affixed on the bottom of the card: "Ronald Regan." The counterfeiter didn't even know how to spell Reagan's name.

The most common autograph-displaying mechanism is the old reliable glass frame. Signed photographs and other items from autograph collections decorate many collectors' walls. Depending on what part of the country, or world you call home, this could lead to deterioration of your prized collectibles. High temperatures and humidity are not friends of paper, particularly paper containing acid from wood pulp. The unsightly result of too much heat and humidity is *foxing,* those unsightly brown spots that, on occasion, pop up on autographed photos and documents. A framed photo even sticks to the glass sometimes. An autograph sticking to glass is not a happy union. In general, a cool, dry area is the best place for a framed photograph to hang. Better still, when enclosing an autograph of any kind in a glass frame—either on a photograph or some other document or paper—you should utilize an acid-free backing and Plexiglas or museum glass.

The most common method of displaying autographs is in three-ring binders. Autographs placed first in Mylar clear acetate folders, which are acid-free, and then in a binder, makes for an easy and comfortable way to thumb through your collection at any moment in time. It's also a way to show off your collection to friends and relatives. Just pass them the binder.

Some autograph collectors go the matting route. Framing shops are adept at enshrining and protecting your autographed photographs and other signed materials. They are educated in what best protects items enclosed behind frames.

A place worth checking out for autographed photo sheet protectors, acid-free paper inserts, binders, and so much more is Light Impressions, one of the world's largest suppliers of archival storage, display, and presentational materials. Museums use them, and so do average collectors in a wide cross-section of hobbies. Visit them online at *www.lightimpressionsdirect.com,* or call 800-828-6216

Knowing What an Autograph Is Worth

Some autographs are very valuable. Again, that means that somebody's willing to pay a lot of money to own a scrap of paper, photograph, or document with another's signature or handwriting on it. There are only six verified examples of William Shakespeare's autograph in existence. If you are one of the ultra-lucky ones, you've got a pretty valuable collectible there. Hold on to it and protect it with your dear life.

ESSENTIALS

If you want to get involved in the autograph hobby, join clubs and visit Web sites and forums devoted to the art of collecting signatures. Listening to the experiences of others will help you immensely in your own collecting efforts. Learn from others' mistakes, but also from their successes.

It's probably a safe bet that you don't have one of the Shakespeare Six, so let's address the autographs that you do own, and what determines their desirability—and value—in the hobby. In the following section, I cover some of the significant factors that determine an autograph's overall worth.

Scarcity

Scarcity in autograph circles, like everywhere else in the collectibles world, enhances an autograph's value. It's the law of supply and demand again. Needless to say, a scarce autograph from a nobody that nobody wants is not valuable, even if it's as scarce as scarce can be.

For certain, any person's death enhances the value of his or her autograph. Why? Because the deceased are not ever going to put pen to paper again and scribble a signature or write a letter. Immediately after a celebrity dies, there is a finite supply of his or her autographs in circulation.

Material

What your autograph rests on plays an important part in its ultimate value. Generally speaking, an 8- × 10-inch signed photograph is worth more than a 3- × 5-inch photograph. A signature on a scrap of paper, on the other hand, is worth less than one on a 3- × 5-inch photograph. This is because the most common autograph is usually scribbled on something thrust at a celebrity somewhere. Hence, they are ordinarily more plentiful than, say, a photograph—and less valuable because of this.

Historical Importance

The most priceless autographs are often intact documents. Signed handwritten letters from the famous folks throughout time are prized, and especially so if there's some fascinating content in the document or letter, or something of historical significance.

Darkness

Signatures or handwritten materials that are bold and dark are worth more than their hard-to-decipher, light counterparts. Pencil signatures are obviously less appealing than are their brothers in ink. Pencil marks, for one, fade away through time faster than Douglas MacArthur's "old soldiers."

Condition

Regardless of the item that your autograph's attached to, it's better that it be in good shape than bad shape. (Now that's a startling pronouncement!) Taking care of your autograph collection and avoiding, as best you can, the pitfalls that befall autographs will greatly enhance both its value and eye-catching appeal. Tears on autographed photographs and documents diminish their overall value, even if it doesn't impact on the writing itself; so do creases and staining of any kind. Then, of course, there's the signature and writing proper and how it's held up with time. Any smearing or fading in it diminishes its desirability to fellow collectors, never mind to you.

FACTS

Fan letters mailed to the late Cesar Romero's home on San Vincente Boulevard in Los Angeles were always answered. One fan sent Mr. Romero a "Bat Laffs" trading card—featuring Romero as the Joker—in hopes of having it autographed. To his surprise, he received a postcard from Maria Romero, Cesar's sister, informing him that Cesar would be happy to sign his card when he returned from appearing in a dinner theater production in Texas. Now that's going beyond the call of duty!

CHAPTER 8
Political Memorabilia

America is not only the land of the free and the home of the brave, it is a sanctuary for collectors of all stars and stripes. But can anything be more quintessentially American than Americans collecting things firmly rooted in American soil? Americana, as it's called, encompasses all materials and characteristics that are American in nature. In this chapter, we start with political memorabilia. In Chapters 9, 10 and 11, other types of Americana collections will be mentioned.

The History of Political Collectibles

The never-ending story of the American political campaign is a blessing for one group of people: collectors in the hobby that celebrates and preserves our American political heritage. I'm talking about political-items collectors, a hearty breed of well-informed patriots.

Standing on the steps of Federal Hall in New York City in 1789, George Washington put his hand on the Bible and was sworn in as the first president of the fledgling United States. It was inevitable that commemorative articles and souvenirs of some kind would soon follow. Items honoring Washington's ascendancy to the highest office in the land did, in fact, hit the streets. Various tankards and pitchers, as well as brass clothing buttons with Washington's revered image and the words "Long live the president!" were manufactured throughout the young nation to honor the father of the country.

ESSENTIALS

If you are interested in collecting items from the American political scene, the first place you should check out is the American Political Items Collectors (APIC) at *www.apic.ws*. This organization provides you with a wealth of information on the hobby, including its history, lingo, and links.

Medalets, or tokens, turned up some thirty-five years later during the hotly contested 1824 national campaign between the dour John Quincy Adams and Battle of New Orleans hero Andrew Jackson. Their grudge match in 1828, with Jackson doing combat this time with the incumbent President Adams, also generated campaign goodies, along with a heaping helping of rancor. These two presidential contests were the first of their kind to feature partisan political materials advocating the election of one particular candidate over another, a precursor of things to come. In addition to tokens, there were garment buttons, flasks, plates, ribbons, and bandanas that dotted the campaign landscape and were gobbled up by the politically charged minions. Many of these historical campaign materials are available in today's hobby trade.

It was 1840, however, which gave birth to the modern campaign, the kind that we all know and love. When Whig candidates William Henry Harrison and John Tyler provoked such fevered support in their effort to unseat the aristocratic Martin Van Buren, the excitement manifested itself in parades, rallies, and more and more campaign trinkets—which trickled down into the hands of John Q. Citizen. This hard-fought election also marked the birth of organized rallies and the introduction of silk ribbon badges, posters, cloth banners, snuff boxes, silk bandanas, and Sandwich glass cup plates—all plugging political candidates. Harrison and Tyler supporters were overjoyed at getting their hands on the bounty of souvenirs from such an exhilarating electoral show, which, by the way, they won.

Four years later, in 1844, lapel contrivances with paper portraits encased behind glass and pewter frames, and some of the first multicolored lithograph prints became a part of political Americana. Lithographs featuring the likenesses of James K. Polk and his running mate George M. Dallas were marketed by a man named Nathaniel Currier, and later by the partnership of Currier and Ives. Now that's a familiar name in collectors' circles!

Other uncommon political materials sprouted up in the mid-1800s. Pocket hand mirrors made of pewter, with the images of 1848 Whig Zachary Taylor and 1852 Democrat Franklin Pierce, both of whom were subsequently elected president, were manufactured for their campaigns. Attractive campaign pieces from the time include lacquered wooden cigar cases with colorful representations of the presidential candidates in their maximum splendor.

Indeed, the images of the presidential candidates portrayed in this period in American history were often sensationalist and heroic, with wartime accomplishments exaggerated beyond recognition, and other biographical tidbits blown way out of proportion, or sometimes created out of thin air. Abraham Lincoln as the rail-splitter from humble, rustic roots is a prime example of the images that the political consultants of the day erected for politicians. Lincoln did spend his early years living in a log cabin, but that's where rural families lived in those days. He wasn't dirt poor. Yes, he did split fence rails in Illinois for a short time, but he'd been a practicing lawyer and a politician for decades, far removed from his verdant prairie days by the time he was running for president.

Fortunately, in this instance at least, the campaign worked like a charm in introducing "Honest Abe" Lincoln to the American people. And it was only fitting that the 1860 election campaign introduced, too, the ferrotype lapel pin. The ferrotype lapel pin was not assembled on a printing press, but rather by a photographic process of exposing a light-receptive surface to a photo negative, then developing the image on a tin sheet. Multiple images were then fashioned from the one sheet, individually cut, with each image mounted in its own brass shell. And lo and behold, a bunch of nifty-looking campaign pins were born.

Political postcards for Richard Nixon and John F. Kennedy

So, with the most contentious and important election in American history—with four major presidential candidates doing battle on the eve of the Civil War—the most significant visual innovation for a campaign pin simultaneously saw the light of day. These pins, with the likenesses of Lincoln, Stephen Douglas, John C. Breckinridge, and John Bell, are the first of their kind somewhat resembling the popular political buttons that would dominate the twentieth century and so many subsequent political-items collections.

The 1860 election also witnessed the increasing popularity of torchlight parades. With more of these boisterous political events coming to towns all across the country, more and more campaign ephemera were produced. Americans relished showing their support for candidates with pins and ribbons of all kinds. Ferrotypes from this time period are trading in today's hobby. They don't come cheap, but they are exceptional and attractive pieces from both a thrilling and tragic epoch in American history. Some of the smaller Lincoln ferrotypes (tintype, photo badges, for instance) can be purchased for anywhere between $400 and $600. Common ribbons with Lincoln's portrait on them usually sell in the range of $1,000 to $2,000.

FACTS

In 1973, President Nixon signed into law the Hobby Protection Act, which states that copies of collectibles, such as buttons and other memorabilia, must be clearly marked as "reproductions," or a comparable term, and in a conspicuous place for all to see. Imitations are a very real problem in many collectibles fields today, and if you have reason to believe you've been had by a violator of this act, or if you just have a question about a particular clause of this act, write to: HOBBY, Special Assistant for Enforcement, Bureau of Consumer Protection, Federal Trade Commission, Washington, DC 20580.

Making Sense of All Those Slogans

Political pins are embellished with many acronyms and slogans. If you encounter these pins in your button hunt, the following sections let you know what they mean.

100 Million Buttons Can't Be Wrong

The 1940 Wendell Willkie presidential campaign saw a slew of pins hit the streets advocating his election over FDR, who was seeking an unprecedented third term. This curious slogan played off of this bounteous fact.

16 to 1

A catchphrase from the 1896 campaign and the currency controversy, which specifically referred to the weight ratio of silver to gold that proponents of this particular coinage course advocated (16 ounces of silver to 1 ounce of gold).

ABJ

ABJ stands for "Any But Johnson." LBJ was President Lyndon Baines Johnson.

ADA

ADA is the acronym for Americans for Democratic Action, an advocacy group best known for publishing scorecards on politicians and rating them on issues that they deem liberal litmus tests. The more of our money a politician spends, the higher his or her score.

AFSCME

AFSCME stands for the American Federation of State, County, and Municipal Employees. How's that for a mouthful?

AuH$_2$O

Remember the periodic table? The one we all had to memorize in high school? Au is the symbol for the element gold; H$_2$O, for water. Gold plus water equals Goldwater, as in Barry Goldwater, 1964 Republican presidential candidate.

Christian in the White House

This was an anti–Al Smith slogan from the election of 1928. Smith was the first Catholic candidate nominated by a major political party, and this fact had a portion of the electorate—who didn't consider Catholics to be Christians—shaking in their boots.

Convict 2253/9653

In 1918, Socialist Eugene V. Debs, a perennial presidential candidate, was convicted and jailed for violating the Espionage Act. In 1920, while serving his sentence, and with a convict number to call his own, he ran for president from his jail cell, or cells, hence the two different numbers from two different penitentiaries.

Eugene and Gene

This was a button for 1968 anti–Vietnam War Democratic presidential primary hopeful Eugene McCarthy. Presumably this informality was an attempt to portray McCarthy as a regular guy, which the poetry-writing, detached pol unmistakably wasn't.

HHH

HHH stood for Hubert Horatio Humphrey. Humphrey was the 1968 Democratic presidential nominee.

I Want to Be a Captain Too

This was an anti-FDR pin from 1940. It referred to the special treatment given to the president's son, who was appointed a Captain in the U.S. Army.

No Man Is Good Three Times

This was a pin that expressed opposition to a third term for FDR. It was used to support his opponent, Wendell Willkie.

Remember October 9

This was an anti-Nixon, pro–George McGovern rallying cry. It referred back to a campaign speech Nixon had made on that date in 1968, in which he said that no man should be re-elected as president if he didn't end the Vietnam War in his first term.

Starting a Collection

Collectors of political memorabilia have many paths open to them in shaping a collection. Collect what grabs you—that's the direction to take in

Richard Nixon re-election poster

this hobby. Be aware, though, that in the here and now, there are more and more items being manufactured specifically for the political memorabilia collector, and not—as was the case in the past—for the campaign enthusiast at the rally, or the devoted worker in the headquarters. In addition to this fact, a somber trend emanating from many political campaigns is the replacement of buttons with stickers. Attend a political rally these days and you will more than likely see stickers anchored to people's clothing, where buttons used to be. It's obviously cheaper to produce stickers, and campaigns aren't overly concerned about what a blow this is to political button collectors.

The nation needs coolness more than clarion calls; intelligence more than charisma; a sense of history more than a sense of histrionics.

Political ephemera: Yesterday's sign—today's collectible

This isn't to imply that new collectors should be discouraged. Not at all. Join campaigns, visit headquarters, write to candidates requesting pins, stickers, and literature, and you can start building a collection with virtually no monetary investment. This is, after all, how many collections get off the ground.

General

No, not collecting generals, although you could do that (Washington, Grant, Eisenhower, and so on) if you so desired. I'm talking about getting

1952
Eisenhower-
Nixon
campaign
brochure

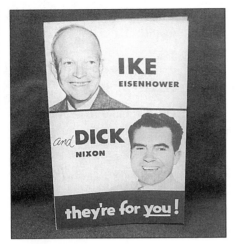

a representative piece or two (or three or four) from as many of the national campaigns as possible. This is the route numerous collectors choose, and for good reason. Many older political items are readily obtainable and fairly priced. The more common pin-backs from 1896 to the present are available to average collectors each and every day in hobby papers, online auctions, and at trade shows.

Your Favorite Son

Franklin D.
Roosevelt
small plaque
(1932)

Some collectors acquire as many buttons and other memorabilia from the campaigns of their favorite politician or political champion as they can. The American Political Items Collectors (APIC) has separate chapters specifically devoted to collectors of Ronald Reagan items, JFK items, and so on.

State and Local

Collectors attached to their hometown or state, or the place of their birth, sometimes devote their collecting energies to congressmen from their district, senators and governors from their state, or mayors from their city. There are many state and local offshoot collector groups within the APIC.

Jugates

Collectors, in general, love *jugates,* which are the buttons, posters, and related items that feature two candidates, most often the presidential and vice-presidential party nominees. Two heads are better than one.

Trigates, by the way, have three candidates on them—often the national ticket duo joined by a state or local candidate, who hopes to boost his or her chances by riding on their coattails.

ESSENTIALS

The Political Bandwagon and *The Political Collector* are both monthly papers that feature classified and display advertising. For a sample copy, send $1.00 to *The Political Collector*, P.O. Box 5171, York, PA 17405. Contact *The Political Bandwagon* at P.O. Box 348, Leola, PA 17540, or e-mail them at *polbandwgn@aol.com.*

Understanding the Terminology

There are several terms that are bandied about in the hobby all the time. You should be aware of these if you plan on wading into the collecting of political items, or are already knee-deep in collecting them.

FACTS

Tokens, medals, and scrip are classified as *exonumia.* And many political-items collectors collect exonumia in the form of campaign medals. *Scrip,* by the way, is any document used as evidence that the holder or bearer is entitled to receive something. Scrip has often proved worthless to its bearers. But collectors today aren't much concerned with the poor souls who got stuck with worthless scrip; they are concerned with whether the scrip has any value as a collectible.

Ambrotype

When a positive photo image is made on glass and set against a dark backdrop, this is called an *ambrotype.* Ambrotypes in political campaigns were very popular in the mid-nineteenth century.

Brummagem

The counterfeits in political memorabilia are often christened *brummagems.*

Campaign ephemera brochures: Anderson, Carter, Wallace, Ford, and Nixon

Carte-de-Visite (CDV)

Very widespread in the 1860s, with many picturing President Lincoln, CDVs are small portrait photographs that measured 2½" × 4¼" and were not—contrary to their name—regularly dispensed as visiting cards. They were too expensive to have them made for that.

Fob

The ornament on the end of a pocket watch chain is called a *fob*. Fobs have long been used in political campaigns. Often you'll see the description *watch fob* to identify an item.

Hopeful

This upbeat word is frequently attached to candidates and their campaign-related materials. Hopefuls are candidates who were long on hope and short on success, who didn't win their party nominations for the job they sought.

O'Clock

To button collectors in any hobby, this description is used to indicate where a defect or mark is located on the button proper. "A smudge at six o'clock" tells you where to look on the button and what to expect when you get there. Of course, knowing how to tell time helps.

Sepia

A photographic image with a brown tone, instead of the more common black tone, is referred to as *sepia.*

Stud

An item that's specifically been designed to be worn through a lapel buttonhole is a *stud.*

FACTS

You might remember those little tin clicker toys from your youth, also known as *crickets* because they sound something like the melodious insect. The 1972 President Nixon reelection campaign produced a clicker that read, "Click With Dick." The most historically important clickers, however, were the ones used in the D-Day invasion of Normandy. As the mass parachuting effort scattered soldiers literally all over the map, they were instructed to use their clickers when they heard someone approaching. A clicker rejoinder would indicate a friend; no response, a foe.

CHAPTER 9
Coca-Cola and Beer Memorabilia

Another part of the Americana collectibles centers around beverages—Coca-Cola and various beers. In this chapter, I give you a history of this collecting arena and let you know how you can get involved.

Coca-Cola Collectibles

Coca-Cola conjures up images of a summer's afternoon at the ballpark, a festive Christmas party, and having a hot dog at the zoo. The soda pop's image is in the same league as moms and apple pie. Even Norman Rockwell illustrations and the drink are associated with one another, and these works from America's more drowsy past are much more uplifting and visually appealing than the muddle of colors and shapes called "modern art." Coca-Cola knows no season of the year, no particular epoch, and no geographical locale. For these reasons, Coca-Cola tastes so sweet to so many collectors in so many different places.

FACTS

Pepsi-Cola collectibles are gobbled up by an unwavering group of aficionados of Coke's chief rival in the soda pop war. Pepsi traces its roots back in time almost as far as Coke. Created by a waggish North Carolina pharmacist named Caleb Bradham, his 1898 popular concoction was initially called "Brad's drink." Pepsi is in the history books for being the first company to record an advertising jingle. Called "Nickel, Nickel," this ditty so captured the public's fancy that it became a hit record.

The History of Coca-Cola

In 1886 an Atlanta druggist named Dr. John S. Pemberton invented Coca-Cola. Pemberton, a former Confederate officer, initially marketed his syrup as a "brain and nerve tonic," which he sold to drugstores. First-year sales for Coca-Cola totaled a whopping $50, offset by advertising expenses of $73.96. Despite the financial loss suffered, the stage was being set for bigger things—much bigger things.

Legend has it that in Coca-Cola's first summer on the market, a customer with a splitting headache walked into a local drugstore, which fortuitously stocked the sweet-tasting syrup, then sold mixed with water. This particular day, the story goes, when the restless customer asked the clerk on duty to prepare him a Coca-Cola drink, the intrepid counterman suggested trying soda water with the syrup, in lieu of the usual tap water.

And so Coca-Cola, the carbonated drink, was born, courtesy of a man with a migraine and a soda jerk's whimsical ingenuity. If it's not true, it sure ought to be.

In 1888 a man named Asa Griggs Candler bought into the Coca-Cola business. The company's ailing founder Dr. Pemberton died later that year. In a few years time, Candler consolidated his hold on the company. He was a hands-on owner after that, who oversaw the entire Coca-Cola production process with an eagle's eye. The Coca-Cola mystery formula was christened "7X," and only a trusted few knew what went into making the increasingly popular soda drink. Candler incorporated Coca-Cola, registered a trademark on its famous script, and sold stock in the company, paying the first dividends to shareholders in 1893.

In 1894, Joseph A. Biedenharn, owner of the Biedenharn Candy Company in Vicksburg, Mississippi, bottled Coca-Cola for the first time. Five years later, the bottling process went big time when two Tennessee businessmen purchased the rights to bottle and sell Coca-Cola nationwide. It cost them one whole dollar for the privilege.

In 1904, bottled and on the move, Coca-Cola was widely advertised as more than mere relief for headaches and frazzled nerves. The "For Headache and Exhaustion" company moniker was a thing of the past. Now it was "Coca-Cola Satisfies."

Candler was a genuine visionary who recognized the tremendous potential of Coca-Cola. He creatively promoted his product, producing fans, calendars, trays, and other items depicting buxom women relishing the cool, gratifying drink. This offbeat approach to advertising was a harbinger of the countless promotions that were on tap over the next century. And more promotions meant more goodies for collectors of Coca-Cola memorabilia, who early on took a shine to the drink and its larger-than-life appeal.

In 1929, soon after pioneer Asa Griggs Candler's death, his heirs sold their sizeable interest in the Coca-Cola Company to Ernest Woodruff and a group of investors for $25 million. To put it mildly, the Coca-Cola enterprise had grown considerably since the first day it was sold as a nickel-a-glass soda fountain drink at Jacob's Pharmacy in Atlanta, Georgia.

For the better part of the twentieth century, the Coca-Cola Company has been cognizant of the mystical grip it has on the American populace. And so, they've issued collectible items through the years designed specifically for collectors as well as for the mere drinkers of Coke, too. Their collectible items complement the vast amounts of Coca-Cola memorabilia in the marketplace. We're talking about everything from advertisements to bottles, clocks to cans, pins to signs, and tins to trucks.

FACTS

The inventor of Coca-Cola syrup, Dr. John Pemberton, did not originate its now-famous name. It was his bookkeeper, Frank Robinson, who suggested the sweet-tasting syrup be dubbed "Coca-Cola." He took the main ingredients used in the production process, the African kola nut and coca leaves, and combined the words. With a little editing, the rest is history. Robinson also thought the Coca-Cola script, which he neatly penned, would look great in advertisements and other promotions.

What People Collect

Why collect Coca-Cola items? Coca-Cola transcends its product. It's a lot more than just a line of soda pop. Coca-Cola memorabilia in collections is a byproduct of what Coca-Cola means to its collectors. Sure, it tastes good, but there's more to its appeal than that. Coca-Cola is a conduit for memories of good times and interesting places.

Coca-Cola collecting is open to everybody. It doesn't matter where you live or what your bank account looks like; you can collect Coca-Cola materials. Coca-Cola is everywhere imaginable, and collecting its cans and bottles is not an expensive undertaking, unless, of course, you want it to be.

The remarkable qualities of Coca-Cola, beyond its secret formula, are that it is perpetually introducing memorabilia into the marketplace. Commemorative cans and bottles plus related premiums are regularly linked to sporting events, charitable causes, and national celebrations. From Major League Baseball opening days to the international spectacle of the Olympics, Coca-Cola is there. From NASCAR auto racing moments to feting the Statue of Liberty on her birthday, count on Coca-Cola being on the scene. Coke has even found its way to political conventions and noted its attendance there on its bottles and cans. Thirsty delegates not only had political memorabilia to take home, but Coca-Cola collectibles as well. And Coca-Cola celebrates itself, too, as it did during its centennial anniversary in 1986.

What this all means is that the average collector can acquire Coke materials rather easily. And these commemorative inspired bottles, cans, and other stuff are, by their very nature, limited in quantity. Hence, some of these items—even recent ones—appreciate in value quickly. It's all about supply and demand again.

So, you don't have to collect vintage pieces of Coca-Cola memorabilia, some of which are quite expensive. In fact, much of the earliest Coke-related collectibles—from trays to advertising signs—are priced well beyond the reach of the typical collector. However, since Coke's been so prolific in its promotions through time, not to mention its soda production, there are ample opportunities and avenues for collectors to pick up a fair sampling of Coke bottles and other materials from the past century.

ESSENTIALS

The genuine Coca-Cola pricing guide is *Petretti's Coca-Cola Collectibles Price Guide* by Allan Petretti. This is a large and expensive book, but worth the price if you collect or plan to collect vintage Coke from the 1880s through the 1960s. It's worth buying this book just to see the pictures—over 6,000 in full color!

Bottle Collecting

Hundreds of different Coke bottles were introduced through the years. They come in different sizes and shapes, and some highlight events. This is surely the most popular Coca-Cola collecting avenue. It's expansive, but not necessarily expensive.

Coca-Cola bottle collecting places a high premium on condition. A bottle's condition is as key to bottle collectors as any other collectible's condition is to their respective collectors. If you happen upon a bottle—vintage or recent—that captures your fancy, study it very closely. If you are purchasing it online or via mail order, sight unseen, pay close attention to the seller's description of it. The fundamental condition factors to concern yourself with are cracks and chips. The extent of these—if any—will lower a bottle's collector value and detract from its eye appeal.

Here's a brief look at bottle condition descriptions and what they generally indicate if you see a bottle described as such:

- Mint: A brand new bottle with no evident defects.
- Near Mint: A bottle that looks to be in mint condition, but upon close inspection an insignificant scratch, cracked surface bubble, or stain is visible to the eye.
- Excellent: A bottle that has multiple minor defects—scratches, cracked surface bubbles, or stains, but no chips or cracks.
- Very Good: A bottle with multiple scratches and stains, some small nicks, but no chips or cracks.
- Good: A bottle with substantial scratches and stains, and some visible chipping.
- Poor: A bottle with both cracks and chips visible.
- Damaged: A bottle with cracks and chips that lead to large pieces missing from the bottle.

Can Collecting

Can collecting is like bottle collecting, only—you guessed it—there's a can on the table. Cans, while not as visually appealing as bottles, have the capacity to showcase more descriptions and colorful images on them. This fact makes commemorative cans very popular with collectors. Coca-Cola's locking arms with Disney to celebrate Disney World's fifteenth anniversary in 1987, and placing Mickey Mouse, Donald Duck, Goofy, and friends on its cans, is just one example of the can collector's potential booty.

Advertising

Coca-Cola has been a remarkably successful promoter of its products from day one. Many collectors seek out Coca-Cola ads from old magazines. Some concentrate on particular themes like "Coke and Christmas." The Coca-Cola Santa Claus, featured in its holiday ads since 1931, is credited with having ushered in the modern image of St. Nick that we've all come to appreciate today.

No alcohol served here, only Coca-Cola. The club is located at *www.cocacolaclub.org* and is a gathering place for Coca-Cola collectors throughout the world. The Coca-Cola Collectors Club will make you privy to the latest news and trends in the marketplace.

Store Advertising

Coca-Cola store signs, whether made of porcelain, tin, cardboard, or light paper, are remarkable collectibles that make for great displaying, too. Some of the older advertising Coca-Cola signs are very expensive, but since there is so much variety in this category, there are plenty of excellent items available to the common collector, even the budget-conscious one.

Clocks

Coca-Cola and clocks—yet another powerful connection made by this soda company. Coca-Cola clocks bring back memories of our favorite pizza shop, the beach concessionaire, and the neighborhood grocery store, which all had Coke clocks gracing their walls. Some light up, some are round, some have a second hand, and some sport the Coca-Cola advertising slogan of the day. The one feature common to them all is that, regardless of the year or style, they wear the famous Coca-Cola logo. The older clocks tend to be quite costly, but collectors can get ahold of some nice 1970s issues, for instance, at reasonable prices. And that seems more and more like ancient history with each tick of those Coca-Cola clocks.

Trays

Coca-Cola serving trays are very popular. If you've got the Coca-Cola Victorian lady tray, dated 1897, it's valued at over $15,000. If you don't have that particular tray, there are plenty of others you can acquire at somewhat cheaper prices.

Trucks

Coca-Cola trucks make up many collections. Many of them are die-cast beauties. And if they are old and in good shape, you can go to the bank on the fact that they are in great demand.

Forgeries: When It's Not the Real Thing

Since Coca-Cola is an international phenomenon now, selling in more than 200 countries, it shouldn't be a shocking revelation when you learn that it is readily available on Fantasy Island. Yes, Coca-Cola memorabilia is being reproduced in significant quantities. Bottles, trays, metal signs, ice picks, calendars, even Coca-Cola coolers have been reproduced and passed off as the real thing. Some reproductions never existed in the first place to reproduce; yet they materialize arrayed with the Coca-Cola logo and fool some collectors. Coke collectors call these particular items *fantasies.*

The fact that so many of these phony items have wormed their way into the collector's market is a fair barometer of the popularity of Coca-Cola collectibles. Reproductions and fantasy items wouldn't be produced if there weren't a hunger—or thirst, in this case—for Coca-Cola items.

There are reproductions that are *legitimate reproductions*—officially sanctioned Coca-Cola retro items that hark back to earlier Coke advertising campaigns. Legitimate reproductions are clearly identified as such. It's the other stuff being manufactured with the intention of fooling you that you've got to be wary of. Some well-constructed fakes have worked their way into legitimate channels and bamboozled even some very knowledgeable collectors. Valuable trays and calendars have been counterfeited with success, so be on the alert before putting down your hard-earned money on any vintage Coke item. Make sure it is what you think it is.

ALERT

Purchase expensive antiques and vintage collectibles—Coca-Cola and otherwise—from dealers with longstanding and solid reputations for trustworthiness. Making sure you get what you pay for is often as simple as that.

Breweriana

Where some people collect Coca-Cola products, others focus on beer-related collectibles, known as *breweriana.* Beer cans comprise many collections in the field of breweriana, which also covers collectors of bottle caps, bottles, mirrors, openers, labels, advertising signs, steins and drinkware, tap handles and knobs, and trays. If you are interested in collecting beer cans, or already do, head over to the Beer Can Collectors of America (BCCA) at *www.bcca.com*.

In 1909 a brewery in Montana contacted the American Can Company and asked about the feasibility of packaging beer in cans. The can company experimented and came to the somber conclusion that beer and the metal can were incompatible mates. The Eighteenth Amendment and Prohibition squelched any potential for fixing the beer and can estrangement for over two decades after that. In 1933, however, with Prohibition repealed and beer freely flowing in the light of the day again, the beer can became reality. The Gottfried Krueger Brewing Company of Newark, New Jersey, was the first to put its beer in cans. A test marketing campaign on its part proved a smash hit, and in 1935, the first ever public sale of beer in cans took place as Krueger's Finest Beer and Cream Ale made history. And from that moment on, beer in cans was an indispensable part of the American culture. The types of cans that constitute beer can collections are classified in four styles.

"BILLY" beer can (1976)

Flat Top

The earliest manufactured cans—by Krueger and friends—are labeled in the collectible trade *flat tops*. The original Krueger cans, followed by Pabst cans that same year, were made of heavy steel with a flat top. These cans were opened by a can/bottle combo opener—ironically, called a *church key* by some—and were the predominant can type in use through the 1960s.

Cone Top

Another can style is known as the *cone top*. These early-year cans were so named for their funnel-like tops and are quite peculiar-looking. Schlitz, for one, utilized this style can, as did many other small brewers of the time. The can shape enabled brewers to synchronize the filling of both their cans and their bottles on the same assembly line. By 1960, the cone top can was essentially put out to pasture, as the big guys in the beer industry had gradually vanquished most of the small breweries in their competitive paths.

Pull Tab

The biggest innovation in can styles occurred in the 1960s when Schlitz introduced the pull tab, also referred to as the pop top. This type of can began the demise of those bulky beer cans that needed an opener, as they were slowly but surely replaced by cans with a handy ring device, where a non-arthritic finger was all that was needed to open it.

Stay Tab

The flip side of pop-tops was that they sometimes fell into the beer and now and then choked a hapless drinker. In addition, they also proved to be environmentally unfriendly, as the discarded pull-tabs were often left in places other than trash receptacles, from sandy beaches to picnic grounds to grassy parklands, leaving an unsightly mess and slicing many a bare foot in the process. In 1975 the Falls City Brewing Company of Louisville, Kentucky, introduced the stay tab can to the marketplace. This can style rapidly won the day. The stay tab can has stayed with us and is what we're all accustomed to today.

QUESTIONS?

Is it better to collect cans and bottles unopened or empty?
The problem with beer cans, particularly those original steel cans with seams along the sides, is rusting and leaking. It happens from time to time, and this—needless to say—doesn't enhance a collection. Most collectors, for this reason—and the obvious reason that they are easier to find—collect empty cans.

CHAPTER 10
The American Way of Life

A huge part of Americana are fields that reflect our American way of life. Whether in the form of advertising, television, or movies, each is uniquely American.

Advertising: The Story of Us

It's hardly just Coca-Cola, Pepsi, and their favorable advertising that have left such big footprints on today's collectible scene. Old advertising memorabilia of all kinds is the stuff of countless collections. The same collector's psychology that draws some people to collecting Coca-Cola and others to collecting Pepsi, draws still others to collecting Cracker Jack items and Mr. Softee ice cream memorabilia. The principle reason why

Vintage metal advertising sign

so many products succeed beyond all expectations, while others quickly fall by the wayside, is directly attributed to the advertising done on their behalf. Very often, a product's advertising campaign is more important than the product itself. Of course, even a genius promotional campaign couldn't successfully market chicken feathers as chicken soup.

Vintage advertising collectibles are intertwined with other collectible categories. A beer stein issued by Budweiser finds itself in the "Stein/Drinkware" classification one minute, and in "Advertising" the next. A Chevrolet pin-back button goes both ways. It can be listed as a "button" or a piece of "Automobilia." It's both. The point here is that advertising collectibles are by their very nature multifaceted. While there are obvious advertising memorabilia like magazine ads and promotional signs from stores and dealerships, there are also tons of giveaways and related premium items from a long list of companies that find themselves clustered under the advertising banner.

If we use eBay sellers as a representative reflection of the kinds of old advertising materials that are in the collector's marketplace, then here's what we are talking about. These are the categories that advertising collectors find themselves in:

- Agriculture
- Banking, Insurance
- Breweriana
- Candy & Nuts

- Cars
- Clothing, Fashion
- Coffee, Tea
- Communication & Utilities
- Distillery
- Food & Restaurant
- Gas & Oil
- Government
- Household
- Retail Establishments
- Soda
- Tires
- Tobacciana

Advertising has been around in various forms for centuries now. Newspapers and advertising have been ink brothers since day one. In

Gas pump metal sign affixed to pumps in the 1950s and 1960s

FOR USE AS A MOTOR FUEL ONLY CONTAINS LEAD (TETRAETHYL)

colonial America, there were retail shop signs and billboards. Early American newspapers ran ads advertising land and a variety of merchandise for sale. It was mainly local merchants advertising in local papers in hopes of connecting with the local citizenry. Times have sure changed.

As far as most of today's collectors' interests go, the advertising they are seeking dates to the mid-nineteenth century and afterwards. As a matter of fact, most collectors of old advertising memorabilia collect twentieth-century materials. With dramatic technological breakthroughs and perpetual product innovations occurring throughout the century, both the advertising and the products appear old in a hurry. Even 1980s advertisements are dated, already far removed from the twenty-first century's approach to selling products.

FACTS

Collecting old advertisements is not only a great hobby, but a learning experience, too. Courtesy of a 1918 advertisement, you can discover the five things it can do for you: It will "steady nerves, allay thirst, aid appetite, help digestion, and keep your teeth clean." And you thought it was just a stick of gum.

Why Collect Advertising?

People collect old advertising for many reasons. The following sections list some of the main ones.

Nostalgia

Collecting old advertising materials is at the top of the list of nostalgia-inspired collections, because it covers a vast array of materials that bring

"First Aid" cardboard advertising sign (early 1900s)

back the best memories from days gone by. A surefire way to start a conversation with a reticent soul is to talk about the past. This might entail chatting about Moxie soda or the Ford Edsel. And, better still, if you're a collector with a piece of the past to exhibit, you'll find you can squeeze words, and maybe even a smile, out of the most bashful of souls.

SSENTIALS

Many people collect antique tins, the containers of many products from the country stores of the past. The best book on the subject for ascertaining values is *Antique Tins: Identification & Values* by Fred Dodge, which offers market prices, useful information on the companies that manufactured the tins, and advice on places to locate these interesting pieces of the past.

History

What we collect is a reflection of who we are. Past advertising is a reflection of what we've been as a society and as a culture.

Beauty

Advertising memorabilia—particularly colorful magazine ads and porcelain and tin signs—is generally quite attractive and ideal for displaying. So it's no surprise people collect it simply because they like the way it looks.

Humor

By today's standards, the old advertising campaigns of the past are often very amusing. Looking at old ads, from the illustrations and pictures to the headlines and text, it's easy to discern how much times have changed, and not always for the better.

FACTS

In Stephen Whitman's candy store in Philadelphia in 1842, the chocolates' mixture box was born. Whitman conceived the idea of putting a varied selection of the most popular chocolates in one box and selling them as a sampler. Years later, the Whitman Company scored yet another first, when it placed a four-color ad in the *Saturday Evening Post.* The color and graphics were so sophisticated and attractive for 1925 advertising, that readers cut out the ads and framed them. Today, the same vintage Whitman's Chocolates ads are framed, but this time by collectors.

Valuable

Old advertising memorabilia is often very rare, particularly store signs in excellent or better condition. Some of these items are very valuable. The serious collectors in the specific advertising collectible fields (for example, 7Up, Nabisco, McDonald's, Sunbeam Bread, Lucky Strike, and so on) are very willing to pay top dollar for a needed piece to round out their collections. Don't let the smaller collectible fields fool you into thinking value is not there. It often is. A rare 1900 Campbell's Soup embossed tin sign sold for $93,500.

Country store product (early twentieth century)

In 1936, Schick Shavers ran an advertisement headlined, "The survivors were shaved with Schick Shavers." Pictured in the ad was the *Hindenburg* as it crashed to Earth in flames. The ad read, in part, "Many of the passengers and crew of the ill-fated *Hindenburg* whose faces were burned were shaved with Schick Shavers during their stay in the hospital. . . . It was quite impossible to use a blade to shave them. But the Schick Shaver glided gently and painlessly over the injured skin, removing the scarred surface."

Shopping at the Country Store

Remember Sam Drucker, Hooterville's town grocer on television's *Petticoat Junction* and *Green Acres*? Sam Drucker ran a country store

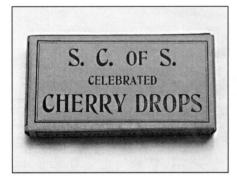

Country store product (early 1900s)

stocked with country store products. In the days before supermarkets, all Americans shopped in these kinds of general stores. That's all there was to choose from. The stores, by necessity, stocked everything, sometimes even including the kitchen sink.

Country store products, as they are often referred to, are the natural by-products of vintage advertising. They are the products themselves that were advertised and sold in those bygone days. Old grocery items from the store shelves of yesteryear find themselves in many collections today.

"Drefs Gout and Rheumatism Pills" canister, country store product (early 1900s)

Are country store products intrinsically valuable? An unopened tin can of Faust instant coffee from 1919, for example, is not usable. Sure, you can try mixing a cup if you like. But it's not recommended. Fortunately, though, collecting is not about intrinsic worth; it's about what people want. And that old, unopened can of coffee is worth something to someone who desires it,

"Chippewa Evaporated Milk" country store product (early 1900s)

not as his or her morning brew, but as an addition to a collection. Here are several factors to keep in mind when collecting country store products—old items sold in the stores of yesteryear, ranging far and wide, from tea to toothpaste:

- Rarity: Is the item hard to come by?
- Condition: Is the item in top-notch condition?
- Demand: Is the product more in demand than other items?
- Eye appeal: Is the product visually appealing?

ESSENTIALS   Check out Mike's General Store at *www.mikesgeneralstore.com* for numerous old advertising signs and antique bottles for sale. Another place to stop by is *www.nostalgiaville.com.* You can take a virtual tour of the Museum of Beverage Containers Advertising or, if you're in the area, visit it at 1055 Ridgecrest Drive in Millersville, Tennessee. Contact them at 800-826-4929.

Turning on the Television

In 1961, FCC Chairman Newt Minnow called television a "vast wasteland." And at that time there were only two major networks (CBS and NBC) and a handful of local channels for viewers to choose from. (So, that begs the question: If it was "vast" then, what is it now?) Slang terms for the television set—*idiot box* and *boob tube*—have even slithered their way into the dictionary.

Yes, a lot of garbage has come down the television pike. On the other hand, television has also brought an army of fine entertainers right into our homes. TV characters and TV families have left indelible marks

Ice bag, country store product in original packaging (1950s)

on so many of us. Television is said to be a "warm medium," in stark contrast to the big screen. And it's true. Sitting around in the comfort of your own living room and watching *The Brady Bunch* is a vastly different experience from venturing out to see the epic movie *Saving Private Ryan* in the theater. The movie situation is an event and an adventure. The TV show is part of our regular lives.

So, naturally lots of collectors are fiercely devoted to television and the memorabilia it's been generating through the years. TV shows from the 1960s and 1970s, in particular, have the widest followings and a vast array of items to hunt for.

Why is this a growing collectible field? It's the aging baby boomer who is driving this collectible craze to new heights. They are a bunch of people looking to physically acquire sentimental memories from the TV shows that they grew up with. It's not coincidence that Hollywood has

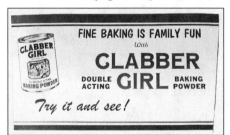

Cardboard advertising sign (early 1900s)

been making full-feature films based on classic TV shows from the past: *The Beverly Hillbillies, The Brady Bunch, Charlie's Angels, The Fugitive,* and so on. There's clearly an audience for them.

And there's an audience for collectibles like lunch boxes and matching thermoses, dolls, coloring books, magazines, board games, paperbacks, trading cards, puzzles, and record albums—all produced thirty or forty years ago to promote their favorite TV shows. Those shows, by the way, run the gamut from *Bewitched* to *Dallas, Bonanza* to *Happy Days, I Dream of Jeannie* to *Kojak, Family Affair* to *The Addams Family,* and *The Partridge Family* to *Baretta.*

An amazing book on this subject is the *Collector's Guide to TV Toys and Memorabilia: 1960s & 1970s* by Greg Davis and Bill Morgan. This book is loaded with market prices of the myriad memorabilia, of course, but it also has tons of color pictures. The authors' mission is to record and photograph every item marketed for the TV shows of that era. That's quite an undertaking, but they've clearly made a good start at doing so.

FACTS

A small, but nevertheless devoted group of collectors collects lunchboxes and matching thermoses. The first kid-style metal lunchbox debuted in 1950 with a decal image of *Hopalong Cassidy*. Lunch boxes remained metal until a group of mothers compared them to lethal weapons, saying that too many kids were whacking each other over the head with them. A *Rambo* lunch box, circa 1985, made history as the last of its kind. Thereafter, kids' lunch boxes would be made of plastic.

The Big Screen: Movie Memorabilia

Movies memorabilia is yet another collectible field that is dominated by America and Americans. American movies are seen all over the world. American movie stars have fans on every continent, but it's Americans who make most of the movies, watch most of the movies, and collect most of the movie memorabilia. The starry-eyed among us are legion.

Movie stars of yesteryear were movie stars—period—and TV stars were TV stars. There was rarely any mixing of the two. Spencer Tracy didn't appear as a grandfather in a 1960s sitcom. Today, however, the movie and television worlds have blurred considerably, and so too have the two collectible fields. A star—particularly a young star in a popular TV series—will often be cast in a feature film. So collectors of today's movie stars have a different task in front of them than, say, collectors of vintage movie memorabilia.

Cinderella Face Beautifier, left, country store product (early 1900s)

Cinderella Face Beautifier, right (side view listing product benefits)

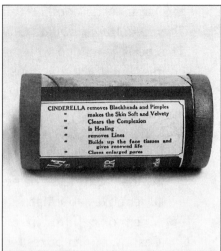

The sought-after stuff from Hollywood's heyday (pre-1980) includes many hard-to-come-by items. Many of these coveted collectibles are even more appreciated because the studios' promotional arsenals have discontinued them. Here are just some of the items that are sought after by movie memorabilia collectors:

- Lobby cards
- One-sheet posters
- Half-sheet posters
- Insert posters

- Press books
- Press kits
- Props and costumes

For the films produced from the 1940s through the 1980s, 11- × 14-inch lobby cards were commonly used in studios' promotional efforts. Lobby cards colored theaters' lobbies for decades. The cards usually consisted of eight different stills from the movie, and sometimes four.

One-sheet posters are another piece of movie memorabilia that collectors cherish. Original promotional posters, usually 27 × 40 inches, are hard to come by. And the older posters in mint condition are rarer still. These posters, however, have stood the test of time and have not been banished by the studios, as so many old-style promotional techniques have been. In fact, not only are movie posters produced today for movies in the theaters, but they are also used to promote video and DVD releases. Half-sheet posters measuring 22 × 28 inches and 14- × 36-inch insert posters are no longer used in movie promotions, but they were popular through the mid-1980s.

Some movie memorabilia collectors diligently search for press books from the movies of the past. These books also departed the scene in the early 1980s. A press book on a particular movie contained articles, pertinent information (plot synopsis, cast and credits, and so on) and advertising samples for possible use in newspapers and magazines. They varied in size, color, and format and are quite an interesting throwback to movie promotions. Some press books were only a few pages, while others were of magazine length. Today, the press kit for a movie is commonplace. It is sought after by movie memorabilia collectors. Press kits contain stills, news releases, cast information, and so on—and they vary in both size and general look.

FACTS

McDonald's has a collector's club all its own. Stop in for a bite at *www.mcdclub.com.* Not only will you hook up with fellow McDonald's items collectors, but you'll get a mouthful of history, too. For example, did you know that the first McDonald's Happy Meals were tested in St. Louis for two years before making their national debut in 1978 under the promotional banner "Circus Wagon"?

Some aggressive collectors seek out original scripts, props, and costuming from the movies themselves. In this area, make sure you are dealing with aboveboard sellers. If you're about to buy the bathing suit worn by Bo Derek in *10,* make sure it's the genuine skimpy article. If you're looking for any of the aforementioned movie items and more, drop by *www.movie-memorabilia.net.*

CHAPTER 11

Pin-Back Buttons and Comic Books

Pin-back buttons are more than just political campaign ephemera—they encompass a lot of uses, from celebration to advertising. And, of course, comic books are a quintessentially American invention. Let's take a look at the details of collecting these Americana.

Collecting Pin-Back Buttons

Pin-back button collecting is most often associated with political-items collectors. And for good reason: Buttons are omnipresent in politics and have been for over a century. They are the chief collectible item in the political materials hobby. But the political pin-back is only a snippet of the whole button story. There are many button collectors who avoid politics like the plague. In the following section, I fill you in on everything you ever wanted to know about this popular collectible field.

FACTS

During the 1950s, a psychologist named Dr. Frederich Wertham created quite a stir with his book, *Seduction of the Innocent*. Wertham believed that the rise in juvenile delinquency was directly correlated with juveniles reading comic books. Can you imagine what Dr. Wertham would think of today's world?

Types of Collections

Some collectors regularly find buttons that neatly fit into their overall collection—which may not be pin-back buttons. For example, an Elvis

Apollo XI commemorative pin-back button

Presley collector might include Elvis buttons in his extensive collection of "King of Rock and Roll" items. A space exploration collector may count NASA commemorative pin-backs among a collection that includes famous astronaut autographs and other related memorabilia. A World's Fair collection embraces buttons as just one of many souvenirs from those historical happenings.

Other collectors collect pin-back buttons and pin-back buttons alone. As you can imagine, there are many possibilities open to the button collector—and many challenges, too, courtesy of the saturation of buttons in circulation. There is often a methodology in the practices of button collectors, many of whom collect within certain parameters.

General

The guideline here is no guideline. There are button collectors who just can't control themselves. If it's a button, they want it—and it doesn't matter if it's got a smiley face on it or a bloodied animal on it excoriating the fur industry.

Advertising

Advertising buttons are a biggie! And this covers a lot of ground. Some collectors find it necessary to further break down this category and collect in subcategories such as food and drink, tobacco, alcohol, and so on. Others get even more specific than that and collect, for example, only bread and bakery buttons, or fast food restaurant pin-backs, and so on and so forth. Then, of course, there's the decision on whether to collect vintage pins or concentrate on newer items, or perhaps both.

Causes

There are always "issues of the day" or statement pins being produced. Whether it was the gold-versus-silver-currency debate of 1896, the Civil Rights Movement of the 1960s, or the Pro-Life Movement of today, buttons were manufactured for the impassioned and continue to be for all issues great and small, right and left, and right and wrong.

Events and Geography

Begin-Sadat commemorative pin-back button (1977)

There is a branch of button collectors who seek out pins only from specific events or locations. There are collectors, for instance, of only World War II–related buttons, 1976 American Bicentennial buttons, and so on. Other collectors concentrate on pins unique to their area of the country or state. There are many sportsmen who collect their state's fishing or game license pins, too.

Disney

Disneyana is a collectible field in and of itself. In the button world, there are loads of Disney pins featuring everything from Mickey Mouse to Peter Pan.

Cartoon and TV Characters

From Hanna-Barbera to the Honeymooners, from Peanuts to Fonzie, this is a vast area of button collecting. Some collectors seek out pins from classic TV shows like *Bonanza* and *The Munsters.* Others find classic cowboys like *Roy Rogers, Hopalong Cassidy,* and the *Lone Ranger* to their liking.

Music

Elvis Presley and the Beatles are the big guys on the overall music-related collecting scene—and this includes pin-backs, too. But let's not forget the easy-listening folks. Perry Como, Tony Bennett, Julius La Rosa, are just a few examples of personalities whose visages grace vintage buttons.

Movies

Movies are a staple of American life. From Shirley Temple to the Marx Brothers, the *Three Stooges* to *E.T.,* there are buttons aplenty to collect.

Holiday

A very festive button collecting route. Santa Claus pins, particularly early twentieth-century varieties issued by department stores at Christmas time, are a surprisingly sizeable collectible button offshoot.

Fraternal Groups

The Boy Scouts, Girl Scouts, Salvation Army, and so on have been around for the better part of a century. This means that there are a lot of their buttons out there, too, and some are quite coveted and rare.

The Condition of Buttons

Like with every other collectible, it is rarity and condition that most determine a button's value. Be aware that pin-back buttons are often tagged with these conditional terms:

- Mint: The button is in perfect condition, like new.
- Near Mint: The button is as close to perfection as possible without being perfect; upon close inspection, it exhibits some slight wear.
- Excellent (EXC): The button reveals light wear, but still maintains its strong original characteristics.
- Very Fine: The button shows light wear and minor aging but still maintains an overall bright and clean appearance with no defects.
- Fine: The button exhibits general wear throughout but does not have any serious defects.
- Very Good (VG): The button reveals a loss of luster and coloring but does not possess any serious defects.
- Good: The button displays overall wear and possibly a critical defect but still maintains its ability to be collected.
- Fair: The button is visibly damaged.
- Poor: The button combines extensive wear with damage.

In this broad button-grading scheme, the descriptive words used to identify a button's condition tend to be rather general. This is why it is important—particularly in the lower button grades—to demand more than a one-word description from a seller. Ask for precise details on the button's wear and defects.

Button Resources

If you are looking to add a pin-back button to your present collection in any of the above categories, or are looking to start a collection from scratch, check out *www.hakes.com,* or request a free catalogue from Hake's Americana & Collectibles, P.O. Box 1444, York, PA 17405. Hake's Americana & Collectibles has been the King of Popular Culture

Collectibles since 1967. For buttons—political and nonpolitical—nobody offers more variety on a consistently updated basis than Hake's. With its perpetual auctions and sales, Hake's is a button collector's

New York World's Fair pin-back button (1964–1965)

utopia. Hake's main feature, and especially welcome in these cynical times, is that all of the materials in auction or on sale are thoroughly described, illustrated, and backed up with a full guarantee—by a real person, Ted Hake himself. You've been implored time and again to deal with reliable sellers—Hake's fits the bill.

Hake's catalogues are loaded with vintage advertising buttons and other advertising premium items such as the following:

- Pencil sharpeners
- Clickers
- Tops
- Flicker Rings

- Whistles
- Lighters
- Mirrors

The *Price Guide to Collectible Pin-Back Buttons 1896–1986* by Ted Hake and Russ King is the best book on the subject of nonpolitical buttons. The book contains updated values and sixteen pages of color photos.

Holding On to Comic Books

Comic books have been around since the end of the nineteenth century, and they occupy a special place in the hearts of all those who read them as kids—and who didn't? Many people acquire vast collections of comic books, some of which are quite valuable.

The Value of Comic Books

Like baseball cards, comic books have secured a certain place in the collectible mystique for being "valuable." If it's laid bare that forty-something neighbor Charlie, who lives with his aging parents, has a comic book collection, the first thought that pops into people's minds is that it must be worth a fortune. It's possible, of course, that neighbor Charlie's collection is worth some serious moolah, if he happens to have some of the rarer issues. But it's also possible that its worth lies solely in the sentimental appeal it has for ol' Charlie. Just as with baseball cards—and most every other collectible—comic books aren't worth anything just for being comic books. What determines a comic book's value boils down to the two factors you've seen repeated over and over in this book, and everywhere else in the collector's realm. Rarity and condition are the two keys that unlock a comic book's value in the hobby.

The Official Overstreet Comic Book Price Guide by Robert Overstreet categorizes comic books in one of the following five categories, based on their year of publication:

- Platinum Age (1897–1932)
- Golden Age (1933–1955)
- Silver Age (1956–1969)
- Bronze Age (1970–1979)
- Modern Age (1980–present)

The comic books of the Platinum Age feature some of the rarest issues in existence and are quite different from the more contemporary issues in both layout and content. Having spawned some of the most sought-after comic book issues in the hobby, the comic books of the Golden Age began to look and feel like the modern issues that we are all accustomed to seeing, many of which are in great demand in today's market.

In the different comic book ages, there are, of course, individual issues that are the stuff of legend. That is, they command the big money in the comic book trade. So, if you have a little extra pocket change that you were planning to invest in the stock market, you might want to seek out some of these comic books and preserve them with your dear life. Here's a sampling and the kinds of prices they've been seeing—in Near Mint condition—in the marketplace:

- *Yellow Kid in McFadden Flats* (Platinum Age, 1897): $7,000–$8,000
- *Buster Brown and His Resolutions* (Platinum Age, 1903): $5,000–$6,000
- *Mickey Mouse Book,* 1st and 2nd print (Platinum Age, 1930): $10,000–$12,000
- *Action Comics #1* (Golden Age, 1938): $180,000–$200,000
- *Marvel Comics #1* (Golden Age, 1939): $100,000–$120,000
- *Superman #1* (Golden Age, 1939): $120,000–$140,000
- *Detective Comics #27* (Golden Age, 1939): $150,000–$170,000
- *Flash Comics #1* (Golden Age, 1940): $50,000–$60,000
- *All-American Comics #16* (Golden Age, 1940): $60,000–$70,000
- *Batman #1* (Golden Age, 1940): $60,000–$70,000
- *Showcase #4* (Silver Age, 1956): $20,000–$25,000
- *Fantastic Four #1* (Silver Age, 1961): $17,000–$22,000
- *Incredible Hulk #1* (Silver Age, 1962): $10,000–$12,000
- *Amazing Fantasy #15* (Silver Age, 1962): $25,000–$30,000
- *House of Secrets #92* (Bronze Age, 1971): $450–$500
- *Giant-Size X-Men #1* (Bronze Age, 1975): $450–$500
- *Star Wars #1* (Bronze Age, 1977): $500–$600

QUESTIONS?

What makes a valuable comic book desirable?
The issue must be hard to come by, in demand, and in top condition. But these comic books are the exception to the comic book rule. The majority of comic books don't sell for a lot of money, nor is monetary value the driving force behind most comic book collections.

Comic Book Care

As a collectible made of paper, comic books need to be given extra-special care. The acid in paper reacts to the fickleness of weather and the changing seasons. Hot humid summers are comic books' enemy number one. Comic books stored in an excessively hot room will quickly turn brown and, over time, worse than that. On the other end of the meteorological spectrum, cold and damp storage locations lead to molding. And some insects are oddly attracted to them, and not for reading purposes either.

Check out *The Official Overstreet Comic Book Price Guide* for the most updated information on comic book prices. If you're interested in acquiring some of the higher-priced issues, you'll at least have some idea what to look for and what to pay for them when you find them.

So, what are your options? Other than not collecting comic books at all, or living in the perfect climate sans humidity and temperature extremes, you've got to do a few things:

- Purchase acid-free backing boards and acid-free comic book bags, and place each comic book in your collection in an individual bag.
- Store your comic books in a cool, dry place, and avoid exposing them to direct sunlight, which will fade colors so quickly that you won't be able to decipher Batman from Superman.
- Handle all your comic books very carefully, because even the tiniest tears, folds, or spots on a comic book's pages can make a substantial difference in its condition grading and consequently its value.

Mile High Comics—dealers of Marvel Comics, DC Comics, Viz Comics, Dark Horse Comics, Image Comics, and others—is also a great source for all the supplies you need to properly protect your collection from the ravages of time and Mother Nature. They have it all: comic bags, backing boards, mylars, mylites, and grading stickers to keep your collection updated and ordered. Visit them online, at *www.milehighcomics.com*.

The Various Comic Book Grades

There's a lot of subjectivity in comic book grading. It's not an exact science. Nevertheless, it's important that you understand what the grade attached to the comic book you are purchasing means.

Mint (MT)

Mint condition is as close to physical perfection as is possible. This means absolute flatness, no surface wear, glossy covers, sharp corners, centered and clean staples, and supple paper. As you might well imagine, not too many comic books meet these rigid criteria. The comic book you pick up in the store is more than likely already in Near Mint (NM) or lesser condition, courtesy of its long journey from the printing press to the wider world.

Near Mint (NM)

Basically, this classification gives the comic book a little leeway in imperfection, such as a minimum of fading from the cover inks. More thorough graders also use NM+ and NM/MT in their descriptions.

Very Fine (VF)

An allowance is made here for covers and interior pages exhibiting slight yellowing—usually off-white. A stress line in the spine is also permissible under this banner. Some variations of this grade are also used: VF+ and VF/NM.

Fine (FN)

Minor spine wear, surface wear, creasing, and yellowing pages are permitted within this description. Overall though, the comic book remains flat, clean, and free of a brown margin. A comic book at this grade is still considered a highly collectible comic book. Also used are grades FN+ and FN/VF.

Very Good (VG)

This is the classification and home for the typically handled comic book, with all the deleterious results: discoloration, browning (but not brittle) interior paper, loose centerfold, and even a minor tear. A comic book in this condition still maintains enough appeal to be desirable to collectors. Variations on this description include VG+ and VG/FN.

Good (G)

This grade is determined by consensus in the hobby as the lowest grade acceptable for collectors. Paper quality is very low, but not brittle. Creases, scuffing, minor tears, and even some soiling is allowed here. However, the comic book is fully intact and readable. Variation in this grade includes GD+ and GD/FN.

They've got pages for TV and movie memorabilia, action figures, Barbies, battery-operated and wind-up tin toys, cap guns, coloring books, games, GI Joes, lunch boxes, and more. This is not an auction site, it's an old-fashioned store, only its location is in cyberspace at *www.toylectibles.com.*

Fair (FR)

A comic book with this description applied to it has been handled extensively with a significant loss of eye appeal. It, nevertheless, still has its cover and all of its original pages, but often the paper is brittle and heavily soiled.

Poor (PR)

Damaged beyond readability. Comics under this wretched distinction are brittle to touch and in rigor mortis. Discoloration, defacing, staining, even missing pages are all allowed here, because, after all, there is no grade lower.

CHAPTER 12
Dolls

The doll has been around in a variety of forms for millennia. Perhaps no inanimate object has provided the human species with as much pleasure as the faithful little doll. Indeed, this unwavering companion has comforted many a lonely heart through centuries of turbulence and change.

The History of Dolls

A variety of crude dolls have been unearthed in the graves of Egyptians going back as far as 2000 B.C. Dolls made of wood, clay, and even bones existed thousands of years ago. These early dolls are known today as *paddle dolls,* courtesy of their paddle-like contours. Paddle dolls were often garnished with painted designs to resemble clothing and strings of clay beads to double as hair. They were not initially children's toys, but spiritual idols created by society's elders to appease their laundry list of gods. The dolls buried with the dead were also expected to come to life in the hereafter—as servants for the deceased. You might want to make an addendum to your last will and testament, requesting that you be buried with your favorite doll.

It appears that pint-sized Greeks and Romans in antiquity knew what dolls were all about and actually played with them. It is believed that young girls left their doll playthings on the altar of Artemis, the goddess of childbirth, when it was time for them to say goodbye to their childhood and cross over into the adult world. That is, they were expected to swap their innocuous, clumsy dolls for the brutish men of the day.

Multitudes of dolls dot the historical timeline. The Renaissance (1450–1600), a period of enormous cultural and intellectual strides throughout the continent of Europe, saw the number of dolls manufactured increase in leaps and bounds. Molded white clay dolls were baked and made in the images of children, little men, and stylish ladies.

In the sixteenth century, simple wooden dolls appeared as toys. German peg wooden dolls, resembling the modern clothespin, also hit the streets. Then along came wax dolls. Munich, Germany, in fact, became the hub of wax doll production in the seventeenth and eighteenth centuries. Wax dolls were fashioned by pouring a piping hot melted concoction into a plaster-shaped cast, then letting it cool and harden. Courtesy of this molding process, dolls' facial features could be more defined and lifelike than with the predominant wood creations. One of the earliest "baby dolls" on record—an early nineteenth-century English creation—was made of wax.

Notwithstanding all this waxy buildup, the doll remained principally a wooden affair until the Industrial Revolution descended upon Europe and mass production became the "in" thing. Then, a pulped-wood amalgam was utilized in doll production, permitting a more thorough molding of dolls' facial features in something other than wax, which had its design limitations and was prone to breaking. Papier-mâché was one such mixture that became popular in Germany, France, and later in the United States.

The next level for the doll—beyond wax and paper product—was porcelain. Understandably, some people don't quite grasp it. How could there be a rock solid porcelain statute or figurine and, simultaneously, a cuddly, soft porcelain doll? It's all about processing. When a mixture of ball clay, kaolin, flint, and feldspar are fired at very high temperature in a *kiln*—a super-hot furnace of sorts—porcelain is the derivative. The first porcelain dolls made were what are commonly called *glazed*. The china doll with its shiny finish is glazed porcelain.

Plastic baby doll

When, however, the same blend is fired a second time and *vitrified* (melted), unglazed porcelain called *bisque* is the result. This melting process also permits colors/tints to be added. And so, when it became feasible to fashion a doll's face into something resembling soft human skin in both color and tone, porcelain bisque became a widely popular doll ingredient.

The French *Bebe* bisque doll, first marketed in the 1850s, was in the vanguard of things to come. *Bebe*, you see, looked like a little girl. The word *Bebe*, in fact, is commonly used to identify French dolls portraying small children. Prior to *Bebe*, dolls were generally patterned after adult personages, and not adolescents or infants. Believe it or not, this was quite a revolutionary move at the time, but *Bebe's* popularity overwhelmed the fuss. Krammer and Reinhardt, a German doll company, took this youthful character bisque doll to the next level, when it produced a series of realistic-looking dolls. The age of the character doll had arrived.

While bisque was making a big splash, rag and cloth dolls were also commercially marketed. Rural mothers, and their city counterparts, too, routinely made dolls for their children from whatever excess fabrics were available to them. *Waste* was not a word common to households' vocabularies in those austere days. A rag doll was often a young girl's first toy—and sometimes her only one. Not surprisingly, businesses elbowed their way into the fabric doll concession, competing with homemade varieties. They knew full well that once a child spotted a doll in a store or in the Sears Roebuck catalogue, mom had a difficult job competing with that, even though every rag doll that she sewed together was a one-of-a-kind, with no two ever the same.

Dolls throughout history have been made with quite an assortment of materials. Besides wood and wood products, porcelain, bisque, and wax, there have been dolls made of leather, rubber, celluloid, hard plastic, vinyl, corn husks, ivory, metals, and combinations of so many things.

With all the technology that's come down the manufacturing pike over the last century, an interesting phenomenon is occurring with many modern doll makers returning to dolly roots and using materials popular in the nineteenth century and early twentieth century in assembling the dolls of the twenty-first century. Everything old is new again.

FACTS

Doll collectors refer to wood dolls from the late-eighteenth-century and early-nineteenth-century England as *Queen Anne dolls.* These early dolls with painted features are very rare and coveted by advanced collectors. Queen Anne, who was the last British sovereign of the House of Stuart, reigned from 1702 to 1714, about a century before the dolls were made. So, somewhere along the way, somebody lost a century when the dolls got their untimely appellation.

Types of Dolls

Collecting dolls is an international hobby that some say counts more collectors in its expanding dollhouse than any other collector field save the champion, stamps. Perhaps it's the nature of the collectible itself that enables its collectors to quietly go about their business of buying and selling, without the fanfare of the baseball card collector or élan of the philatelist.

 **ESSENTIALS**

If you are a doll person, or thinking about becoming one, visit *www.our-world-of-dolls.com.* Covering a variety of collector interests in the hobby, you'll find plenty of links here to doll clubs and organizations, collectors' sites, calendars of doll shows and doll-related events, and even listings of doll hospitals.

Dolls cover a lot of ground. Some collectors consider the doll to be anything manufactured in a human form, including an army of action figures and figurines. A GI Joe is a doll, but you won't likely find it in a doll-collecting category. It's more apt to be classified as a toy in the overall collectible sphere.

Dolls distinguish themselves in many ways:

- Age: Is the doll an antique or is it a modern issue (a doll made within the last twenty-five years)?
- Composition: What is the doll made of (wood, papier-mâché, a composition, bisque, hard plastic, wax, and so on)?
- Special effects: Is the doll endowed by its creator with features that make it rather unique, such as talking, flirty eyes, gusset joints, mohair, or anatomical capabilities ranging from eating to wetting?
- Maker: Who manufactured the doll?

In the following sections, I provide a representative sampling—by no means exclusive—of some of the specific doll types that are of sustained interest to doll collectors.

Alexander Doll Company

Beatrice Alexander Behrman—known as Madame Alexander—began manufacturing dolls in 1923, and the company is still at it today. Through the years Madame Alexander dolls, as they are known, have produced dolls in the images of such famous individuals and characters as Shirley Temple, Scarlett O'Hara, Alice in Wonderland, and even a celebrated group of infants known as the Dionne quintuplets. The earliest of these dolls were made entirely of cloth, then a composition, followed by plastic. Madame Alexander dolls are credited with introducing into circulation the first American-made fashion dolls, with *Cissy* in 1955. Others soon followed: *Cissette, Elise, Lissy,* and *Wendy.*

The 1950s have been termed the Golden Age of American dolls, thanks in no small part to the Madame Alexander line. Madame Alexander dolls produced over the years have utilized minimal variations in facial features, but tremendous disparity in costuming of silk, satin, velvet, and accessory items. The original costuming or wrist tag is therefore essential in identifying an older Madame Alexander doll. Check out the Madame Alexander Doll Club at *www.madc.org* for the answers to all your questions regarding both old and new issues of this very popular long line of dolls.

Artistic Dolls

These are modern dolls issued for art's sake, and not for little girls to cuddle and play house with. These dolls are usually one-of-a-kind or very limited in number, unique to a particular artist, and often purchased for investment reasons.

Barbie

Who would have ever imagined that Ruth Handler's notion of a small fashion doll would take off as it did and become an international sensation? Barbie was initially marketed as a young girl's play toy, but like so many other things in this unpredictable world, it's become a collectible item extraordinaire and thus engendered contemporary collectors' Limited Edition Barbie dolls. Barbie is so popular today that she even has a physically challenged doll friend confined to a wheelchair.

Bru

This French company, founded by Leon Casimer Bru, produced bisque dolls from 1867 to 1899. Today, Bru dolls represent some of the most sought-after in the hobby. Bru is an enchanted name in the world of antique dolls, courtesy of the dolls' many innovations and eye-catching styling. In 1873, Bru patented the *Smiling Poupee* doll replete with a swivel head, which could be placed on a variety of body styles. In 1878, the company introduced a nursing baby doll with a bottle that could ingest liquid, and then the *Bebe Gourmand,* which could devour food, with its digestion occurring through a hollow leg and expelled at the foot. These were novelties that established many doll trends. Just think about the baby doll and its bottle and how commonplace that pair has become since the day Bru went public with his winning combination over a century ago.

Cabbage Patch Kids

In 1977, the Cabbage Patch doll was created by a man named Xavier Roberts, who first sold them at craft shows for more than one hundred dollars each. Roberts first called his dolls Little People. The dolls were ultimately mass-produced by toy companies Coleco and Hasbro in 1982, and were an astonishing fad item that Christmas. Everybody was talking then about Cabbage Patch Kids and their peculiar looks and accompanying birth certificates. These unique dolls, put up for "adoption," as it were, have made the Cabbage Patch name one of the most recognized in the world.

The Cabbage Patch Kids fad phenomenon led to some very strange rumors about the dolls. It was reported that toy manufacturer Coleco was mailing out death certificates to children who had returned their dolls to them for repair. Other reports claimed that mini-coffins were being sent back to kids with their damaged dolls, so that an appropriate funeral could be held. Some gossip even purported that children were receiving "child abuse" citations from Coleco for mistreating their dolls. The Cabbage Patch saga was all fiction. Be careful what you believe.

Effanbee

Founded in New York City by Bernard Fleischaker and Hugo Baum in the early twentieth century, Effanbee has been a trendsetter in the American doll industry. Its *Patsy* doll was the first of its kind American baby doll to be the size of the genuine article—a real baby. This imaginative company also introduced doll playmates for *Patsy,* and a wardrobe, too. *Patsy* was Barbie before Barbie, with different looks and wardrobe styles through the years. Effanbee was also the first to go public with a drink-and-wet doll.

Ideal Novelty and Toy Company

Morris Mitchom is most remembered for naming the stuffed toy bear, the Teddy Bear, named after President Theodore Roosevelt in 1902, who, by the way, loathed being called Teddy. The controversy that still rages today is whether Mitchom actually created the stuffed toy bear itself. In any event, Mitchom's company did more than manufacture stuffed animals. It made dolls of famous people like Shirley Temple and Judy Garland, and also produced the first hard, unbreakable plastic doll in 1909. Its fashion dolls of the 1950s and 1960s include the popular *Revlon Family* of dolls.

Jumeau

This French doll maker from the mid-nineteenth century was run by the Jumeau family. Emil Jumeau, an architect by trade, applied his considerable design talents to dolls and the result was the *Jumeau Bebes.* He also had a talent for production and marketing in an age before big toy conglomerates ruled the distribution roost. Emil's wife, Madame Ernestine Jumeau, further enhanced the work of her husband by crafting attractive and fashionable couturier dresses for their line of dolls. These dolls are considered works of art in today's trade and are very valuable.

Nancy Ann Storybook Doll

Nancy Ann Abbott founded an American doll company in 1936. It shut its doors in 1964. It is perhaps best known for producing both high-quality painted bisque and hard plastic dolls, along with elegant clothing. Today's collectors prize these dolls, which include *Little Sister* and *Big Sister*.

Raggedy Ann

In 1918, Johnny Gruelle, a political cartoonist and children's book illustrator, published *Raggedy Ann Stories,* a book about the adventures of a rag doll, *Raggedy Ann,* and subsequently her little brother, *Raggedy Andy*. A doll was created to aid in the selling of the books. Although the books were popular, the dolls—replete with black eyes and triangle noses—were much more so, and have been for quite some time. On the market since 1920, when the P. F. Volland Company first produced them, Raggedy Ann dolls are as popular today as they were fourscore and a few years ago.

Raggedy Ann doll

Vogue

Jennie Graves began her business by designing doll clothing. She imported the dolls themselves from German doll companies. When Germany became politically unstable in the 1930s, Graves opted to manufacture her own dolls in addition to their outfits. The result was the founding of Vogue dolls in 1948. She introduced the *Ginny* doll, and later gave *Ginny* a family of her own: *Ginnette, Jill,* and *Jeff*.

Doll Terminology

In a world inhabited by billions of people, millions of dolls, and thousands of doll collectors, it is essential that you acclimate yourself within the doll realm. If you collect dolls, or are a wannabe collector of them, get to know their widely diverse characteristics. And what better way to do this than to commit to memory the terms commonly used on the doll scene to identify them and their many differences. The followings sections cover some frequently used doll terms and what they mean.

ESSENTIALS

The most popular doll collecting magazine is the *Doll Reader,* which regularly provides valuable and timely information on both antique and modern dolls. Check out *www.dollreader.com* for subscription information. Another worthy and choice magazine is *Doll World,* which is strong on doll and costume history. For more information on this magazine, visit *www.whitebirches.com.*

All-Bisque

An all-bisque doll is one consisting entirely—from head to toe—of unglazed porcelain. Many dolls are branded *bisque* with just a head of bisque and body parts consisting of other materials. These dolls are not all-bisque, unless so noted.

Applied Ears

A doll with applied ears has gone through a production process that molds a doll's head and ears separately. That is, the ears of the doll are added to the head, instead of them being part of the head.

Ball Jointed

A procedure utilizing small balls at the doll's arm and leg joints, enabling them to move back and forth.

Brevete

Brevete is the French word for "patented," often stamped into their antique dolls. It is sometimes seen abbreviated to *B.T.E.*

Book Value

Book value is the value of any collectible as determined by the most recent market transactions. Price guides in various collectible circles list book values of particular items to give collectors an idea of the worth of them. These numbers are designed to reflect the latest market prices and demand of the collectibles. Often, inexperienced collectors are unpleasantly surprised when they go to sell their doll, in this instance, and find that they can't get the book value for it—or even close to it. It's important to understand that the book-value dollar figure is not set in stone and is dependent on a variety of factors, particularly condition, and being in the right place at the right time. If somebody paid $5,000 for a particular doll, that somebody might not be around to cough up a similar amount for the same doll again. Yet, that particular sale could well be determinant of the book value in a price guide.

Composition

Composition is a mixture of resin, sawdust, starch and other materials used to make doll bodies and sometimes both their heads and bodies. Before hard plastic dolls became the rage, composition dolls were very popular.

Celluloid

Celluloid is a plastic used in manufacturing dolls from the 1920s through the 1940s. The downside of celluloid was that it was highly flammable and thus a potentially dangerous ingredient in doll making. It was gradually phased out with a nonflammable, alternative plastic.

Closed Mouth

A closed-mouth doll is one assembled with no visible teeth. Antique bisque dolls with closed mouths are generally considered more valuable than are their open-mouth sisters. Silence is golden in this instance.

Character Dolls

A character doll is one fashioned in the image of a living child or adult.

Crazing

Crazing is a group of tiny intersecting cracks that often develop with age on the surface of composition and china dolls.

Dollhouse Doll

Dollhouse dolls are ones constructed and scaled to fit into a dollhouse.

Domed Head

A domed head on a doll is closed and domed on top. This is in contrast to the open-head doll.

Flange Neck

A flange neck is a doll's head and neck that juts outward to facilitate its attachment to a cloth doll body.

Flirty Eyes

Flirty eyes are eyes that move up and down on a doll.

Googly Eyes

Googly eyes are round eyes on a doll that are bigger in proportion to the remaining facial features, and often glance from side to side.

HTF

HTF is an acronym for "hard to find." This acronym is repeatedly seen in doll descriptions on auction sites, and in doll magazines and price guides. "Hard to find" usually means more valuable, if you happen to be one of the lucky ones who make the find.

Intaglio Eyes

Intaglio eyes are eyes that are molded into the doll's head and painted. Inset eyes are also set into the doll's head but do not move.

Kid

Kid is a soft leather made from the skin of a goat and put to use in crafting French and German fashion doll bodies.

Mohair

Mohair is angora goat hair used for doll wigs. This hair was popular with antique doll makers and the buying public, too, who loved the soft, natural-looking wigs made from this distinctive hair.

Molded Ears

Molded ears are just the opposite of applied ears. They are part of the head, just as surely as is the nose and mouth.

Open Head Doll

The open-head doll has the crown cut out in order to allow the eyes to be inserted from the inside.

Open Mouth

Open-mouth dolls are dolls made with—you guessed it—open mouths. Their mouths reveal teeth and sometimes even tongues.

Portrait Doll

A portrait doll is a late-nineteenth century and early-twentieth century doll that depicts a personage.

Provenance

Provenance is the historical information as to the origins of antique dolls. Knowing the provenance of your doll—and every other collectible— is always a big plus. If you're looking to sell, it obviously benefits you to know the full history of your doll. If you're looking to buy, you want to know precisely what you are buying.

Presentation Box

The presentation box is the original packaging of antique dolls and all their accessories. A presentation box greatly enhances the value of a doll, just as similar original packaging enhances other collectible items.

Shoulder Head

A doll with a shoulder head has its head and shoulders in one piece, attached to a body.

Sleep Eyes

A doll with eyes that close when it is laid down is said to have *sleep eyes.*

Socket Head

A *socket head* is a doll's head that is assembled to fit into a body in much the same way that a light bulb fits into a light socket.

Stationary Eyes

A doll that has eyes that don't open and close is said to have *stationary eyes.*

Swivel Head

A swivel head is one that utilizes distinct shoulder plates, enabling it to move back and forth.

Vinyl

Vinyl is the most-often-used plastic in doll manufacturing since the 1960s. Vinyl can be both hard and soft.

The Value of Dolls

So what determines a doll's value? The biggest factor is condition. Even minor flaws in a doll can greatly affect its value in the trade. Chips, cracks, stains on clothing, damage to hair, and other wear dramatically reduce a doll's appeal to collectors. Antique dolls are naturally allowed more leeway in their overall condition. It's assumed that a 100-year-old doll will exhibit some aging blemishes and a variety of faults. A contemporary doll, on the other hand, is not afforded such generous latitude. Newer dolls are expected to be in mint condition if they are to have any secondary market value at all.

Rarity in a doll can sometimes trump condition as the chief driving force for demand and value. A hard-to-find doll is likely to be coveted by many collectors, thus pushing up the price. So, a little wear and tear will not impact as negatively on the price as it would on a more common doll.

In the doll world, more than in most collectible fields, restoration plays a significant role in doll values—especially antique doll values. The restoration process, which includes restoring or repainting a doll, has unpredictable results on a doll's price in the marketplace. Sometimes restoration increases the value of a doll, and sometimes it does just the opposite. The workmanship of the restoration is fundamental. Antique dolls are regularly restored, and many are significantly upgraded in both their appearance and value. The flip side, however, is shoddy repainting and poor cleaning jobs, which substantially detract from both a doll's visual appeal and price tag.

So, when buying a doll—particularly an older doll that has been restored in some way—it's important that you carefully consider whether the restoration process enhances the doll's overall worth or diminishes its collectible desirability. It's fair to say that—if given the choice—most collectors prefer dolls "as is" and untouched by any form of restoration,

Howdy Doody bobbing head

because this removes any of the valuation intangibles that can't help but come with the territory of restoration.

Another big factor impacting on a doll's value is its *completeness*. That is, does the doll have all of its original parts? Completeness refers to the doll's entire outfit from head to toe; clothing to shoes. And very importantly, a doll in its original box completes the completeness picture.

Dolls that are Mint in Box (MIB) are most prized. The realities of everyday living tell us that most people, for example, who receive a doll as a Christmas or birthday gift, dispense with the box forthwith. The doll's box is not generally seen as an important piece of the collectible puzzle, and is more often viewed as a pesky scrap of cardboard taking up valuable space that belongs in the recycling bin. Nevertheless, the original box matters in doll prices. Some sellers place dolls in boxes that are not their original cartons. This is known as *empty box selling* and doesn't upgrade a doll's value in the least. It has to be the box that it was sold in, be it 120 years ago or yesterday, for it to count.

Another value barometer rests on the markings that were made on many antique dolls at the time of their manufacturing. Date, country of origin, and so on were often stamped on a doll's back or neck. These marks of time and place are great value enhancers, in that they provide the very important background of the doll, and thus remove many of the doubts that are wont to swirl around older dolls and their authenticity.

Considering the popularity of dolls, authenticity is a very vital concern. Imposters are out there. So, the more information you have on a rare doll, the less chance there is that you'll get swindled and duped into plucking down big bucks for a reproduction. A price too-good-to-be-true on a rare doll usually indicates a too-good-to-be-true rare doll that's more than likely not rare at all.

There are additional factors that influence a doll's value that are very subjective. Doll fads, for example, which generate buying frenzies and meteoric price rises, often distort real value for a period of time. In fads, though, the law of gravity always applies: What goes up in price must come down.

The doll collector's domain is unique in so many ways, not the least of which is the numerous doll hospitals that exist to fix and heal the hurts of all your injured and damaged dolls. An experienced and well-regarded doll hospital, as well as old-fashioned doll seller, is Judy's Doll Shop at *www.judysdollshop.com* located at 1201 Highway 70 East, New Bern, NC 28560. Call Judy at 252-637-7933.

Here are a couple of books that'll surely help you in your doll education. *Antique Trader's Doll Makers & Marks: A Guide to Identification* by Dawn Herlocher will provide you with doll manufacturers' histories, doll mold characteristics, and lots of tips on avoiding purchasing forgeries. *Doll Values: Antique to Modern* by Patsy Moyer is likewise an indispensable companion loaded with color photos, doll and manufacturer histories, and, of course, what you really want this kind of book for—doll values.

CHAPTER 13
Figurines

Collections plus figurines equal shelves. This triumvirate goes together as harmoniously as do the three Gibb brothers in creating the Bee Gees sound. Curio and cabinet shelves the world over are loaded with figurines depicting humanity at its most idyllic and benevolent. Some figurines are more elegant and sophisticated than are others. Some are glazed and shiny; others are more muted and quietly recede into their surroundings. But they're collected all over the world.

M. I. Hummels

M. I. Hummel figurines and plates are one of the most popular collectibles in this domain, especially in America, "the land of collectibles," and in Germany, the land of their birth and original production home. Hummels, as they are both affectionately and informally known, have been called the world's "most beloved collectible," and few would dispute this sentiment, because each genuine M. I. Hummel figurine has a unique charm and innocence all its own. A Hummel's smooth and careful detail is second to none.

M. I. Hummel figurine, left

Take care of your collection! Vintage Hummels gone to pieces, right

The Hummel History

The story of the Hummel figurine befits its captivating and carefree air. First introduced at the Leipzig Spring Fair in Germany in 1935 by a businessman named Franz Goebel, the Hummel immediately got noticed. Goebel was the head of W. Goebel Porzellanfabrik, a well-known porcelain firm, and was always on the lookout for fresh artistic talent to develop new figurines for his company. He found his talent this time, not behind a canvas on a street corner in Munich, or in an art studio in Berlin, but in the Convent of Siessen. Goebel spotted the works of Sister Maria Innocentia Hummel in books and art cards that the religious order sold to raise funds for their teaching and missionary efforts. He was most impressed, believing that the talented nun's artwork—evoking the true spirit of childhood—would make for a great line of figurines, particularly in the unsettled and increasingly downcast political climate of pre-war Germany. And so he approached Sister Hummel with his idea of converting her drawings into figurines. To his utmost delight, she warmly embraced his vision.

M. I. Hummel "For Mother"

Sister Hummel was not only receptive to the project, but she worked closely with the Goebel painters to find colors for the figurines that closely matched her drawings. She also made sure that all of her entitled royalties from the Hummel figurines bearing her name went into the coffers of the Convent of Siessen.

It was more than a decade after their debut that the Hummel phenomenon took flight. Two monumental things happened: The horrors of World War II slowly lifted, as did the materials' restrictions that were in place during the conflict. War was replaced with a hunger to rebuild and forget the horrendous devastation. And what better contrast could there be to a vanquished brutal tyranny than a gentle Hummel figurine?

The international attraction was also set in motion when American soldiers returned to the states after their post-wartime service in occupied Germany with Hummel figurines in their luggage. These statuettes of innocent, young children in Bavarian garb were the perfect gifts for soldiers' moms, wives, and girlfriends. And they were the origins of many collections, too. The American fascination with the Hummel was at hand.

Tragically, Sister Hummel contracted tuberculosis and died in 1946 at the age of only thirty-seven. Fortunately for admirers of the Hummel figurine, the talented artist was prolific throughout her short life and left behind a wealth of her artwork. These original materials remain to this day the bedrock for each and every M. I. Hummel produced.

How Hummels Are Made

Original Hummel figurines aren't found on the shelves of any of those discount stores that seem to be sprouting up in every mall and on every Main Street in America. And for one very good reason—they're not cheap. You don't always get what you pay for in the collectible world, but in the M. I. Hummel's case, you usually do.

If you look into the painstaking process that goes into producing an individual Hummel figurine, it's easy to see why they are both a moderately-priced and coveted collectible. This is not one of those pedestrian figurines that methodically winds its way along a conveyor belt and has paint squirt at it as it passes from point A to point B. Quite the contrary: Each and every Hummel figurine is treated with the utmost care by real human beings with real eyes for craftsmanship. The Goebel Porzellanfabrik firm is still the one and only manufacturer of the M. I. Hummel, and it has a longstanding reputation of quality that it does not take lightly.

The twinkle in the eye of a Hummel's conception is the initial selection of a Sister Hummel drawing or painting for consideration as a future figurine. An accomplished sculptor is then asked to carefully study the original two-dimensional artwork and perfect a multidimensional clay model of it. With this accomplished, the sculpture is then presented to the Artistic Board of the Convent of Siessen, which still plays an integral part in the Hummel creation process.

If the sculpture gets the thumbs up from the board, the sculptor locks arms with a mold-maker and the two determine the number of pieces that the clay figurine should be cut into to facilitate the best mold-making procedure. After some trial and error, a series of plaster molds are agreed upon.

With the molds at the ready, liquid ceramic (kaolin, feldspar, clay, quartz, and water) called *slip* is poured into them. The plaster molds absorb the moisture from the slip as it slowly thickens. The result is various empty ceramic shells resembling the parts of a figurine. The superfluous slip is now poured out and the shells are pieced together using the excess slip as glue. Seams are carefully smoothed over at this time. The payoff is a fully assembled figurine that is set to dry for approximately a week.

Next comes the figurine's firing at super-high temperatures in a kiln. Its first entry into the pool of fire transforms the figurine from its slightly moist primary state into a chalky white bisque state. The piece is now given a liquid glaze tinting and returned to the kiln for round two. This second firing allows the glaze to melt into a fine glassy coating. Initial painting begins here, and then it's into the kiln yet again to bind the colors to the Hummel for perpetuity. Sometimes a figurine goes into the kiln two or three times, just to affect this essential color bond and to create a smooth matte finish.

The last chapter in the Hummel-making process involves extensive hand panting. A sample is prepared by a master painter, attempting to mimic the precise hues of the original Sister Hummel artwork, and this is sent to the Convent of Siessen for final approval. A staff of artists then goes to work painting each Hummel figurine by hand. Yes, every figurine that survives the trial of fire is hand-painted. This means that each and every Hummel figurine is unique. And with countless checkpoints along the way, the quality of the Hummel is assured.

FACTS

Ceramic pieces are usually glazed, which makes them waterproof and more resistant to wear. The glaze itself is a liquid compound that when applied to an item forms a glasslike surface. The myriad techniques used in this sometimes complicated and multifaceted process make for the vast and varied types of ceramic wares that exist. There is also a method called *underglaze*, in which colors are applied to bisque, dipped in a glaze, and then fired a second time. This gives the painted colors permanence.

Your Hummel Collection

Hummels are a valuable collectible, both monetarily speaking and—more importantly—sentimentally speaking. A couple of places worth checking out for M. I. Hummels, both young and old, are *www.someonespecial.com*, which also stocks a variety of other collectibles. Another seller of M. I. Hummels, as well as various imports from Germany and Austria, is *www.deutscheshaus.cc*.

If you collect Hummel figurines or want to start a collection, get an idea what the going prices are. You'll find plenty of invaluable information in *The No. 1 Price Guide to M. I. Hummel: Figurines, Plates, More* by Robert Miller. This book contains hundreds of photos that will surely assist you in identifying a Hummel, its date of manufacture, and current book value. Another well-regarded book on the subject of Hummels is *Luckey's Hummel Figurines & Plates: Identification and Value Guide* by Carl F. Luckey.

In the world of Hummels, there are bogus figurines being passed off as the real thing. There are also perfectly legal imitators. What you're looking for as collector of M. I. Hummel figurines is the definitive signature and trademark that tells you that you're getting the genuine article and not an ersatz hunk of clay. Some Hummel figurines are marked "B. Hummel" or just "Hummel." These are obviously not M. I. Hummels, but they nevertheless confuse some people, who think they are. Years ago, Schmidt Brothers, Inc. forged an agreement with the Hummel family before Sister Hummel was ordained, and when she was known by her given name, Berta Hummel. Thus, the "B. Hummel" labeling. Another company, Verlag Ars Sacra, maintains rights to the original artwork of Sister Hummel, and they are known for producing postcards, books, collector spoons, and miniature clocks. Keep all this in mind in your Hummel quest. There's nothing wrong with collecting any of these materials. Just know from whence they came.

For M. I. Hummel figurines, it's the Goebel trademark (used on all their products, not just Hummel figurines) coupled with the signature (M. I. Hummel) that'll tell you an awful lot. With the trademark and signature, you'll know that it's a Goebel-produced original and you'll get a hint as to the year of the Hummel's issuance, too. The Goebel trademarks have changed over the years and varied quite a bit. Look for them on the underside of the figurines. Here's a simple roster of the kinds of trademarks used and the years they were active:

- Crown: 1935–1949
- Full Bee (bumblebee inside a "V"): 1950–1959
- Stylized Bee (small bee inside a larger "V"): 1960–1963
- Three-Line ("by/ W. Goebel/ W. Germany"): 1964–1972
- Goebel/V (in large lettering with small bee inside a "V"): 1972–1979
- Goebel (in large lettering alone): 1979–1990
- Goebel/C (with "Germany" and small bee): 1991–2000
- Bumblebee (with "Germany" and bumblebee): 2000–present

Armani Figurines

Giuseppe Armani has established quite a reputation for himself. And this reputation as a remarkably gifted artist has given rise to collections in all parts of the world. The "Armani" name conjures up images of rich detail and beauty. No, we're not talking about an Armani suit jacket, tie, and pair of pants. We're talking about a finely honed Armani figurine. Armani sculptures are becoming increasingly popular as more and more collectors in this collectible jurisdiction appreciate the unmatched style of this adroit artist from Calci, Italy.

FACTS

Giuseppe Armani's works are quite renowned and the artist is celebrated in varied circles. In 1996, Armani presented his one-of-a-kind sculpture "Madonna with Child and Young Saint John" to Pope John Paul II. That same year, he gave President Clinton his "Wild Hearts" creation. Clinton liked it so much that it remained on view in the Oval Office for all who visited to admire.

The Armani Story

Giuseppe Armani was an artist in the making the moment he emerged from his mother's womb and let out his first yelp in 1935. Maybe his mother and father didn't realize right then and there, but they did shortly thereafter. As a little boy, young Giuseppe drew everything he saw, from the inanimate (trees and buildings) to the animate (Uncle Tony and the village grocer). It was clear that Giuseppe Armani was destined to take his talent to the wider world.

And he did, thanks to a few fortunate twists of fate. A local priest proved instrumental in advancing the young man's career when he organized an exhibition of young artists. There, Armani's sculpture of an anatomically precise male torso was lauded by art critics for its amazing detail. To make a long story short, Giuseppe Armani took his talent and ran with it. Through the years, Armani publicly exhibited his many sculptures of clay, alabaster, and marble, while his reputation blossomed.

In 1975, the Florence Sculture d'Arte offered Armani the opportunity to work exclusively for them, giving him an absolute free hand to do with his artistic impulses as he saw fit. The end result has been more than a quarter of a century of Armani figurines, distinguished and adored for their impressive realism.

ESSENTIALS

If you're looking for places to buy, or just browse, it is imperative that you stop by the Collectors Gallery at *www.collectorsgallery.com*. Here you'll find figurines and more figurines for sale, but you'll also unearth links to some of the most prominent clubs in the various hobbies.

Collecting Armani

Giuseppe Armani was a prolific artist from the first day he picked up a pencil. His family was astounded at his unrelenting capacity to draw and draw and draw. Well, it carried over into his adult life. All you've got to do is look at the categories of Armani figurines to see that this man is one productive artist. And an artist not bound to a particular theme. Armani figurines are found in categories such as: "My Fair Ladies," "Disney," "Millennium," "*Novencento*," "Avant-garde," "Flower Ladies," "*Via Veneto*," "Spring Melodies," "Premier," "Seasons," "Clowns," "Professions," "Weddings," "Maternity," "Events," "Social," "Religious," "*Capodimonte*," "Florentine Garden," "Golden Age," "Wildlife," and "Children."

If you're interested in purchasing Armani figurines, or just want to get on a mailing list keeping you abreast of all the information on the newest Armani items, check out *www.collecto-mania.com*. You'll also find Hummels, Lladro, Harry Potter collectibles, and nativity set-ups here.

Precious Moments, Dreamsicles, and Cherished Teddies

Precious Moments debuted in 1978, the work of artist Samuel Butcher. The small porcelain bisque figurines portrayed little boys and girls engaging in the impulsive activities of youth—jumping rope, riding a skateboard, and the like.

Butcher was a former minister, and a deeply religious man. He named his creations Precious Moments because he believed the figurines embodied the spiritual message of "love, caring, and sharing." And they reflected his strong beliefs in their names ("Blessed Are the Pure In Heart," "I Believe In Miracles," "Prayer Changes Things," and so on), if not precisely in their design.

There have been more than 1,000 different Precious Moments figurines marketed through the years. And each year the company retires several of its statuettes to make room for new issues. This fact alone has begot a busy secondary market for Precious Moments figurines, which has grown exponentially through the years, as more and more of the older issues are available only in the trade. If you're a Precious Moments collector, or want to be one, visit *www.preciousmomentscommunity.com.*

Dreamsicles is a collectible figurine that is sometimes confused with Precious Moments—but not by their respective collectors. There is a considerable following for collectors of Dreamsicles pieces—from figurines to plates to key chains.

Dreamsicles was the brainchild of artist Kristin Haynes. In 1991, she introduced the world to an army of cherubic-like characters replete with large eyes, round noses, plump cheeks, and bashful smiles. The warm and reassuring images of guilelessness became so popular that Haynes, who initially produced and marketed the items herself, turned to Cast Art Industries to manufacture the Dreamsicles line. Through the years, Dreamsicles have featured its cherubs and little animals marking events common to all of us: the first day at school, playtime in the schoolyard, frolicking with friends, marriage, and so on. They've become one of the leading collectibles in the giftware industry. With their individual castings, finishing, and hand painting, you are assured that no two Dreamsicles will ever be alike. If you're interested in learning more about Dreamsicles, go to *www.dreamsicles.com.*

People love inanimate bears in our cartoons (Yogi Bear), teddy bears, and made of bisque, too, as in the Cherished Teddies Collection, which were first marketed in 1992. Like Cabbage Patch Kids, each Cherished Teddies figurine comes with a Certificate of Adoption, which can be completed by its owner and mailed to the Cherished Teddies Adoption Center.

Cherished Teddies by Enesco are the creations of artist Priscilla Hillman, who has breathed life into a line of charming little bear figurines. She's even given them a town all their own, aptly called Cherished Teddies Town. These bears are made of cold cast resin and are hand-painted with oil-based lacquer paint. If you want more of the bear facts, check out *www.enescoclubs.com* and follow the directions to Cherished Teddies Town.

ESSENTIALS There are numerous collectible-related Web sites in virtual reality. Here are a couple of places that you should surf on over to: *www.whaticollect.com* and *www.worldcollectorsnet.com*. Both sites connect collectors from all fields—from dolls, autographs, glass, and trading cards, to places of interest in their respective hobbies.

Nodders

These figurines are interchangeably referred to these days as nodders, bobbing head dolls, and bobble heads. I'm talking about those

Enesco ceramic parrot with bobbing head

eccentric doll-like figures that firmly stand on a base but have their heads attached to a spring mechanism of some kind. This enables the heads to bob up and down, or side to side, when touched by a human hand, or all by themselves during an earthquake or some other natural disaster.

The *nodder* was in fact its original moniker, because when the dolls first appeared on the scene in the late 1800s, their heads nodded from side to side. The earliest of nodders depicted animals, comic characters, and zany images of human beings at work. Remember the nodding dogs and tigers that used to be rockin' and a rollin' in a car's back window? They were all nodders.

The bobbing head dolls—up-and-down head nodding—arrived on the scene in the 1950s and fast became favorites with the public, particularly in the sports worlds of baseball and to a lesser degree football. In 1960, Major League Baseball produced a series of 6½" bobbing head dolls, one for each of its then sixteen teams. The dolls were made in Japan of papier-mâché. Their design featured smiling little boys or a mascot adorned in the team uniform—cap to cleats. The initial series of these dolls was anchored to a white base. These original baseball bobbing heads in mint (quite rare), or near mint, condition are highly sought after by collectors.

FACTS

Some of the most popular bobbing head dolls are the earliest Major League Baseball authorized issues. In 1960, MLB issued team dolls on a white base. In 1962, similar team dolls were done, except with a green base, plus player bobbing heads featuring stars Mickey Mantle, Willie Mays, Roberto Clemente, and Roger Maris. If in mint condition, these dolls command big bucks, with the Clemente doll reaping $2,000 and more.

The bobbing head doll was not just a sports affair in the 1960s. Character bobbing heads appeared at the same time, imitating favorite comic strip and cartoon figures of the day like Dick Tracy, Felix the Cat, Bozo, Popeye, and Porky Pig. Even flesh-and-blood celebrities and TV characters—like the Beatles, Dr. Kildare, Ben Casey, and comedian Charley Weaver—found their way onto bobbing heads. Occupations were also featured on the dolls, from flighty astronauts on down the line to country doctors. Historical figures weren't ignored, from good guys Ben Franklin and JFK, to tyrants Mao Tse-Tung and Fidel Castro. Everybody and everything was a candidate for bobbing head status. And yes, of course, the product-advertising world couldn't resist getting in on the fun, and so Mr. Peanut, Colonel Sanders, and Bob's Big Boy got in on the action.

The bobbing head has made an extraordinary comeback in the twenty-first century. The old papier-mâché dolls have blazed the trail for ceramic and lots and lots of plastic offspring. Today, the new breed of bobbing head is more often than not referred to as a *bobble head*. It's back, beloved, and collected in increasing numbers. And yes, the new bobble heads on the block are likely to wear better over time—materially speaking, that is—but they don't quite sport the charisma of their vintage predecessors.

ESSENTIALS

What are you waiting for? Get shaking. And head on over to *www.nationalbobbinheadclub.com*. This is the National Bobbin Head Club's official Web site. If you're a bobbing head collector, or thinking about becoming one, it's worth checking out.

Major League Baseball, for one, has seen team after team offer the dolls as promotional freebies to attract more fans. Stadium gift shops' bobble head sales have skyrocketed. And this rebirth in bobbing head

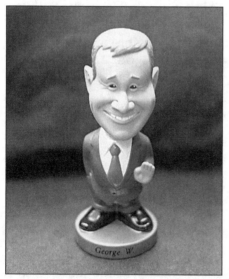

Presidential bobbing head: "George W."

interest, much like its original heyday in the early 1960s, has infected the world beyond sports. The Hormel Company has introduced a Spam bobble head, hoping to link a beloved little nodder with its perplexingly popular meat-like spread.

Why this bobbing head reawakening? Well, it was just a matter of time before these interesting dolls experienced a rebirth of interest. They've never disappeared from the market because there's always been a cheerful quality about bobbing heads that draws people—kids and adults alike—to tap them on their tops. Their wobbly quality makes even the most unsavory personages collectible while in a bobbing head state. You can put out on display a Fidel Castro bobbing head and chuckle at its intricate silliness. Regardless of whose face it's wearing, the bobbing head doll is a benign presence. And that's part of its appeal.

When the New York Mets sold out of their entire 3,000-doll inventory of Mike Piazza bobble heads on their very first home game of the 2001 season, it surprised even the marketing mavens who are paid big bucks not to be surprised. It was a sign of the times. Heads were indeed turning, or, in this case, bobbing.

Collecting bobbing head dolls is a fun hobby. Bobbing heads look quite dignified on display and make for great conversation pieces. Collectors are afforded many options in the hobby. The nodder is waiting for you in online auctions, specialty stores and Web sites, at antique and memorabilia shows, and—yes—they're seen on occasion at the tried-and-true flea market. Keep your eyes peeled and you'll get the nod to go ahead and make a buy to add, or start, a collection of bobbing head dolls.

ESSENTIALS

If you're interested in collecting the bobbing head dolls of today, a visit to *www.funko.com* is well worth the trip. The "Wacky Wobblers" from the hip cats at Funko include quite a cast of characters, and they're regularly releasing new bobbing heads into the wider world. Another place to scope out is *www.trendco.com*.

If you fancy yourself an investment collector, and are not attracted to bobbing head dolls for their special charm, this isn't the collectible for you. Sure, there are many valuable bobbing head dolls, particularly the vintage issues. But, even though the bobbing head is flying high again as a choice collectible item, it's still not a hobby teeming with the kind of big-dollar numbers that garner so much attention in so many other collectible fields.

The varied original bobbing head dolls from the 1960s—the most popular decade for vintage collectors—and many earlier issues are available in today's trade in hit-or-miss conditions. The papier-mâché composition of most of these dolls has ensured that the preponderance of those extant are suffering the ravages of age. Hairline cracks are common, as are broken springs and faded color. Alas, some are even chipping away, with pieces gone with the wind.

Naturally, this deteriorating condition predicament has given rise to repair artists, who have moved in with a vengeance to patch up the bobbing heads in need of serious upgrading. Fixing problems of this kind creates new ones. Restoration is fine if the restorer is doing it for his or her personal collection. And if the restorer wants to sell a bobbing head doll that's undergone a transformation of any kind, it is imperative that this information be made public knowledge.

When you're considering purchasing a vintage bobbing head doll, start with the obvious. Examine it closely for cracks. A couple of cracks are generally tolerated and expected with older bobbing head dolls, particularly those made of papier-mâché. If the cracks become chips—then that's another ball of wax. Any missing pieces dramatically diminish the money value and certainly the doll's ocular seductiveness. In addition to cracks and chips, also pay special attention to loss of coloring and flaking due to the sands of time and the unhealthy climes the bobbing head has suffered through.

If you're dealing with a reputable seller, and you're satisfied with the bobbing head's overall condition—make the transaction. If you're buying from an unknown source, look for repainting and other acts of repair on the doll. Get inside the head of that bobber if you must and check for a sprinkling of excess paint or a lump of overflow papier-mâché. These are the inevitable footprints of post-manufacturing tampering. And then there are cracks, which may be covered up discriminatingly on the outside of the head, but reveal themselves on the inside. It's merely a question of using your eyes and having the basic knowledge of what to look for, which you now have.

CHAPTER 14
Books

Bibliophiles, lovers and collectors of books, have been around longer than most other collectors have. That's because mass-produced books have been around for centuries—since the middle of the fifteenth century when Johannes Gutenberg converted an ordinary winepress into a movable-type printing press. And people have been collecting them almost as long.

The History of Books

Many have called the printing press, invented by Johannes Gutenberg, the most significant invention of all time, the invention that radically altered the world. Born in 1395 in the German city of Mainz, Gutenberg labored as a goldsmith and a gem cutter, all the while acquiring knowledge of the properties of metals.

With financial backing from a partner, Johann Fust, Gutenberg perfected a movable type cast in metal that could be evenly spaced and set on a printing press. This was a revolutionary advancement in 1440, the year Gutenberg completed his wooden printing press and consummated its marriage with his new-fashioned metal type. This new type consisted of the metals lead, antimony, and tin and was fashioned into 290 separate symbols. Gutenberg even formulated special ink from boiled linseed oil and soot to enhance the visual appeal of the mass printing of words, which turned into pages and pages, and then whole books. He so finely tuned his newfangled invention that it enabled him to squeeze water out of the paper, while simultaneously printing on it.

Clay type had been invented and utilized in China 400 years earlier, but it was quite inefficient and cumbersome compared to the durable metal type employed in the Gutenberg machine. Prior to the Gutenberg innovation, books were around in awkward forms, mostly created by and for the Church. The book production process involved a craftsman carving out a block of wood and leaving raised the section to be printed. One page of text would often require that several blocks of wood be joined together. It was a very time-consuming process to say the least—not to mention that the wooden blocks did not pass the durability test.

The first printed Bible to see the light of day, the Gutenberg Bible, was printed in 1455. It contained forty-two lines per page and it took Gutenberg over two years to complete. It also was the first "modern" book ever printed in Europe—a triumphal first undertaking indeed. At the time of the first Bible's publication, Europe was in the midst of great changes. The entire continent was emerging from the Middle Ages. With a populace hungry for knowledge, Gutenberg's contribution to this period of history—the Renaissance—was immeasurable. His printing press slowly but certainly ushered in the era of mass production of books and the secularization of learning and enlightenment, which would ultimately lead to schooling and media.

FACTS

Before movable type became omnipresent in the printing process, books were regularly handwritten. Every single word and every single letter were copied onto parchment or *vellum* (animal hide). Scribes methodically went about their jobs of reproducing the printed word. As you can imagine, errors were made in the transcription process. It was kind of like the game we played as kids called Telephone, where a message was passed from one person to the next, and by the time it reached the last person, it bore little resemblance to the original message. The moral of the story is, don't believe everything you read or hear.

Why Collect Books

Thomas Jefferson once said, "I cannot live without books." The author of the Declaration of Independence and third President of the United States, Jefferson was a true Renaissance man. He was an inventor and an architect; a writer and a scientist; a connoisseur of fine wines and a farmer. He also was a prolific bibliophile. Jefferson's first rather considerable library was completely incinerated in a fire in 1770, yet he was able to amass another one. During the War of 1812, the British burned the U.S. Capitol and the Library of Congress's 3,000 books along with it. Jefferson generously offered the federal government his own personal library as a replacement. He was paid $23,950 for 6,487 volumes, which effectively more than doubled the size of the previous government library. But Jefferson wasn't done collecting books. By the time of his death in 1826, he had accumulated several thousand more.

Are you one of the soldiers in the book battalion who regularly comb bookstores and flea markets looking for—what else—books? If you are, you are among a collector set who collects, first and foremost, to read their finds, and secondly, to add them to their very own growing libraries. If you engage in this activity, you are collecting used books (reading copies) as opposed to antiquarian books, which are considered the truly desired collectible books.

The numerous collectors of used books are worth mentioning, even though most of these books are worthless in a strictly monetary sense. For the highfalutin set, these book buyers are not collectors at all, but accumulators of things. Just don't tell that to them.

These collectors are often disciples of books and reading alike. They search high and low for books of particular interest to them. And you know what? This ignored element of the book-collecting hobby, while simultaneously gratifying and educational, has absolutely nothing to do with future resale value—and that's a refreshing thought. Instead, it's about locating a diamond in the rough—a book that will educate or entertain, and many times both.

Paperback
books

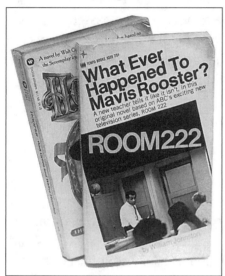

There are more and more book superstores sprouting up all over the place. Regrettably, these book-selling behemoths are chasing away many independent booksellers, who just can't compete with the discount prices that the big boys offer their customers. And, if that isn't bad enough for the neighborhood bookstore, there's Amazon.com, which offers all the latest book titles at cut rate prices, and will even do searches for out-of-print books, if you so desire.

Yes, bigness and technology have dramatically altered the book trade. And since there's no putting this genie back in the bottle, we might as well take advantage of these new opportunities to locate and buy books. Search the Internet auction and Web sites. Books are all over the place. And don't forget the old tried-and-true places to find books—the flea markets and garage sales, and the many sellers of used books. People don't put out books with the trash. It's considered sacrilege. So, this means that unwanted books are going to find themselves in foster homes all over the place, like at flea markets, libraries, Salvation Army outlets, and used bookstores.

Book lovers find gems in all these places. Used book collectors usually concentrate their time and resources in areas of special interest to them. Some people read everything and anything they can get their hands on. But most people don't, and concentrate on their special interests: paperback romance novels, Civil War, biographies, historical fiction, mystery novels, autobiographies, and so on.

Books are fascinating collectibles in a whole host of ways. Foremost, there is quite a selection of them to choose from—both in print and out of print. And there is tremendous variance in both style and content. A smart fellow once opined, "Variety is the spice of life." And there's no better place to rendezvous with variety than at a library or in a bookstore.

FACTS

Reproduction of books prior to the Gutenberg advancement was done by hand transcription and cutting a page of text into wood. This wood cutting method was a labor-intensive undertaking that necessitated great skills from the craftsmen involved in the job. Some of these pages were illuminated, with striking illustrations and ornamental adornments. As a matter of fact, some of the earliest printers who utilized the Gutenberg press attempted as best they could to maintain the elegance and pattern of the illuminations.

Types of Used Books Available

Generally speaking, today's newly published books fall into one of three categories: hardcover, trade paperbacks, and paperbacks. The trade paperback is fast becoming the most oft-purchased book around. These are the glossy softcover editions that are noticeably larger than the common paperback. They are sometimes referred to as *quality paperbacks*. What you most appreciate about them—particularly in this day and age—is their cost. They are significantly cheaper than their hardcover brethren.

A visit to any secondhand bookstore will reveal to you that the sleek trade paperback of today is a relatively recent phenomenon (post-1960s). There were predominantly paperbacks and hardcovers before then, with little in between. The oversized paperbacks of yesteryear didn't much distinguish themselves. Old bookstores' shelves are mostly loaded with hardcover books and sometimes racks of unassuming yellowing paperbacks.

"Wehman Bros." series of mini-books. (circa 1906)

Book hunters uncover all sorts of secondhand treasures in their searches. This is what makes the hunt so exhilarating. They find books that the general buying public was never meant to see, such as *advance reading copies* and *advance reviewer copies* of books that were sent—prior to publication—to booksellers, book clubs, book reviewers, and other publicity people. These books, in many instances, were uncorrected proofs with different bindings and covers—and sometimes entirely different typefaces—from the subsequent published versions of the same titles. These are intriguing book discoveries that open a window for the everyday reader into the book publishing process. For book aficionados, it's particularly fascinating to discover a book in its advance state. It adds a little extra spice to the book hunt.

Other unusual finds include book club editions. These books were often printed with a lesser quality paper and binding materials than the trade editions, which are the books that are sold to bookstores for sale to the public. Book club books are offered to their members at discounted prices—hence, the economical manufacturing features. Other oddities include books that were once library books put out to pasture in used bookstores.

FACTS

Rare books, first editions, signed books, illustrated books, plus articles and features of interest to collectors of books of all kinds are here at *www.alibris.com. Ex libris* is Latin for "from the library of" or "from the books of."

The Qualities That Make Books Valuable

Okay, you've got a library of your own. Your bookshelves run over into your closets and maybe your attic and garage, too. The collector aristocracy might say that you don't have a collection at all, but merely an accumulation of books that have 25-cent flea market stickers written all over them. And maybe this is the case—but maybe it's not: You just might have a desired book in your mix. You might even have a sleeper in there—a book that nobody gives a second thought about right now, but that will become a treasure in twenty or thirty years' time. In the collectible arena, you never quite know what's around the corner.

ALERT

If you have a book that means a great deal to you, be sure to encase it in a dust jacket protector. Brodart Company Library Supplies and Furnishings at *www.brodart.com,* or 800-233-8959, has these book saviors—and more—for sale.

In any event, taking proper care of your collectibles is always in your best interest. Books are no exception. Letting them sit on a shelf for years is not the equivalent of taking good care of them. So, even if their monetary value is the farthest thing from your mind, take care of your books—if for no other reason than that they look better in superior condition and are much more readable that way.

The Value of Books

There's one big misimpression that swirls around books. It's the same one that often dogs other collectibles. The myth is that old books are intrinsically valuable just because they are old—and for no other reason than that. Although wisdom sometimes does come with age, sometimes it doesn't. Not every senior citizen is blessed with the wisdom of Solomon. And similarly, not every old book is wanted by collectors and worth a pile of money.

It's a fact of life for many people that what comes with age is aging (wrinkles, hair loss, tooth decay, age spots) and little else. The same is true of most books. An old book is often a dusty, yellowing, brittle, deteriorating sheaf of papers. You certainly know these books when you touch them. They leave an invisible, musty film on your hands that even the toughest industrial soap in the world can't seem to wash away.

Since books have been around for centuries, there are loads and loads of them—that much is certain. Consequently, not every old book is in demand by book collectors. Take the Bible as an example. Millions of American families own copies of the Bible, or have at some point in their lineage. The Bible is a family heirloom in many instances. Great-great-grandma's family Bible became Great-grandma's, then Grandma's, and now it belongs to you. The fact is that there have been more Bibles published in more forms than any other book in the history of the world. And more people holding onto them means that there is a generous bounty of Bibles amidst both the saintly and the sinners alike. And yes, while many of these copies of the Bible have great spiritual and sentimental value to their owners, most editions do not sport high price tags in the book trade. Pre-eighteenth-century Bibles are another Bible story. But really, the Bible's not supposed to be about dollars and cents, right?

Fittingly, though, the Bible is illustrative of the overall book collectible marketplace. What determines a book's value in the collectible marketplace are the usual suspects: condition and scarcity, coupled with a keen understanding of the book's past sales history and perceived desirability to collectors. There are books that are a century old, two centuries, and even three, which are not especially coveted by collectors. Hence, they don't have much, if any, monetary worth. This is just the nature of books. But then, this isn't a hobby driven solely by dollars, even though there are many extremely valuable rare books.

The first test that a book must pass before it ever can be considered a desired collectible is the condition test. Even some of the rarest books around lose most of their appeal to collectors when they are in poor or damaged condition. Restoring dolls may be commonplace, but restoring books is not so easily accomplished. Antiquarian books need to be in as close to their original condition as possible to maintain collector appeal. This means that they need to have their original *dust jacket* (the removable paper cover often used to promote the book in some way, or catch a browser's eye), no torn pages, damaged covers, mold and mildew, insect remains, and other signs of the book death rattle.

This is merely the first test an antiquarian book needs to pass. It's like passing the eye test on the way to getting your driver's license. The hard part comes when you nervously get behind the wheel and hit the road. For books, there are a variety of distinctive components that cultivate collector demand. I cover some of them in the following sections.

SSENTIALS At *www.software4collectors.com*, you'll find a complete software program designed with the book collector in mind. Libraries use this program to organize their books, and you can do the same.

Age

In and of itself *old* doesn't equal *valuable*. There are, however, some books from certain periods of time that are popularly collected. Any books printed prior to 1501 are desired because of their extreme rarity.

This applies also to English books printed before 1641. American books published before the turn of the nineteenth century and pre-1850 books from west of the Mississippi are very alluring to antiquarian collectors.

First Edition

First editions of books are generally more sought after than later ones. How do you know if you have a first edition? Many books indicate on the page following the title page that it's a first edition or first printing. You will sometimes see a list of numbers and letters. First editions will begin with "1" or "A"; second editions, with "2" or "B"; third editions, with "3" or "C"; and so on. Remember that even though the terms *first edition* and *first printing* are sometimes used interchangeably, they don't mean the same thing. A first edition can have more than one printing, and sometimes it has several. A subsequent edition, as opposed to a printing, usually indicates that the original book content has been modified in some way.

Scarcity

In the antiquarian book collector's market, scarcity looms like a colossus, perhaps more so than in all other collectible hobbies. A book, for instance, printed in a limited edition in some capacity is obviously more sought after than the same book plucked from its 50,000 first edition print run. There are lots of twists and turns in the book production process concerning its various editions and print runs. This is why it is particularly key to have the knowledge of a book's history at your disposal, if this is at all possible. There are countless instances of first editions with very large printings, that also did limited editions, many of which were autographed by the author. Limited editions are often impressively bound and uniquely styled. Add this nifty look to their small circulation numbers and you've got a tailor-made, coveted collectible.

First Books

Famous authors weren't always famous. Unless you're born into a royal family, fame usually has to be earned. And so an author's always got a first book that he or she has published. Many times these original efforts garner little or no attention. It's akin to the Hollywood celebrity who began his or her acting career in commercials peddling Skippy Peanut Butter or shilling for Burger King. First editions, therefore, of these very first books often prove quite a collectible find, particularly early novels by unknowns who strike it big later on down the literary road.

Sign of the Times

Books with author signatures have more collector value than books without them. And better still, personalized inscriptions from the author trump even those solitary signatures. And better yet still, if the personalized inscription is made to another famous sort, you've reached the pinnacle. Alert time! For collectors who acquire anything with a signature or inscription—need we say it—make certain it's genuine and not the work of a ubiquitous scammer.

QUESTIONS?

What does the term *incunabula* mean?
Books printed prior to 1501 and utilizing Gutenberg's movable type are referred to in the antiquarian book trade as *incunabula,* plural for the Latin word *incunabulum,* which literally means "cradle." If you've got any *incunabula* on your bookshelves, you've got some valuable books indeed.

Awards

Literary folks and other artistic types love dispensing awards to one another. And even though many of these so-called awards are politicized and elitist in nature, they nevertheless impact on a book's desirability to collectors. Here are just some of the annual awards that are bestowed on writers: the Nobel Prize for literature; the Pulitzer, given to writers of American nonfiction, literature, and other categories; the National Book Award, for writers of American nonfiction; the Newberry Medal, for American writers of children's literature; the Carnegie Medal, for English writers of children's literature; the Caldecott Medal, for writers and illustrators of children's picture books; the Nebula and Hugo Awards, for writers of science fiction; and the Edgar Award, for writers of mystery novels.

How to Care for Books

Anything made of pulp products is a prime candidate for decaying as the clock ticks and the calendars turn. And books certainly fit the bill. Books are like people with weak immune systems; they are susceptible to so many maladies.

Book preservation authorities implore book collectors to be eternally vigilant in watching over their book collections. And this means regularly inspecting books for bugs and rodents and the onset of mold and mildew. There is a point of no return in insect and mice infestation and in the progression of fungi. If these problems are not detected early, the ravaged book may well be a candidate for book cremation. Early detection is therefore essential.

The best place to store or display books is a location with low humidity. If you wonder what humid air can do to a book, take a softcover book to your favorite seaside spot. The moisture-laden sea breeze may be refreshing and uplifting for you when you deeply inhale, but take a look at your book after a few days of lying out. The book's cover will quickly get the bends, and its interior pages will slowly but surely turn from white to off-white, and eventually yellow. The paper will be increasingly brittle to the touch.

Then, of course, there's the sun. A book's spine will fade fast when exposed to direct sunlight. And if you display your books in an enclosed bookcase, be sure to stack them vertically and allow for some ventilation. Shelves without backboards are best. Condensation in hermetically sealed bookcases and cabinets—where air cannot circulate—happens all the time. And condensation is fine in the refrigerator and on the morning grass, but it damages books. Antiquarian books, especially, should be loosely shelved to allow for proper circulation. A scattering of whole cloves on bookshelves is an effective tool in staving off the onset of mildew. If you notice the beginnings of any these unwelcome fungi, lightly spray a soft cloth with a disinfectant and carefully wipe the affected area.

Also, don't wrap books in newspapers and the like. Newspapers are very acidic. Don't store them with newspaper and magazine clippings and any bric-a-brac. The only companion a book ever really needs is you. Dust your books regularly with a feather duster. Dust is not a friend of you or your books.

Speaking of you and your book, how you handle a book matters. Mom taught us not to grab. Well, this is particularly sound advice when reaching for a book in your collection. Grabbing it from its top begins the inexorable weakening of the book's spine. When you need a book for whatever reason, the best advice is to push in the two books on either side of it, and then pull out the book you want by grasping it at mid-spine, and not from the top. Bookends are also useful in preventing warping.

Use kid gloves when handling a book. Clean hands are always a plus. And don't lick your fingers when turning a book's pages. Mr. Smith, your high school trigonometry teacher, may have done that when handing out his mimeographed test papers, but saliva is highly acidic. Okay for trigonometry tests—unwanted ephemera—but bad for books. And kind of gross, too.

SSENTIALS

To remove bad odors from old books, pour either odor-absorbing cat litter (scent-free) or baking soda into a large plastic container with a snap-shut lid. Put the smelly book in a smaller plastic container of its own, without a lid. Place the uncovered smaller plastic container into the larger plastic and snap the lid shut. Leave the book in the container for weeks if necessary.

The Grades of Books

When looking to buy or sell a book, you should know what a book's condition description means. Here's a simplified version of various book condition terms:

- New/Very Fine (VF)/Mint: These three descriptive terms should only be applied to books that are in pristine "hot off the press" condition, but even new books usually don't make these grades because of damage done in shipping the books from the printer to the bookstore.
- Fine (F): A book in this condition is as close to Mint as is possible without perfect crispness; a lack of defects and a tight binding are a must.
- Very Good (VG): A book in this condition shows small signs of wear, but no tears on binding or interior pages; it no longer lies flat when open.
- Good (G): A book in this condition is typically a used book with all its pages intact, as well as possibly loose bindings and tears on dust jackets.
- Fair (FR): A book in this condition is well worn, and handled, with all its text pages intact; it may be missing some of its interior end pages, and its bindings and dust jackets may be noticeably worn.
- Poor (P): A book in this condition has text that is still intact and legible; the copy could be soiled and spotted with serious binding defects.

FACTS

The general consensus of what makes a book a desired collectible, as opposed to a mere accumulated collectible, implores us to exclude a whole host of books in the big-game collectible hunt. The undesirables are as follows: mass printings of any book, most paperbacks, encyclopedias, dictionaries, romance, popular fiction without dust jackets, textbooks, common family Bibles, and *Reader's Digest* condensed books (translation: the vast majority of everything ever published). But remember—there are always exceptions!

CHAPTER 15
Photographs and Postcards

Go through the basements and attics and drawe rs of any American household, and you're likely to come across dozens of old photographs and postcards. Americans have a love affair with the camera, so it only makes sense that many collect images— whether in a photo album or on postcards.

Say Cheese! Collecting Photographs

Collecting vintage and historic photographs is a growing hobby, thanks in no small part to Internet auction sites, which offer up a steady diet of old photographs of all varieties. Daguerreotypes, ambrotypes, tintypes or ferrotypes, carte-de-visites, cabinet cards, stereotypes, and many others are sold every day to everyday folks like you. Tracking down these visions of history has never been easier.

The Science of Photography

The science of photography is not very easily explained in layman speak. Most of us don't give much thought to the principles at work when

Early twentieth-century photograph (studio portrait)

we push a button on this contraption called a camera. But when you step back and ponder what's happening when you click away, it's truly a fascinating process. A moment in time is frozen—for all time, optimistically speaking—on a photograph.

Silver nitrate, a light-sensitive chemical, played the role of a lifetime in the birth of photography. When exposed to light, silver nitrate transforms itself from a light silvery gray to black. Experimenting souls resolved that if something—glass or paper, for example—were coated with the chemical, and then exposed to light and shadow, it would develop an image on it, as the components of the silver nitrate turned black. This was a considerable deduction that changed the world forever! The only stumbling block was that the image, when brought into the light of day, turned completely black. With great alacrity, the unexposed portions of the silver nitrate spread like wild fire, annihilating the image.

The bug that needed to be worked out was how to preserve the developed image without losing it to the forces of light. Fortunately, a

Frenchman named Louis J. M. Daguerre figured it all out. In 1839, he fixed the problem and made photography and photographs possible. Soon after, an Englishman, William H. F. Talbot, with an entirely different solution to the impasse, also solved the riddle of the unexposed silver nitrate.

Daguerre's subsequent photographic images were called *daguerreotypes.* His photographic invention, very simply put, involved a polished, copper plate of metal—a mirror-like surface—treated with silver nitrate and made light-sensitive by exposure to iodine. Daguerreotype images were developed within the camera device itself. No negatives were involved; meaning that every positive image produced was one-of-a-kind. Daguerreotypes often resulted in strikingly sharp and detailed images. These were the very first photographs.

Talbot's photographic brainchild was called the *calotype,* and sometimes the *Talbotype.* His method revolved around a paper print developed from a paper negative. The calotype never took hold in America, but it was popular in England in the 1840s. The downside of the calotype was its paper quality, which ensured that the details of the photographic images were much less sharp than the daguerreotypes'. Let's just say that the calotypes' negative was its biggest negative as a photographic method.

FACTS

The name Matthew Brady is synonymous with historical photographs. Brady, a portrait artist, is best known for his Civil War photographs. Ironically, he was losing his eyesight during the war years, and his competent assistants Alexander Gardner and Timothy O'Sullivan took most of his photographs for him.

Why People Collect Photographs

People collect photographs from the past for the same reason that they take photographs in the present: to note and remember moments, events, and people. Photographs—particularly old ones—are collectible treasures because they are more than mere articles from the past. They've captured the images that are literal windows into all of our yesterdays. It's the closest thing we have to traversing the time barrier.

Vintage-photograph collectors are more than just interested in old photos because of the fascinating antiquated photography processes that produced them. They are interested in history. And when they study a photographic image from the nineteenth century, for instance, they step into a time and a place that no longer exists—if only for a fleeting moment.

ESSENTIALS

If you happen to be a collector of archival materials (documents, photographs, and other materials from historical moments in the past), you have the added burden of preserving history as well as your own collection. Look into the best products available for protecting archival materials from their enemies. Check out *www.superiorarchivalmats.com* or 888-857-1722.

It's commonplace for people to get swept into an old picture. Looking at the main subjects of pictures, the clothes that they were wearing, or the hairstyles of that moment in time, is a fascinating journey. Or perhaps it's something in the background of the photograph that catches your eye, like a store window's advertising, or cars on the street that all look the same. Or maybe what grabs you is that there are no cars on the street because the automobile hadn't been invented yet.

Type of Photographs Collected

Nineteenth-century French composer Hector Berlioz once remarked, "Time is a great teacher, but unfortunately it kills all of its pupils." Collectors of vintage photographs are well aware of time's exacting price. But they also celebrate time, by preserving its images, notwithstanding its unrelenting march into the future of the unknown.

The types of pictures of the past that are most often sought and collected include those covered in the following sections.

ESSENTIALS

Collectors of vintage photographs should visit the photography museum at *www.photographymuseum.com.* This site has a wealth of advice and counsel on how to preserve your photographs.

Ambrotypes

Ambrotypes were the first inexpensive alternatives to the pricey daguerreotypes. Frederic Scott Archer, a sculptor by trade, introduced this new photographic process in 1855, and it fast became the preferred method of photography for portrait galleries, supplanting daguerreotypes. Courtesy of its moderate cost, ambrotype portraits became accessible to the professional and working classes of the day. Ambrotypes were essentially derived from a glass plate negative against a black background, creating what appeared to be a positive image when viewed in the proper light. The peak moment for ambrotype photographs occurred around 1860 at the start of the Civil War. Ambrotype photography, however, waned with the introduction of the carte-de-visite, which became the rage in the mid-1860s (see the next section).

ESSENTIALS

For any collector of vintage photographs or photographic equipment, a stopover worth making is at *www.superexpo.com/aphs,* the American Photographic Historical Society. Here you'll find an updated calendar of photographic events and oodles of information on how to locate pictorial treasures anywhere from flea markets to photo fairs.

Carte-de-Visite (CDV)

Introduced in 1854 by a French photographer named A. A. Disderi, this photographic method involved the manufacturing of multiple images on a single glass plate and transferring them onto a card stock. Disderi, a court photographer for Emperor Napoleon III, also devised a camera with four lenses capable of producing a negative with four images on a single glass plate. This was a key technological advance for portrait photographers, who could now reproduce their photographs and offer multiple copies of pictures to their customers. Between 1860 and 1865, the Civil War years, carte-de-visites, which measured 2½" × 4¼", ruled the photographic roost, with every family worth their salt having their very own carte-de-visite picture album.

Cabinet Card

The cabinet card, mounted on paper stock, replaced the carte-de-visite. These images were larger (4¼" × 6½") than the carte-de-visites, enabling the photographers of the day to work with a larger area. Cabinet cards grew in popularity and dominated the photograph playing field in the 1880s, and then slowly rode off into the sunset as more and more photographic alternatives and advances were introduced.

Tintype

Of all the earliest photograph types, the tintype sported the longest legs. Introduced in 1856, the tintype, or *ferrotype* as it is sometimes called, was still regularly produced at the turn of the twentieth century, and even later at country fairs, traveling carnivals, and beach boardwalk parlors into the 1930s. The tintype photograph got its name from the fact that its image was produced on a metal plate, in contrast to the ambrotype, which used a glass plate. The appearances of both the tintype and the ambrotype are very similar. Both images are whitish gray. The tintype process, however, used iron to buttress its image. If you are unsure if what you're looking at is a tintype or something else, get hold of a magnet. Iron is attracted to a magnet; ambrotypes will not respond to one, nor will daguerreotypes, which are made with copper.

Stereotype

The stereotype was yet another innovative and popular classification of photography. There were many stereotypes manufactured from the mid-1800s to the mid-1900s, and they distinguished themselves by their two roughly identical images mounted side by side. When seen through a stereo viewer these two images appeared three-dimensional.

ESSENTIALS

The ideal storage environment for most photographs is at a temperature of 68 degrees and relative humidity in the range of 30 to 40 percent. Contemporary color photographs and their negatives do well in a cooler setting (30 to 40 degrees). If you can't offer your photographs a storage utopia, just do the best that you can.

Wish You Were Here! Collecting Postcards

People collect postcards for the same reason that they send them. It's an appropriate event and people marker. When you're on vacation with the family, the trip wouldn't be complete without combing a postcard rack at the souvenir shop in town. And how many times have you bought a bunch of extra postcards to keep for yourself? Many times, of course. After all, postcards are cheap. Ten postcards for $1 is not uncommon. Sometimes you can even get fifteen for $1. After a couple of decades of vacationing, you've probably accumulated quite a postcard collection. And it's a collection with a very personal touch; one that documents your life and—hopefully—some of the best times.

Postcards

Postcard collecting is ideal for kids as well as adults. Get your kids started now, if they haven't already begun a collection themselves. Wherever you go, pick up a postcard or two. They are ideal learning tools. If your work takes you to different places, bring back some postcards from each stopover. Airport gift shops are full of them. You'll be pleasantly surprised at how much your youngsters will appreciate them, and how much it'll spur them on to want to know more about the people, places, and things that grace the postcards.

Of course, for many serious postcard collectors, current postcards may or may not be a part of their always-growing inventory. For sure, though, their postcards go back in time. Postcard collectors have so much to choose from. The styles through the years vary a great deal and the subject matter is limitless. Postcards have been on the scene in the United States since the middle of the nineteenth century, and they span the globe. These two historical facts open up endless avenues for postcard collectors to travel down.

ESSENTIALS If you're looking for antique postcards, you should check out *www.vintagepostcards.com.* They specialize in vintage postcards of all sorts. A page of postcards even showcases "postcards about postcards." For example, "Brook's Store, Headquarters for Souvenir Post Cards" from Hoboken, New Jersey. Cost: $100.

The History of Postcards

One of the earliest American postcards on record sports a December 1848 postmark on it. From 1848 to 1893, privately issued postcards were produced, but they are very rare finds in today's postcard hobby. During this period, only the federal government was permitted to use the term *post card* on a piece of mail. Non-government postcards of this time were imprinted with such things as *souvenir card, correspondence card,* and *mail card.* And it cost twice as much to mail a non-government postcard in those days.

The postcard was around and available, but as a widely used mailing preference, it remained rather obscure. That is, until it received national attention and acclaim at the World's Fair in Chicago in 1893. Two types of postcards were sold at this hugely attended and exciting event celebrating the technological innovations of the day. There was the government-issued postcard, which required a one-cent stamp for mailing, and there were numerous souvenir postcards from the fair, which required a two-cent stamp.

These early postcards have been classified as part of the Pioneer Era. The pioneer postcards (1893–1898) in effect greased the skids for the many, many private issues to follow. In the last decade of the nineteenth century, the postcard maintained a rather mysterious appeal to the folks who encountered them for the first time. Sending something other than a letter—with an image on it, no less—was a dazzling alternative. But for the men and women on the cusp of the twentieth century, the postcard as a routine mailing option was a novel breakthrough. Since communication with friends and relations far away was done exclusively by letter writing, the picture postcard was big stuff—a new dimension in reaching out and touching someone.

Thanks to a benevolent Act of Congress, on May 19, 1898, a law was passed that permitted entrepreneurs to sell and identify postcards as mailing instruments, ushering in the Golden Age of Postcards (1898–1918). The postcards, however, had to be identified as private mailing cards (PMCs). The Private Mailing Card Era within the Golden Age spans the years of 1898 through 1901. It cost one cent to mail a postcard back then, and quickly businesses took to selling postcards to a citizenry that slowly, but increasingly, were eager to send them—and to collect them, too. Most of these early postcards were printed in Germany, as their more advanced lithography printing technology won the day. This remained the case until the outbreak of World War I in 1914 or thereabouts, when many printers in the United States got the hang of it. On these early postcards, writing—other than addressee information—was expressly forbidden on the backs of them. Messages were scribbled on the front of the postcard, beside the image, where often a small blank space was provided. These early postcard backs are referred to today as *undivided backs*.

Undivided-back postcard: (A) undivided back, (B) front side, with space for writing

In 1901, the word *postcard* was officially relinquished by the government. Private producers of postcards could now use the term on their productions too, just like the government, which had maintained a monopoly on the term for decades. And so was born the Post Card Era, covering the years 1901 through 1907. Today, the two words *post card* have become one in the dictionary, and *postcard* is acceptable and widely used.

The Divided Back Era was quietly ushered in with a simple line on the postcard's back, partitioning the address side on the right, from the writing side on the left. This inaugurated the longstanding postcard tradition of messages consigned to their backs in blissful coexistence with the addressee info. This era (1907–1914) also witnessed millions of postcards wind their way through the mail. With images running the gamut of humanity, the postcard had arrived.

It reached new heights, however, in what is known as the White Border Era, which lasted from 1915 to 1930. It refers specifically to postcards printed with a white border surrounding their images. The white-border postcards were very similar in appearance with their postcard predecessors, the divided backs, except for the border addition on their fronts, and sometimes a more detailed description on their reverse, identifying their varying images (for example, "The Boardwalk at Atlantic City"). The white border will assist you in determining a postcard's age.

With new printing possibilities coming into play, the next style of postcard is consigned to what is called the Linen Era. Once it was feasible to print on card stock with a high rag content (cheaper paper), that's the route the postcard went down. You can recognize these particular postcards for their layered linen-like texture and oftentimes garish colors. This postcard period generally spans the years 1930 to 1944, but many were manufactured after that. This postcard timeframe also coexisted with two colossal events in American history, namely the Great Depression and World War II. So, if you have a war-year postcard from the 1940s, it's more than likely printed on rag stock. Perhaps the most fascinating aspect of these particular postcards is the robust colors used in their printing, including some hues that don't necessarily jibe with reality. If you come upon an older postcard with an image of a man who looks like he's sporting cherry red lipstick—and it's not intended as a humorous postcard— you've likely got hold of a Linen Era issue. Some of the postcards from this historical period used the white border, while others were *full bleed,* meaning that the image covered the entire surface—without a border.

The ever-shifting postcard winds blew in a style that proved to be so popular that it is still around today. It's known as the Photochrome Era, which overlapped with linen-like postcards for a time in 1939, when the

Union Oil Company launched these high-quality color photo postcards in their western service stations. It was after the war, in 1945, however, when they became very widespread and popular with consumers. And, generally speaking, these photochrome postcards are the ones you are plucking off the racks in gift shops and gas stations today.

Vintage postcards are often found stamped and postmarked. If you come upon a stamped and postmarked vintage postcard, don't remove the stamp. Old postcards are usually worth more with the stamp still attached to them.

How Collections Begin

How do postcard collections get started? There are so many reasons why collectors seek out the particular postcards that they do. A trip to Australia might foster a love affair between you and the people and places in the Land Down Under, which might, in turn, manifest itself in an Australian postcard fetish that leads to a collection of Australia-issued postcards throughout the twentieth century.

Your mother's small hometown of Bangor, Pennsylvania, in the state's Slate Belt, and the fond memories you have of visiting your grandparents there, could jumpstart a postcard collection of small American towns. There are plenty of vintage postcards from places that once teemed with industries like steel, coal, and slate that today are shadows of their former vibrant selves. Postcards from these old towns celebrate and remember the importance of these hamlets in building America.

Maybe you were born and raised in Los Angeles, California, and you've seen the city's geographical expanse and population balloon over these past few decades. A postcard history of the City of Angels might just be the perfect match for you.

Other postcard collections revolve around the images themselves. Here are some popular postcard categories: angels, art deco, animals, children, ethnic, famous, greetings, humor, medical care, military, novelties, real photographs, topicals, transportation, views, and vintage.

And these categories themselves have copious subcategories in the postcard-collecting arena. Listing them all is impossible.

A great book on postcard collecting A to Z is *The Postcard Price Guide* by J. L. Mashburn. This is a comprehensive reference book that'll not only give you an idea of what your postcards are worth, but also provide you with historical background coupled with loads of photographs. The author is a collector, dealer, and historian, the perfect triad for a writer of this kind of material.

ESSENTIALS

For collectors of postcards—and stamps and assorted ephemera, too—there's an online auction site that should appeal to you. Playle's Auction Mall at *www.playle.com* regularly features thousands of postcards in its auctions.

Postcard Terminology

There are many postcard terms frequently seen in the hobby. Getting acquainted with them will assist you greatly in your postcard chase.

QUESTIONS?

What is the study and collecting of postcards called?
It is referred to as *deltiology,* a word that traces its roots to the Greek word *deltion,* which literally means "small writing tablet." Get it? Small writing tablet equals small writing surface on a postcard.

Artist Signed

Postcards are described as such when they exhibit a facsimile signature of an illustrator. If a byline of any kind connotes the artist of the postcard image, it is dubbed *artist signed.*

Die-Cut

You've probably seen the term *die-cut* mentioned in reference to other collectible items ranging from baseball cards to old advertising signs. Add postcards to the list. *Die-cut* refers to things precisely shaped by a manufacturer to resemble the contours of something like a car, animal, or human being. In the postcard realm, it means postcards that aren't in the traditional rectangle form, but shaped like a tiger or Santa Claus or an angel.

Embossed

Postcards with designs that are raised above the surface in some fashion are referred to as *embossed*. They are usually easily distinguished from their non-embossed companions. If you don't know if you have an embossed postcard by sight, run your clean fingers across its front. The surface will be raised up to some degree, and not smooth to the touch.

Hold to Light (HTL)

HTL postcards are schizophrenics that transform themselves before your eyes. A manufacturing process enables these postcards—when held up to light—to appear entirely different (day to night, for instance).

Installment

Installment postcards are ones with several different images or designs that are meant to be mailed—one a day—to a lucky recipient, who ultimately will get the picture when the final card in the installment arrives. The postcard images form one picture when they are all placed together.

Mechanical

Postcards that feature moving parts. This style is usually equipped with a tab to pull or a wheel to turn. The end result of all this pulling and turning is a shifting or changing image.

Oilette

An oilette postcard is one that resembles an oil painting. It's even replete with brush strokes.

Oversized

The postcards of today are generally 6" × 4". The common postcard from the Golden Age of postcards was 5½" × 3½". Postcards bigger than

6" × 4" are considered oversized by the post office and require a regular mail first-class stamp.

Series

Different postcards issued with a common theme, be it an event, topic, or work of a particular illustrator, are referred to as series postcards.

If you collect postcards, drop by *www.deltiology.com* and *www.postcard.org*. These sites will provide you with links and information on upgrading and enhancing your collection.

Topics

Many people associate postcards with pictures. That is, shots of the beach, the mountains, historic buildings, and other scenic wonders. But that's only a sampling of what makes it onto postcards. Topics are postcards that are not views, but devoted to specific subjects. Dogs, hula-hoops, gas stations, curvaceous females, and the game of baseball are just a few examples of topics on postcards.

CHAPTER 16
Records

Discophiles—collectors of records—have seen to it that the old vinyl records will not spin themselves into oblivion. These collector enthusiasts cherish the quality and sound of their collectibles. And, never fear, you can still find turntables on which to play those totally terrific tunes the way they were meant to be played. You just have to look a little harder sometimes.

The Condition of Your Old Records

Old records, like so many other collectibles, are not valuable just because they are old. There are many people who come upon a cache of records at a garage sale, or rummage through a box of them at a flea market, and become transfixed when they see the copyright dates—1940s and 1950s. But in the record-collecting hobby, demand reigns supreme, and chronological age alone does not equal desirability in and of itself.

The first hurdle for an old vinyl record to leap over is the condition hurdle that all collectibles must encounter on their way to a resting place in somebody's collection. And a record's condition takes on added importance because of its unique nature. After all, it's not an item that's going to be displayed on a shelf. It's not going to go in an album and be thumbed through. No, it's an album unto itself that's meant to be heard and not necessarily seen.

What then determines a record's condition? First, there is its jacket, which houses it. If clothes make the man, then the jacket makes the record. It's one thing to buy a doll without its original box. If, however, you encounter a box of records minus their jackets, you're not likely to go near them with a ten-foot pole. Why? Because they are in all likelihood scratched and possibly warped beyond playability. Their value, for these reasons, is very small.

Most records that you see for sale are in their original jackets. It's the condition of these jackets that collectors usually fret over, because the value of the record is greatly impacted by them. A tattered and torn record jacket immediately diminishes its appeal to collectors, and it is often indicative that the record inside is in a similar sorry condition.

The actual record's condition is next on the chart. Here is what record collectors look for, and the grading system that they employ:

- Sealed: This is a record that is unopened and in its original shrink-wrap.
- Mint: A mint record is like new in all respects, but it isn't sealed.
- Very Good Plus (VG+): This is a record that's been around the turntable a time or two but has been treated with due deference and

still plays smoothly without any crackling and popping sounds or skipping; the record also maintains most of its original bright sheen.

- Very Good (VG): This is a record that has been used but that shows some signs of wear; the record plays, but surface noise is audible as the record spins.
- Very Good Minus (VG-): This is a used record that exhibits more wear with even more overt defects in the sound quality.

Any record grade below VG- is generally considered unacceptable for collectors, unless, of course, it's one of those rare songbirds out there.

SSENTIALS   Mylar is chemically inert and won't damage your photographs, books, and other things made of paper. Avoid those vinyl protective sheets that reek of plastic. Mylar materials have no such odor.

What Impacts a Record's Value

Rare vinyl records in pristine, or in some cases merely playable conditions, often command big bucks in the collectible marketplace. Many records were released in limited quantities. Original releases, in particular, are highly coveted by record collectors. Don't confuse reissues with first pressings. You could easily get hoodwinked if you do. In addition, there are many records from solo vocalists or groups that are out of print today. That is, there are no audiocassettes or CDs of their original music. A hardcore fan and collector is therefore left with no alternative but to search for the original record album, and hope that he or she finds one in playable condition. And when more than one of these collectors goes on a hunt for a hard-to-find item—the price goes up.

Other factors that impact a record's value in the trade include the era in which the record was pressed. If you are in any way familiar with old vinyl records, you've no doubt come across records that are thick, heavy, and with deep grooves. You could throw these records across a room and not break them (although it's not recommended that you do). These hardy records invariably were produced prior to the early 1960s, when the bulk of records lost the battle of the bulge. They went, in essence, from Big Macs or Whoppers to regular burgers. Thinness led to more easily broken and otherwise damaged records. This thickness-versus-thinness issue plays a big role in the hobby, because of the durability aspect. Durability and desirability are partners.

Another important factor impacting the value of a record revolves around its recording: monophonic versus stereophonic. Monophonic recorded albums are the more desirable records, and the sound quality is especially pleasing to the ears of discophiles. Stereophonic recordings became the in thing in the late 1950s, slowly but surely phasing out monophonic recordings. What's the difference between the two? Simply put: *Monophonic* means that audio waves are mixed together and released through a single audio channel. Practically speaking, this means that you, as a listener, will hear a harmonious sound in any location in the room in which you are playing a monophonic record. *Stereophonic* recordings utilize two particular audio channels with two microphones recording onto two individual tracks, so as to match the left and right ears of the listener.

SSENTIALS

Check out Off the Record at *www.otrvinyl.com,* which specializes in out-of-print records in all styles and genres. You'll also access links that dispense tips on old vinyl record collecting and the importance of record preservation.

Record Terminology

You've heard these record terms over and over. But do you know precisely what they mean? Here are several thumbnails from the record-collecting scene:

- 45: The RPM of seven-inch records.
- COH: Short for *cut-out hole,* the practice of punching a hole in an album cover to identify it as a promotional copy.

- EP: Short for *extended play* and usually associated with seven-inch record albums.
- Inner sleeve: The protective covering inside the album cover that enshrouds the record itself.

Promotional copy LP with cut-out hole (COH) for the Broadway musical *1776* (1969)

- LP: An abbreviation for *long play;* specifically, a twelve-inch vinyl record album.
- RPM: An acronym for *revolutions per minute,* which is a measure of the rotational speed of a record.
- Single: A record with one—and sometimes more than one—song that doesn't qualify as a comprehensive album; 45s are most often associated with singles.
- SS: A reference to an unopened record album package that is "still sealed" and in its original shrink-wrap.
- S/T: Short for *self-titled;* a record album with a title identical to the name of the artist.

QUESTIONS?

Are record collectors given a name?
Yes, someone who collects phonograph records is a *discophile.* But this title also has been applied to collectors of CDs. After all, CDs are discs, too. And, by the way, discophiles are sometimes called *phonophiles,* who engage in the practice of *phonophily.*

CHAPTER 17
Depression Glass, Pottery, and Plates

G lassware, pottery, and plates run the gamut from pieces made thousands of years ago, to plates made in modern day to commemorate a particular event. But the one thing they have in common is that people all over the world collect them.

Depression Glass

Glassware collectors are legion. And there are so many styles of glass, ranging in value from the rare and pricey—which find themselves in countless museums and in the homes of the rich and famous—to the affordable, which welcomes a broad spectrum of collectors into its glassy heart. Depression glass is a glass-specific collectible that is at once diverse in its collector roster and in its multicolored and varied glassware. Then, of course, there are the values in the marketplace attached to this inimitable glassware, which range far and wide, too.

The History of the Glass

The distinct name applied to this popular collectible is derived from its manufacturing heyday during the Great Depression years. In the hobby parameters, however, Depression glass includes pieces produced in the mid-1920s—when things were roaring—as well as throughout the war years in the 1940s. So, it's not exclusively the Depression years that produced this desired glass collected by so many people today.

FACTS

During the Depression, a movie ticket cost a quarter, and on giveaway nights, you walked home from the movies with colorful glassware in your arms—the very stuff that's called Depression glass today. Other businesses used this glassware to attract customers, too. Flour companies offered free cake plates in their twenty-five-pound sacks. Gas stations gave away glass bowls to their customers with a fill-up. Who would have imagined that this mass-produced glass would become a such hot collectible years later?

Nevertheless, one of the appeals of Depression glass for today's collectors is in fact its historical context. This glassware was affordable to the average family during the bleakest economic times that this country has ever experienced. The five-and-dime stores in those bygone days teemed with it, while many businesses offered it up as advertising premiums because the masses couldn't get enough of the stuff. Gathering varying pieces of this intriguing glassware in its multitude of forms, colors, and patterns was a welcome respite from the trials and tribulations of everyday living.

What Sets This Glass Apart

The most distinctive characteristic of Depression glass—and central to its mystique both then and now—is its vast array of colors. Indeed, its popularity revolves around these manifold hues. Every plate, cup, creamer, goblet, vase, milk pitcher, and fruit bowl has a personality all its own. Depression glass was colored amber, blue, red, green, yellow, pink, orange, and just about every color in between. And yes, even clear crystal rolled off of the assembly line.

Yellow and amber were the most commonly manufactured colors. More than any of the others, these two colors were desired by the public. Their great numbers in today's secondary marketplace attest to this fact. Yellow and amber harmonized with the home décors of the day.

For today's collector contingent, demand for yellow and amber pieces of Depression glass is not especially high, which means that a beginning collector, or one with limited financial resources, can find plenty of bargains in picking up this historic and fetching glassware. It's the cobalt blue, red, green, and pink colored glass that, generally speaking, is in greater demand. Hence, these wanted pieces are more costly and valuable. Limited numbers in circulation mean higher prices.

Some collectors seek out the manufacturers of the glass itself: Cambridge Glass, Federal Glass, Fostoria Glass, Hazel Atlas Glass, Hocking Glass, Imperial Glass, Jeanette Glass, and Mac-Beth Evans Glass. There's a nifty Web site for Hazel Atlas Glass Collectors at *www.hazelatlas.com.*

Included under the Depression glass umbrella is an offshoot that's been dubbed *Elegant glass.* What distinguished Elegant glass from garden-variety Depression glass was its manufacturing process. Elegant glass was fashioned by companies that—quite literally—provided a helping hand in the glass-making process. That is, each individual piece of Elegant glass was hand finished when it was removed from its mold.

Grinding bottoms to ensure perfectly flat surfaces, intricate glass cutting, acid-etching of patterns, and fire polishing to remove mold marks were the kinds of things regularly done to Elegant glass, but infrequently to Depression glass, which remained very true to its original mold.

Carnival glass "pickle plate"

In the larger picture, the collecting of this particular glassware amounts to collecting an important fragment of American history. As just mentioned, Depression glass is the product of an epoch when momentous historical events like the Great Depression and World War II dominated the day. And so, when this stirring historical background is added to the vibrantly colored, transparent glassware itself, it elevates Depression glass as a collectible. Because of its astonishing popularity during days that otherwise were the antithesis of bright color and variety, Depression glass has a solid hold on its many collectors.

What You Need to Know to Start Your Collection

Collecting Depression glass requires a little study on your part. It is not a one-dimensional hobby. Glassware collecting, in general, asks that its collectors do a little investigating. And this means locating the right books, finding helpful Web sites, and joining collector clubs and sharing information with your companion collectors.

Depression glass was manufactured in numerous colors and patterns. This means that there is quite an involved Depression glass marketplace. All sorts of colors, shapes, and patterns figure into the market mix. Separating the common piece from the rare one is not always a simple task.

Although Depression glass was a mass-produced product, specific pieces were very limited in their production. For today's collectors the challenges lie in finding these quality pieces of the glass that are not only rare but in choice condition as well. And then there are the fakes to contend with.

Finding glassware in mint condition is not as easy as it might seem. If the glassware was used at any point in its existence—as plenty of Depression glass was in its day—it is not likely to be completely free of defects now. A fruit bowl that cradled apples and oranges in its utilitarian role during the Great Depression is bound to have a scratch or two by now. Scratching, chipping, and cracking are not the bosom buddies of glassware.

Before pulling the trigger and buying any collectible piece made of glass, employ the one finger test. This entails running your finger (any one will do) around the edges of the item that you are contemplating purchasing. You can sometimes detect a chip or other defect in this way. Next, put the light test into action. Hold the item you're interested in up to a light. You can often notice scratches and cracks that you wouldn't ordinarily see while the glass is sitting on a table, or even when it's comfortably resting in the palm of your hand.

When push finally comes to purchase, buy from established sellers with reputations for honesty and reliability. Businesses that have been around for a while are generally safe bets for smooth transactions, and, if there is a problem, very professional in making the proper amends.

ESSENTIALS

Depression glass makes for a wonderful collectible. For a mother lode of information, visit the Depression Glass Shopper: The Depression Glass Super Site at *www.dgshopper.com,* and shop 'til you drop.

Mail order and online transacting are obviously more risky ventures than in-person buying, where you can see and touch the particulars of interest to you. If you've done your homework, though, you'll be fine with whomever you're dealing with. Always remember that successful collecting requires patience and the making of deliberate decisions.

A good place to begin your education, or further it, is the *Collector's Encyclopedia of Depression Glass* by Gene Florence. This comprehensive book provides you with information on the various colors and sizes of the glassware. You'll be apprised of what's commonly available in the trade and what's hard to come by. There's even a section on the numerous reproductions that confuse and often scar the collectible hunt.

How to Care for Your Glass

Caring for your Depression glass collection is now the order of the day. Some collectors use this nifty glassware as it was intended. The creamer dispenses cream; the cake plate has a piece of cake atop it from time to time; the vase has water and flowers in it; and the cups sometimes are called upon to hold a spot of tea. If your Depression glassware is more than just doing display duty, then it is imperative that you take certain steps to protect it from the common afflictions that mar glass products.

Dishwashers are more popular than ever these days. As you might suspect, these machines are not friends of Depression glass. It's a safe bet the original owners of the glass did not use dishwashers to clean their glassware—since the dishwasher didn't become popular in homes until the 1950s (although it was around in commercial establishments for decades before then). They were their own dishwashers and are rolling over in their graves at the thought of a hulking contraption cleaning—and damaging—their precious glassware.

Putting this glass in a dishwasher isn't a wise move, because of the excessively hot water used in them. Extreme heat leads to cracks. Warm water—not piping hot—and a gentle dish detergent perform the cleaning job nicely. It is also a good idea to line your sink's bottom with a dishtowel, as the glassware shouldn't be permitted to bounce up and down off of a solid surface. Depression glass is very hard and prone to chipping and cracking. Also, don't wash the stuff with the rest of your dirty dishes. When Depression glass ends up swimming in the same dirty dishwater with ceramic cereal bowls and coffee mugs, it feels grossly out of its element and sometimes just goes to pieces.

Steel wool is also a no-no in cleaning Depression glass. It's an open invitation to scratches. And come drying time, use a linen dishtowel, which will prevent lint pieces from tenaciously clinging to the glassware like barnacles do to a ship's bottom.

Storage of Depression glassware should always be upright. Upside-down storage sometimes initiates complex chemical reactions that only scientists fully grasp. Translation: The glassware gets a musty smell. And don't stack plates on top of one another or put one bowl into another or in any way allow one piece of glass to touch one of its glass peers. Use paper towels or some other soft product to separate them. This will prevent needless scratching and chipping, which can occur very easily.

If you are displaying your Depression glass, keep up with the dusting. While the dishwasher may not be grandma-approved, the old-fashioned feather duster most assuredly is.

SSENTIALS

The Glass Encyclopedia, at *www.encyclopedia.netnz.com,* is a reference bonanza for the varieties of glass that make up collections the world over. If you have a collectible piece of glass hanging around the house and you don't know anything about it, it is more than likely contained in the Glass Encyclopedia.

Pottery

Pottery is one of the oldest art forms known to human history. Over 6,000 years ago in Ancient Egypt, people discovered that when fire and clay joined forces, they could create pottery. Pottery is one of those rare art forms that has survived the test of time relatively intact. Whether pottery is handcrafted in an artist's studio, a residential basement, or at a factory, people want the stuff today just as much as they did a long time ago. And that's where the collector comes in.

FACTS

Christopher Columbus discovered the New World in 1492 and subsequently has had more things named after him than any other figure in human history—countries, cities, parades, you name it. Even pottery produced in the Americas prior to his arrival on the scene is called *Pre-Columbian.*

The Pottery We Collect

Earthenware pottery is porous. This means that it's fired in a kiln at low heat and is very permeable. It has a softer body than its kiln kin—stoneware and porcelain. It is earthenware, however, that leads the way in the pottery field. The dishes in your kitchen cabinet are more than likely made of it, unless, of course, you use paper plates all the time. Because of its permeable nature, earthenware requires glazing to be waterproofed. And the various glazing colors and techniques play an essential part in the look of pottery and in its subsequent appeal to collectors.

Collectors of pottery find themselves searching high and low in a whole host of categories. Different countries, ethnic cultures, time periods, and styles are just some of the distinctions made in pottery. Art pottery is especially popular. Decorative pieces of all sorts have been produced through the years and many of these styles are in great demand. The one dark cloud in the pottery-collecting hobby is reproductions. This is not a collectible field to dive into headfirst. A little diligence on your part is a must.

QUESTIONS?

How can you tell the difference between porcelain pottery and earthenware and stoneware?
Porcelain is translucent. Also, if you tap the item in question and it makes a ringing sound, you have a porcelain piece on your hands. If you hear nothing but a hollow thud, porcelain it ain't.

The following sections include some popularly collected American-manufactured pottery. But it's worth noting that pottery's long arm also reaches into private homes and small studios. And the products that come out of these cozy lairs often find their way onto the collectors' radar screen. In fact, some of this pottery is in very big demand, particularly if the potter achieved some acclaim at some point in time. It's something akin to a now-famous author's early books, published when he or she didn't have a pot to cook in—books that nobody much wanted. But now, those formerly untouchable books, which didn't exactly fly off the shelf when they initially saw the light of day, are coveted in book collectible circles. Pottery made yesterday by an unknown, who by some twist of fate gets known today, makes the previous day's formerly undesirable pottery very desirable.

Cowan

This Ohio pottery operated between the years 1909 and 1931. It is recognized for its unique glazes and designs of noted artists, including the founder, R. Guy Cowan. If you're a collector, or just want to know what all the fuss is about with this pottery, visit *www.cowanpottery.org*.

FACTS

Very often in the collecting of pottery and its related fields, you'll come upon references to *hairlines* and *cracks*. Hairlines are very confined, almost invisible cracks that are at least a quarter of an inch in length. Some hairlines run through entire items. This is one important condition qualifier that you should keep your eyes open for—wide open. In addition, any piece of pottery that's been glued back on should be termed *broken* as opposed to *cracked*.

Fulper

Fulper began pottery-making in the early 1800s and turned to artware in 1909. This pottery is known for its hand-thrown assembling, vibrant glazes, and intricate decorating by studio artists. A company called Stangl took control of Fulper after a fire devastated its plant in 1929. Collectors generally prefer the pieces fashioned prior to the change in ownership.

Grueby

Grueby began spinning its wheels in the last decade of the nineteenth century. This pottery is most known for tiles and hand-thrown art pottery in the Arts and Crafts style. The Arts and Crafts method is recognized for its matte green glaze.

QUESTIONS?

What is a pinhead chip?
A pinhead chip is an infinitesimal chip in a piece of pottery that is no larger than the head of a pin. It sometimes is called a *flea bite* or a *chigger bite*.

Hull

Hull is another Ohio-based pottery that was in the business from 1905 to 1985. Hull manufactured a whole host of products including artware vases, dinnerware, kitchenware, and cookie jars. These items are very popular with today's collectors.

McCoy

From Roseville, Ohio, this company's existence spanned the years 1910 to 1981 and churned out quite a variety of stuff—all of which is feverishly collected today. Among many things, it is known for its leaf and berry motifs and earthy tones of brown and green. If you're interested in this popular brand of pottery, surf on over to *www.mostlymccoy.com.*

Rookwood

In business for almost a century, from 1879 to 1967, this Ohio pottery produced fine art pottery that is in great demand today. Its flat, textured glazing on soft-colored clays makes these items quite appealing to collectors. Some of the oldest pieces from Rookwood are extremely valuable.

Roseville

From 1892 to 1954, this company with locations in both Roseville and Zanesville, Ohio, produced copious art pottery lines. It's been called by some the Pottery Barn of the 1930s and 1940s. Today's collectors covet these attractive and quality pieces.

Van Briggle

This Colorado pottery opened its doors in 1901 and is alive and well today. Its earliest pieces were stamped and dated up until 1920. They've subsequently reissued some of their early designs, which can be very confusing to novice collectors. Before buying Van Briggle pottery, it is critical that you know whether you're looking at an original item or a reissue of the same style. Remember that while they may look the same, there's a big difference in their worth to collectors.

Weller

In business in Zanesville, Ohio, from 1882 to 1948, this company produced many lines of art pottery. They also manufactured figural pieces. Why not take a moment and pop on over to *www.wellerpottery.com* and see what you've been missing all these years.

Collected Dinnerware

Plates and their companion pieces mean a lot to a lot of people. For dinnerware collectors, dinner served on something with character and beauty is a must. These folks believe that attractive plates, cups, and saucers add further flavor to a repast, whether it's a choice French recipe or a kabob cooked in Ron Popeil's Showtime rotisserie oven. The following sections list some of the preferred dinnerware sources that have fashioned what many collectors desire today.

At *www.collectics.com* you'll find glass and crystal, pottery, jewelry, and a whole lot more. This site offers a mix of educational information on a variety of collectibles, plus ample buying and selling opportunities.

Blue Ridge

This hand-painted pottery operated for about twenty years, from the late 1930s to the mid-1950s. In conjunction with Southern Potteries, this company put out over 2,000 unique patterns of dishware. Most of the patterns sport attractive floral designs. If you're interested in learning more, visit *www.blueridge.com.* You can even subscribe to the *Blue Ridge China Quarterly* if you like.

Coors

This company produced a line of artware and dinnerware known as "Rosebud." This vibrantly colored pottery was made prior to 1939 and is in great demand today.

From the 1890s through the 1930s, America imported many items of pottery from Japan, which were branded *Nippon,* the Japanese name for Japan. The pieces were of very high quality and are quite valuable today. Unfortunately, they have been reproduced through the years since, and the reproductions are not of comparable quality. Buyer beware.

Franciscan/Gladding McBean

Franciscan/Gladding McBean is a company known for its embossed dinnerware. "Desert Rose" is one of its popular lines.

Haddon Hall dishware

Hall

Established in 1903, this china company is still going strong a century later. It's famous for its restaurant ware and teapot designs.

Homer Laughlin China

Founded in 1871, this company is still around in the twenty-first century. Among the dinnerware patterns manufactured by them are "Fiesta," "Serenade," "Harlequin," and "Virginia Rose."

The next time you see a piece of pure white ceramic ware, the kind called *bone china,* keep in mind what went into the making of it—bone ash. Oxen bones are popular. Bone china is softer than hard-paste porcelain, but firmer than soft-paste porcelain.

Metlox

Metlox was prolific through much of the twentieth century in churning out dinnerware. They also produced popular cookie jars.

QUESTIONS?

What is a glazed flake?
A chip in the transparent glaze of a piece of pottery that does not make its way through the colored underglaze and onto the surface proper is called a *flake,* or sometimes a *glazed flake.*

Russel Wright

Russel Wright is a designer operation that contracted out its work to other companies. Wright designs on dinnerware always sported the Wright name. Wright is famous for trailblazing amorphous shapes and surrealistic influences in dinnerware.

Vernon Kilns

The Vernon Kilns doors were open from 1931 to 1958 in the Golden State of California. They are known for producing dinnerware and souvenir plates.

QUESTIONS?

What is enamel?
Enamel is the blending of glass and metal at very high temperatures. Enamel wears many faces. It can be translucent or opaque. It may be colorless or multicolored.

Watt

This pottery company, located in Ohio, began churning out kitchenware and dinnerware when flapper dancers were doing their thing. They closed shop because of a fire when President Johnson was in office. Watt is known for its glazed solid colors and warm-hearted, hand-painted designs with moon and star patterns, arcs, loops, and diamond and grooves.

How to Clean Your Pottery

If not excessively manhandled, pottery is a collectible that essentially maintains itself. Archeologist digs unearth so many intact pieces of pottery—and in snappy condition, to boot—because the baking process that these items have been put through ensures their durability, come hell or high water.

FACTS

Pottery that expresses itself as crockery, jugs, and such are called *stoneware*. Stoneware is a heavy pottery that is utilitarian in nature. Wedgwood, an English pottery that's been around since 1759, has produced a ton of stoneware through the centuries. *Lusterware* is a type of pottery that sparkles with iridescent glazes. This lustrous look is the result of adding metals to the glaze and firing away. Different metals will make for different looks.

Pottery doesn't require a lot of care. Just do a few common-sense things and you and your pottery will be happy together for a long time. For example, dusting your pottery is always a good idea. Aside from the aesthetic benefits, dust buildup is both unhealthy for you and your collectible.

You are the only dishwasher your pottery ever needs or should see in its lifetime. Crazing (the small cracks in the clear overglaze of a piece of pottery) occurs sometimes when exposed to too much heat. When this happens, the defect manifests itself with stains creeping into the once-virgin glaze. You'll encounter various terms used in describing the extent of crazing. If you absolutely have to wash your pottery, do it by hand and in lukewarm water. Use a mild soap—no harsh detergents. And never leave pottery soaking in a pool of dishwater.

Crazing occurs on recently manufactured items just as frequently as it does on older pieces. So, trying to judge the age of an item based on the extent of its crazing is, well, crazy.

FACTS

Earthenware, the most popular form of pottery, is not vitrified. The vitrification process, which it does not undergo, leaves ceramic objects with a glassy and impermeable surface. Earthenware, for instance, can be cut with a file, but true porcelain—which is vitrified—cannot.

Collector Plates

Edwin M. Knowles collector's plate, "Edna Hibel Mother's Day" (1989)

In 1895, Bing and Grondahl manufactured a blue-and-white porcelain plate for the Christmas holidays that they christened "Behind the Frozen Window." Since that time, the limited edition collector plate has been with us in some capacity. It wasn't, however, until the latter half of the twentieth century that collecting these captivating pieces really picked up the pace as a variety of manufacturers joined in the fun.

The Popularity of Collecting Plates

According to some surveys, the numbers of collectors collecting limited edition collector plates is in league with the collectors of stamps, dolls, and coins. Collector plates are extremely popular and truly a worldwide collectible. There are many people who have a collector plate or two, but don't consider themselves collectors.

The expanding renown of this collectible field is a relatively recent phenomenon. As more and more people have become attuned to collecting the collectible as opposed to collecting memorabilia, they've set their sights on the many items manufactured specifically for collecting purposes. These are items—like limited edition collector plates—with a value attached to them and a presumption of increasing worth with passing time due to their limited numbers in circulation.

As a collectible, collector plates have a bewitching ambience surrounding them. This is probably because they encompass such an expanse of topics and present them all in such a finely crafted and richly colored fashion. After all, who and what hasn't decorated a collector plate? Ordinary people are all over them—and in many cases—doing very ordinary things. Old people and young people; the handsome and homely, and the famous and the infamous grace collector plates. Religious icons and images are also popularly pictured on these plates. You know you've arrived when you make it onto a collector plate. Unfortunately, many people are no longer of this earth when they get the honor. Historical events are also commemorated regularly on collector plates. TV, cartoon, and movie characters embellish them, too. And let's not forget the animal kingdom and nature, which generate big collector plate demand. From the soaring eagle to the lumbering manatee, there are colorful artist renderings of these impressive—but markedly different—creatures. Collector plate depictions are as endless as time itself.

FACTS

When manufacturers apply a hand application of metals such as gold and silver to the rims of collector plates, it's called *banding.* Banding not only adds to their visual appeal, but to their value as well.

There are three commonplace methods of displaying collector plates: wall hanging, cabinets, and stands. The most popular method is wall hanging, but there are cabinets and individual plate stands that also enable you to prop the plates on tables for the world to see.

Planning a Collection

The art of collecting collector plates is best practiced by what is called *specializing.* Specializing is important in any and all hobbies that are simultaneously diverse and vast in scope. For instance, a *Star Trek* fan may wish to collect *Star Trek*–related collector plates. An admirer of Native American culture and tradition has a wealth of collector plates to choose from honoring warriors and maidens alike. A Civil War buff is afforded opportunity after opportunity to locate collector plates commemorating both the important players and the dramatic events in this monumental historical drama. Maybe you're a feline fan who just wants to collect cat-related collector plates. No problem—you'll find plenty of them if you do a little looking around.

Aside from the varying subject matter, there are series of collector plates issued all the time by manufacturers. Many collectors concentrate solely on these series. Others only acquire plates issued annually as part of a series.

Edwin M. Knowles collector's plate, "The Gettysburg Address" (1986)

Still another collector avenue that some determined souls travel down is the acquiring of only specific manufacturer-issued plates. This collector approach is the preferred method by collectors who value a certain harmony in their plates. Manufacturers ordinarily maintain a consistent style and look in all their collector plates. That is, you can tell a Hamilton collector plate from a Bareuther one. If congruity appeals to your decorative sensibilities, this is a collecting routine worth considering. Contrarily, collecting all over the map means an all-over-the-map collection. And since most collectors like to display their plates, this method of collecting will win them no *Good Housekeeping* medals. Of course, for some collectors it is great variety that appeals to them above all other considerations.

Collecting collector plates by specific artists is also practiced. Many collectors just love a particular artist for his or her use of color and attention to detail. Certain artists magnificently capture certain emotions on a plate, which in turn touch certain emotions in a collector.

FACTS

In many collector fields, the terms *edition* and *limited edition* are bandied about with great frequency. *Limited edition* conjures up dancing images of dollar signs in collectors' heads, but it simply means that the manufacturer predetermines how long a period of time a particular item will be produced, or, the precise number that are going to made. *Edition,* all by its lonesome self, embraces the total number of pieces produced for a particular design in a series.

Where to Buy

It's a name synonymous with limited edition collectible items—particularly plates. It's called the Bradford Exchange. Search for their many collector plates at *www.collectiblestoday.com*. You'll find the many different types and styles of collector plates categorized by subject. And the alphabetized list tells you all you need to know about the diversity of artist depictions that find their way onto these sought-after collectibles.

Theodore Roosevelt commemorative plate (1904)

Here are the Bradford Exchange collector plate subject categories: angels, architecture, cherished teddies, children, Coca-Cola, cottages, country, country décor, cultures, Princess Diana, Disney, Elvis, entertainment, fairy tales, family, fantasy, history/patriotic, holidays, inspirational/expressions, Lena Lui, lighthouses, M. I. Hummel, Marilyn Monroe, marine/sealife, millennium, Native American, nature, Norman Rockwell, pets, Precious Moments, professions, religious, Sandra Kuck, Thomas Kinkade, Victorian, Warner Brothers, and wolves. No matter what kind of plate you're looking for, you'll find it at the Bradford Exchange.

CHAPTER 18
Jewelry

Men and women have been collecting and indeed wearing jewelry for centuries. Some people acquire pieces of jewelry strictly for status reasons. Other people seek out particular pieces to enhance their appearance. Others wear jewelry to serve a function (tiepins keep our ties in place, cuff links hold our shirt cuffs together, and watches tell us the time of day).

The History of Jewels

You can call your jewelry what you like, but remember that in this collector realm there are certain periods of time that are of key importance to collectors. Whether you are a buyer or a seller, it behooves you to know from whence your jewelry came.

The Georgian Period

A few guys named George dominated the eighteenth century in Great Britain—guys, that is, with royal blood running through their veins and crowns on their heads. This age of jewelry is known as the *Georgian Period* and spans the years 1714–1830.

The Georgian Period did not distinguish itself with a particular jewelry style. The items manufactured during this time did, however, frequently focus on aspects of nature. Birds' feathers, brilliant flowers, leafy contours, and even irritating insects inspired the craftsmen of the day. The jewelry of the Georgian Period was primarily dainty and very light. Many pieces, in fact, were set on spring mechanisms and vibrated. This entirely handmade jewelry was customarily set with gemstones. But less precious gemstones were also used, including coral, garnets, turquoise, and even paste on occasion.

The Victorian Period

The Victorian Period supplanted the Georgian Period with the coronation of Queen Victoria in 1837. This period spanned the years 1837 to 1900. The Queen herself was a jewelry horse who loved wearing the stuff. And since she was financially secure, she had many options in picking out jewelry. Victoria herself was instrumental in the particulars of many designs that saw the light of day.

Her reign began when the Industrial Revolution was sweeping across the continent of Europe. New mass-production capabilities changed the face of jewelry as it did virtually everything else. The movement away from an agrarian society to an industrial one put more cash in the hands of more people, thus sparking demand for jewelry from a segment of society that previously couldn't afford anything that even remotely sparkled. This same mass production and machinery also made the mining of various stones and metals used in jewelry a lot simpler and more efficient. This meant that more precious metals, for instance, could be unearthed and, hence, be available to more people at prices they could afford in myriad forms of jewelry.

The Victorian Period is perhaps best known in jewelry-collecting circles for pumping out great quantities of jewelry—and in great varieties as well. Queen Victoria left this earthly plane in 1901, taking her period with her.

FACTS

During the mid-nineteenth century, people began saving a few snippets of hair from their dearly departed loved ones. Craftsmen then took the hair and fashioned a glass brooch with it as the centerpiece. An inscription was engraved on the back identifying and memorializing the deceased. As the years wore on, and more people died, *hair jewelry*, as it's now called, took on new forms in bracelets and earrings. Hair jewelry from the nineteenth century is highly valued by collectors.

The Edwardian Period

Fortunately, Queen Victoria had a son who was ready, willing, and able to join in the pomp and circumstance. His name was Edward VII, and he and his better half, Queen Alexandra, popped the cork on the Edwardian Period, which spanned the years 1901 to 1910. New jewelry fashions ruled right alongside Edward during this very upbeat time. Diamonds became a girl's best friend. The diamond jewelry from this period is considered stellar by today's seasoned collectors. The high production standards in place while the nattily dressed Edwardian women strutted about in their lace and silks made for top-notch jewelry that stands the test of time. Other stones—amethysts, emeralds, and opals—were also popularly used in association with diamonds to add, as it were, extra sparkle to the overall jewelry picture. The outbreak of World War I abruptly ended the buoyant Edwardian Period and its patented carefree style.

Amidst both the Victorian Period and the Edwardian Period there existed countervailing jewelry trends. One such trend was known as the *Arts and Crafts Movement,* which more or less dates from 1894 to 1923. This movement was a concerted effort to return to the quality craftsmanship of the past, which many disciples of Arts and Crafts lamented as a lost art, thanks in no small part to machinery. Arts and Crafts jewelers, of course, made everything by hand and used generous amounts of silver. This was done intentionally to emphasize the craftsmanship as opposed to the monetary value of the piece of jewelry. They also worked mostly with uncut stones. Glistening enamel pieces were often the byproducts of their labor. But the Arts and Crafts style—generally speaking—is not regarded as top-quality jewelry, even though its ostensible aim was to produce such materials. Hammer marks are often visible on some of this jewelry—not a pretty sight.

Leading a parallel existence with the end of the Victorian Period and all through the Edwardian Period was a style dubbed *Art Nouveau,* which was widely seen between the years 1890 and 1915. This acutely artistic style was intricate and curvy in design and craftsmanship. Valuable gemstones were used, but so were things like ivory and horn. Nature themes and natural colors figured prominently in Art Nouveau.

At *www.jewelrymall.com* you'll find links to online jewelry stores and generous amounts of advice and information. Essential buying tips are provided here. Remember, the jewelry collectible field—like so many others—can be a minefield. Restoration and fakery are rampant.

The Art Deco Period

The natural successor to Art Nouveau arrived on the scene in the aftermath of World War I. It was a vastly different world that greeted the Art Deco Period (1920–1935). The term *Art Deco* refers to the style of decorative art that dominated the years between World War I and World War II. The jewelry produced during this period was both very colorful and extensively patterned. Geometric shapes and zigzags circuitously found their way onto jewelry and they've never quite left it. Art Deco used a lot of colored stones and introduced plastic and chrome into the jewelry manufacturing process.

FACTS

Jewelry doesn't have to be made of gold or a hard diamond to be both collectible and valuable. Costume jewelry made of everything from plastic to glass to sterling silver made quite a splash in the 1940s and 1950s, and this very diverse jewelry is extremely popular with collectors today. Check out *www.sparkleplenty.com*, where you'll be surrounded by costume jewelry made of *bakelite* (synthetic resins or plastics), rhinestone, copper, and all the nontraditional stuff that makes up these hip pieces.

The Retro Period

World War II saw material shortages put a virtual end to luxury-item production, which included most jewelry. The Retro Period of 1935 to 1949 is considered America's coming-out party as far as jewelry is concerned. Prior to that time, jewelry design and production was predominantly the province of the French and English. Stars of the stage and screen are widely credited with popularizing the "American look" of jewelry, which often was very sizeable, to say the least, and adorned with snappy stones set in gold on rings, bracelets, and brooches.

QUESTIONS?

Where can I find more information on buying jewelry?
Search for jewelry at the Federal Trade Commission Web site (*www.ftc.gov*), and you'll discover links to articles and information on buying jewelry and precious metals. You can also call the FTC at 202-FTC-HELP and ask for information on jewelry.

Jewelry Lingo

If a piece of jewelry in your collection was manufactured prior to 1830, you have a piece of *antique jewelry*. This delineation mark coincides approximately with the start of the Industrial Revolution in Europe, which many collector historians in all fields consider a defining moment in time, impacting on the production processes of just about every item imaginable. A more generous view of what's antique jewelry and what's not says that anything fashioned prior to the turn of the twentieth century can claim that impressive distinction. Jewelry made from the early twentieth-century to the present—in demand by collectors—must content itself with the distinction *collectible jewelry.*

The jewelry world, like any other, is full of special terminology. Keep the following list handy when you're talking jewelry, and you won't lose your way:

- **Amethyst:** A variety of crystallized quartz that is a popular jeweler's stone and ranges in color from a deep purple to light lavender.
- **Base metal:** Any fusion of alloys of non-precious metals.
- **Bleaching:** A process used to lighten or whiten ivory or pearl.
- **Brilliant:** A diamond, or other gemstone, cut in a particular rounded form with numerous facets creating a distinct brilliance.
- **Carat:** A unit of weight used to measure gemstones; each carat equals one-fifth of a gram or 200 milligrams.
- **Corrosion-proof:** Jewelry that is resistant to rust and other forms of corrosion.
- **Crystal:** A quartz (the most abundant and widely distributed of all minerals) that is transparent or very close to it; it is colorless or slightly tinged.
- **Diamond:** Native crystalline carbon that is coveted by jewelry collectors because of its very hard and durable quality, not to mention its high refractivity, brilliance, and rarity; scored on the 4 Cs scale: carat size, cut, color, and clarity.
- **Diffusion treatment:** A process that adds color to the surfaces of colorless gemstones.
- **Doublet:** A fake, phony, fraudulent gemstone made by piecing together two disparate kinds of materials to create the illusion of the genuine article.
- **Emerald:** A green gemstone that is known to have many naturally occurring flaws (which don't negatively impact the gem's value nearly

as much as flaws on other precious stones do); the brighter the green, the more valuable it is.

- **Fetish:** A charm, pendant, or bracelet depicting an animal or human form.
- **Findings:** The myriad fasteners and other components that go into the manufacturing of jewelry.
- **Flawless:** A descriptive word applied to jewelry that exhibits none of the common flaws; a competent jeweler will look closely for cracks, carbon spots, cloudiness, and other imperfections, and if the piece of jewelry under examination passes every one of these tests, it is deemed flawless.
- **Fracture filling:** A camouflaging method that fills up cracks in diamonds.
- **Full cut:** Rounded diamonds with numerous facets.
- **Gemstone:** Diamonds, rubies, sapphires, amethysts, bloodstones, moonstones, sunstones, turquoises, emeralds, topazes, and other industry products that possess both rarity and splendor and, hence, the value to make the cut as a gem.
- **GIA:** The acronym for the Gemological Institute of America, which is an independent grading laboratory that is very well respected in jewelry circles.
- **Gemstone treatments/gemstone enhancements:** The various treatments—irradiation, diffusion, dyeing, heat, coating, and so on—utilized in fortifying the appearance and durability of gemstones.
- **Genuine:** The word applied to all pieces of jewelry that are not synthetically produced.
- **Gold:** A precious metal that does not oxidize or tarnish like most of its metal cousins; in jewelry, gold is most often alloyed with lesser metals because, in its pure form, it is soft and supple and does not wear well over time.
- **Gold-plate:** A thin layer of gold applied to a base metal; gold-plating on jewelry wears away over time, depending on how thick the plating is and, of course, how often the piece of jewelry is worn.
- **Handmade:** Jewelry that is fashioned from start to finish entirely with the human hand and without the mechanized arms and legs of machinery.

- **Heating:** A very hot process employed to alter the color of particular gemstones.
- **IGI:** The acronym for the International Gemological Institute, an independent grading laboratory.
- **Impregnating:** The process of adding colorless oils or waxes to conceal a litany of imperfections and enhance colors of jewelry that desperately need a pick-me-up.
- **Irradiating:** A method applied to enhance colors and remove certain imperfections in diamonds and other gemstones.
- **Karat:** A measurement that clues you in on the proportion of gold that's mixed with other metals in jewelry; a 14-karat gold piece, for instance, has 14 parts of gold mixed with 10 parts of a base metal, an 18-karat gold piece is mixed with six parts of a base metal, and a 24-karat gold piece is classified as "pure gold."
- **Lucite:** A transparent and very durable plastic that can be molded and carved.
- **Non-corrosive:** A piece of jewelry that is not susceptible to rust and other corrosive enemies.
- **Paste:** Imitation gemstones.
- **Pearls:** Exquisite gems that are produced in oysters and other creatures from the mollusk family when a certain irritant gets into their shells. If the pearl is formed inside the shell, it is deemed an *Oriental pearl,* while a pearl that forms attached to a shell is called a *blister pearl;* the most common kind of pearl, the *cultured pearl,* is produced with help from humans who introduce that pesky irritant into the shell, instead of waiting for it to occur naturally.
- **Pewter:** Jewelry—or any item—with at least 90 percent of tin in its makeup.
- **Platinum:** A precious metal usually mixed with comparable metals.
- **Rhinestone:** A glass stone—its main purpose in life is to imitate a diamond.
- **Ruby:** A very precious gemstone, red in color, that can sometimes surpass the diamond on the value front.
- **Quality marks:** Product marks to indicate what a piece of jewelry is made of; they can be in the form of words, numerals, symbols or any combination thereof.

- **Sapphire:** A gemstone that's often blue in color, but that can come in colors varying from white to pink to green to orange.
- **Sterling silver:** A piece of silver that is at least 92.5 percent silver; a piece that has 80 percent or less of silver is identified as being *silver parts.*
- **Turquoise:** A semiprecious gemstone that hails from desert climes all around the world.
- **Vermeil:** A product with a base of sterling silver and coated with a gold or a gold alloy surface.

Items of costume jewelry for sale are often described as being a "diamond," "emerald," or "sapphire," when in fact they are not precious stones at all. Be aware of this. It's often just references to the *color* of the stones on the jewelry. Look for the "genuine" label. If a piece of jewelry is not identified as such, it's likely not genuine.

How to Care for Your Jewelry

There are many methods used in cleaning jewelry. Talk to a professional jeweler if you have any doubt as to what cleaning method is right for your particular piece of jewelry.

Some people use toothpaste to clean their jewelry. There are liquid jewelry cleaners available in stores that remove oils and dirt. These methods require a little elbow grease on your part, aided and abetted with a small brush or an actual toothbrush. There are also miniature, ultrasonic jewelry-cleaning machines that are effective cleaners of hard stones.

Store your individual pieces of jewelry separate from one another. Don't throw everything into one big heap in a jewelry box. Keep your jewelry away from direct sunlight. Even gemstones fade when exposed to too much of the sun's mighty rays.

And by all means, take off your jewelry when you're washing dishes or working in the garden. Activity of all kinds may be good for your cardiovascular health, but jewelry is inanimate; it doesn't benefit by participating in a softball game or swimming meet. Don't bathe or shower with your jewelry on, either.

Do not, under any circumstances, attempt to clean pearls, opals, emeralds, or any fragile pieces of jewelry, on your own. Professionals are the only ones who should clean these types of jewelry.

What Impacts a Jewelry's Value

If you're collecting jewelry, you probably want to know what your collection is worth. In the following sections, I provide information on the key factors that impact on a piece of jewelry's demand in the marketplace and its overall value.

If you own what you believe to be a valuable piece of jewelry or other collectible item, you might want to visit the International Society of Appraisers at *www.isa-appraisers.org*. They maintain a substantial database of appraisers. And one's bound to be near you.

Certification

Gemstones certified in one of the three most respected independent grading laboratories immediately move up a peg on the value ladder. The troika I'm talking about is the Gemological Institute of America (GIA), the International Gemological Institute (IGI), and the European Gemological Laboratory (EGL). Sure, it costs a few bucks for the service, but if you've got a valuable piece of jewelry, it's worth getting one of the three's authoritative imprimatur.

The Mohs' scale of mineral hardness was devised by German mineralogist Frederich Mohs in 1812. The higher the number on this 1-through-10 scale, the harder is the stone. Diamonds score the highest (10) and are deemed the hardest known natural substance. Anything that rates below a 7 (including coral, opal, pearl, and turquoise) is considered a candidate for prime scratching.

Craftsmanship

You definitely don't want to see hammer marks on your jewelry. Comparable pieces of jewelry vary greatly in price based solely on the details of the craftsmanship.

Condition

Jewelry needs to be inspected very carefully. There are the obvious defects—chips, dents, cracks, and corrosion. But there are many other condition concerns that matter, including reconstruction efforts.

Color

The value of so much of costume jewelry, in particular, is impacted by the fashionable color of the moment. Color also plays a vital part with gemstones, with differing shades and varying levels of brightness significantly impacting on their values.

SSENTIALS

Do you know what your birthstone is? They have their roots in ancient astrology, but here's a modern list of birthstones:

January: Garnet	July: Ruby
February: Amethyst	August: Peridot
March: Aquamarine	September: Sapphire
April: Diamond	October: Opal
May: Emerald	November: Citrine or topaz
June: Pearl or moonstone	December: Turquoise or zircon

Design

Particular designs from particular time periods are in greater demand than others. Know the history of your jewelry, or of a piece that you're considering purchasing.

Demand

Demand for a particular piece of jewelry is often subject to the fickleness of fads and fashions. Some types and styles of jewelry are in vogue one day and forgotten the next. There are, however, certain kinds of jewelry that are resistant to shifting consumer whims and are always in demand and valuable.

Gold and silver are measured in what is called *troy weight*. This is a method that includes pennyweights, ounces, and pounds. The following chart helps you know what you're seeing when you encounter gold and silver measurements in jewelry. Here's how to do the conversions:

24 grains = 1 pennyweight = 1.5552 grams
20 pennyweights = 1 troy ounce = 31.1035 grams
12 ounces = 1 pound troy = 373.24 grams

Naturalness

Certain gemstones come from laboratories, while others come straight and direct from Mother Nature. It's not nice to fool with Mother Nature, who wins the gold medal in value all the time.

Rarity

Rare is a dominant player in jewelry values—not only with regards to specific types of jewelry, but also in the composition of the materials that go into making them. The rarer, the better.

Size

Size matters in a lot of things. In the big jewelry picture, bigger is better and more valuable. But aesthetically speaking, bigger is not always the best way to go. So values range accordingly, depending on the item.

The Internet is loaded with jewelry sellers. Look carefully before you leap into any jewelry purchases in cyberspace. A good place to start your search for bracelets, loose diamonds, earrings, neckwear, rings, watches, and clearance specials is *www.auctionjeweler.com*.

CHAPTER 19
Antique Furniture

Antique furniture is one of the most popular of all antiques collected today. Many people have antique furniture that's been passed down through their families for generations. Others are looking to acquire a piece from someone else's family. Either way, it's a hobby filled with enthusiasts, as this chapter illustrates.

Furniture Terminology

Pull up a Baluster back chair, kick your shoes off if you like, and relax for a moment while I give you some widely seen terms in the antique furniture sphere. Who knows, a word or two just might help you the next time you go antique-hunting:

- **Amaranth:** The rich, violet-colored wood—sometimes called *purple wood* or *violet wood*—that was utilized in the veneering process in the eighteenth century.
- **Apron:** A piece of wood that runs horizontally below a tabletop or the seat of a chair, used purely as a decorative device.
- **Armoire:** A large decorative cupboard replete with shelves and hanging space; often referred to as a *wardrobe*.
- **Art Nouveau:** A far-ranging artistic style, popular in the late nineteenth and early twentieth century, that is known for its long lines ending in sharp twists and curves that resemble a variety of plant forms; this atypical style was a revolt against the commonly mass-produced furniture of the time.
- **Baroque:** Popular from the late sixteenth century through the early eighteenth century, a furniture design that emphasizes an extravagant and dazzling form, in which the scale and proportion knew no bounds and was not averse to grotesque ornamentation.
- **Baluster:** An upright columnar support on a piece of furniture.
- **Bat wing:** Hardware from the eighteenth century that was shaped like a bat's wing.
- **Boullework:** Usually brass or some other intricate inlay of wood used to decorate the surface of furniture.
- **Cabriole leg:** A leg on a piece of furniture that curves outward, forming something of a knee, then curves inward forming something of an ankle.
- **Canape:** A French sofa with a tall, full back.
- **Case pieces:** A range of furniture designed with storage space.
- **Chest-on-chest:** A case piece with a second piece placed atop it, forming, in effect, one piece.

- **Chinoiserie:** An oriental pattern painted on furniture and raised above the surface.
- **Chippendale:** Furniture from the years 1754 to 1790, based on the designs of Thomas Chippendale.
- **Commode:** A low chest of drawers.
- **Corner chair:** A chair with offset legs designed to fit compactly in a corner; also known as a *roundabout*.
- **Cornice:** Elegant moldings atop case pieces.
- **Davenport:** A small and very constricted writing desk from the mid-1800s, the features of which include an angled writing area with drawers and cupboards below it.
- **Dental molding:** Patterned rectangular trim.
- **Divan:** An upholstered bench or sofa without a back and arms.
- **Empire:** Massive-sized rectangular furniture from the years 1810 to 1840, which was manufactured with rich woods like mahogany, rosewood, and ebony.
- **Federal:** Furniture manufactured in the earliest years of the new republic called the United States of America, between 1780 and 1830.
- **Finial:** A shaped ornament used as a decorative embellishment for furniture and usually placed on top of things.
- **Gate-leg table:** A drop-leaf table with stretcher-connected legs, which behave as swinging gates to support the surface top; similar tables without the stretcher-connected legs are called *swing-legs*.
- **Gilding:** Decorations utilizing gold, popular in the eighteenth century.
- **Gothic:** An artistic style using pointed arches and foils.
- **High boy:** A tall chest of drawers that is most often in two sections.
- **Imbrication:** A design resembling fish scales.
- **Intaglio:** Engravings cut into the surface of wood.
- **Inlay:** A decorative application that is shaped in flat surfaces of wood by cutting out patterns and filling them in with wood of dissimilar colors; sometimes done utilizing bands of color called *string*, pictorial forms called *marquetry*, and geometric shapes called *parquetry*.
- **Kas:** A grand wardrobe with very weighty panels, although it is ordinarily shorter and wider than the traditional wardrobe.

- **Lolling chair:** An armchair with a high carpeted back and seat; also known as a *Martha Washington.*
- **Lowboy:** A low case piece with high legs.
- **Lyre:** A design of a stringed instrument often found on Empire furniture.
- **Marlborough leg:** A straight leg that winds its way down to a block foot.
- **Neo-Classical:** The term applied to a revival of interest in the popular designs of the past such as Renaissance and Empire.
- **Ogee:** An S-shaped molding seen often in furniture.
- **Olive wood:** A very solid, close-grained wood with a greenish-yellow hue and diffuse dark markings.
- **Ottoman:** A low stuffed bench without a back or arms.
- **Pad foot:** A flat, oval foot on chairs and other furniture that often sport padding on their bottoms; sometimes called a *club foot.*
- **Patina:** An oft-used descriptive word that describes the color and texture changes that occur to antique wood (and other antiques) after years of exposure to the elements.

ESSENTIALS

A fine and very informative book on the subject of antique furniture from the seventeenth century through the middle of the twentieth century is *The Antique Hunter's Guide to American Furniture: Tables, Chairs, Sofas, and Beds* by Marvin Schwartz. There are loads of pictures and helpful hints to assist you in evaluating antiques just like a pro.

- **Paw foot:** A foot designed to resemble an animal's—often a lion's—claw.
- **Pediment:** A capping top put on chests and bookcases.
- **Piecrust table:** A small, rounded table with scallop-like edges that look something like a piecrust.
- **Pier table:** A table designed to stand against a wall; often built with a mirror along its bottom.

- **Pilgrim:** Furniture from the seventeenth century, the era of the Mayflower and other pilgrim passages.
- **Queen Anne:** Furniture from the period 1725 through 1755.
- **Rococo:** A spirited furniture style with lots of curves and forms.
- **Rose-head nails:** Hand-forged nails shaped in the eighteenth century that closely resemble roses.
- **Saber leg:** A furniture leg that juts inward in the shape of an S.
- **Scroll foot:** The foot of a piece of furniture that looks something like a rolled-up scroll.
- **Settee:** A very small sofa—the width of two chairs—with an upholstered back; its seat is light and open with arms to each side.
- **Shaker furniture:** Simple, pragmatic furniture without embellishments, made by a religious group known as the Shakers.
- **Sideboard:** A dining room piece with both a low and a wide chest of drawers and compartments.

Chapter 20

Buying and Selling on eBay

eBay has become renowned in the span of just a few short years. The online auction site is recognized even in the most non-computer-literate circles imaginable. The marketplace in cyberspace is huge and growing. It's also fraught with numerous obstacles. Your understanding of how eBay works inside and out will make it less likely that a naughty eBayer will get the best of you.

How Computers Have Changed Our Lives

Although it seems like the Internet has been around since time immemorial, it was virtually nonexistent at the beginning of the 1990s. In 1980, high school typing classes were still using the old manual typewriters with bells that alerted students to tap the handle and move onto the next line. And students back then were required to bring along their own correction tape, which was a coated piece of thin plastic used to cover up their many typing boo boos. It was around this same time that the electric typewriter began making inroads into the long established and traditional method of typing. And this newfangled machine was considered a remarkable technological breakthrough at the time—not only because it was faster, but also because it featured this beyond-belief backspace device that corrected mistakes without the need for messy correction tape or gooey liquid white-out.

Today, not only are old manual typewriters desired memorabilia, but the electronic typewriter has all but disappeared, too. It appears that there are more typewriters in museums than in people's homes. Typewriter manufacturer Brother is still around, but the computer and the word processor reign supreme. The amazing element in the history of the typewriter is how quickly it has become a dinosaur. For here was an omnipresent device that was all over the office place and was standard equipment on par with the toaster in so many homes. Typewriter companies thrived into the early 1990s. And now, a decade later, the typewriter has all but left us as a contemporary contraption and lives on more often in staid collections than in active service of typing letters and documents.

The moral of this typewriter tale is that technology has reached a point of snowballing acceleration. This means that its huge hand is reaching into every niche of our lives and it is changing the way we do things without so much as a moment's notice. And there's no avoiding its onslaught.

Initially, as is always the case with great change, there is great resistance. When computers started working their way into more and more homes, it was viewed as a young person's contrivance that old folks would find difficult, if not impossible, to get the hang of.

The predominant mentality was that "it's hard to teach an old dog new tricks."

And at first, this was indeed the case. Young people learned the ins and outs of the computer with the ease of learning to boil water on a stovetop. The older generations, on the other hand, approached the computer with trepidation, looking at it as a cold machine that would surely make their lives worse and not better. It was seen by many people as a step backwards; as surrender to the impersonal world of computer programming and software, of e-mailing instead of letter writing, and of chat rooms instead of real-life conversations.

But as time marched on and computers became unavoidable, the resistance began to crumble. And now Grandmother has one and is sending e-mails to Uncle George and making greeting cards to send to Cousin Felicia.

When eBay first appeared in cyberspace, not too many people batted an eye. Initially it existed in virtual anonymity. A small group of combination computer aficionados and collectors, though, immediately saw something in the auction site that most of the world was still ignorant of, and that's that eBay was surely the wave of the future. It just made sense, because it accomplished something rather remarkable. It was a place that brought the world of collectors and their many collectibles closer together. And it was a place that would complement, and in many cases supplant, the antiquated ways of buying and selling collectibles.

Some Things Never Change

Before we proceed any further in this new millennium of collecting, it's time to clear something up. Yes, the money factor and Old Man Value play a vital part in the present collectible obsession that grips so many of us. But the reality is that the majority of people who fashion collections do so solely for their own personal gratification and for no other reason than that. It brings pleasure into their lives—end of story. These collectors have no plans—and no plans to make plans—to sell off either a part of or their entire collection at any point in their lives. When these collectors make a collectible find, it is their intention that the piece will remain with them until death do they part. These collectors add to their collections and rarely, if ever, subtract from them.

There is so much attention paid to the "selling" half of the "buying and selling" side of collectibles that sometimes we lose sight of the core modus operandi of the average collector. While a portion of collectors both buy and sell, most collectors just buy and never sell.

There are about six billion people in the world. And the number keeps on keeping on. The same can be said for the collector. The aggregate number of collectors is a work in progress. In the 1970s, in particular, there were a lot of doom-and-gloom predictions about a population time bomb about to go boom that would lead to a worldwide food supply catastrophe. Well, a funny thing happened on the way to this apocalypse. New technology made it possible to produce more and more food on less and less land.

What does this anecdote have to do with collecting? Only this: There are many doom-and-gloom predictions being made about the collectible frontier and how it has expanded to the point of committing hara-kiri. Some pundits predict that the tawdry side of profiteers in the collectible industry and the infamous fraud, are bound to make the collectible frenzy recede—and dramatically so! Often cited as evidence is the baseball card delirium in the early 1990s, which saw numerous new companies jump into the manufacturing arena and produce card sets, only to go bust a few years later.

These ups and downs are par for the course, and they will even become more frequent. But with eBay growing in leaps and bounds, and becoming more reliable everyday, it will ensure that this new age method of buying and selling collectibles is not going to die a slow death. In fact, eBay has been on a learning curve through its first few years in existence. It's now a safer haven in which to transact business than it was when it first started. There are plenty of cyber potholes to avoid, but the Internet is a limitless marketplace that more and more collectors are finding to their liking, even with the obvious negatives.

Many of the collectors who initially eschewed the online auction as no place to conduct business, now find that it's not half as bad as they had first imagined. And, besides, they realize that if they don't play the game on eBay, they'll be missing out on a whole lot that would just pass them by. So, basically, it's play in the big game or miss out on the excitement. It's a New World of collecting for sure. Many of the old ways are still thriving—the retail shops, the flea markets, and the collector shows—but why not taste them all?

How to Register with eBay

Registering with eBay is a snap. Go to their main page at *www.ebay.com* and click on the Register Now button. You can register with eBay as long as you're eighteen years old (twenty-one years old in some states) and have a valid e-mail address and a street address.

If you're planning on simply being a bidder in search of collectibles to add to your collection, you don't have to provide credit card information. If, however, you are preparing to actively participate as an eBay seller, you will need to provide eBay with a credit or debit card and bank account information to verify that you are who you say are. You can also leave this credit card information on file with eBay, which will periodically charge you for the fees that you've accrued by listing your items and for the commission charges on the items that you've sold.

FACTS

eBay is not the only online auction site that's thriving. Yahoo! (*www.auctions.yahoo.com*), BidBay.com (*www2.bidbay.com*), and Amazon.com (*www.auctions.amazon.com*) are all in the mix. If your tastes are more refined, you might want to head on over to *www.sothebys.com.* For all sorts of information on the various online auctions—including a discussion board—head on over to *www.auctionusers.org.* You'll find links here to auctions that you never knew existed and all sorts of helpful tips in navigating around them.

If you don't have a credit card, or you don't want to provide eBay with one, you will have to verify your ID before being permitted to sell anything in auction. This more-stringent policy has been adopted to root out fraudulent sellers. When you provide verification, you will have the option of keeping money in a special account with eBay, which you can mail to them in the form of a check or money order. But you will have to wait for the money to be in the account before you can start selling anything on eBay. And you must always keep this account in the black or risk getting shut out from selling. Another option available to you is called *direct pay,* which permits eBay to debit your bank checking account on a monthly basis.

The Fee Schedule

eBay does charge fees for its services. It's not a nonprofit organization; it's a moneymaking entity just like you are when you're selling items on its sprawling site. But the eBay fee schedule is quite reasonable considering the many services that it provides. As a seller, you have access to a potentially huge audience for any kind of item that you feature. Compare the minimal fees charged at eBay with the cost of placing an ad in a newspaper or magazine. Also consider the time lapse between placing one of those ads and seeing it in print versus filling out an online Sell Your Item form and selling on eBay.

The basic eBay fee schedule revolves around two things: an insertion fee and a *final value fee* (commission fee). When you place an item in auction, the first thing you have to do is set a minimum bid or reserve bid, which is the lowest amount that'd you be willing to accept for your item. This figure will determine your insertion fee.

Insertion Fees

Minimum Bid/Reserve Price	Insertion Fee
$0.01–$9.99	$0.30
$10.00–$24.99	$0.55
$25.00–$49.99	$1.10
$50.00–$199.99	$2.20
$200.00 and up	$3.30

The next fee is one that you will only incur if your item sells—which is what you hope happens. This is called the *final value fee,* which is eBay's commission on the sale, and it is based on the final price of the auction. The final value fee is computed as a percentage of this price.

Final Value Fees

Final Selling Price	Final Value Fee
$25 or less	5 percent of the closing value
$25–$1,000	5 percent of the initial $25, plus 2.5 percent of the remaining closing value balance
$1,000 and up	5 percent of the initial $25, plus 2.5 percent of the initial $25–$1000, plus 1.25 percent of the remaining closing value balance

QUESTIONS?

What's a big ticket item?
If you're fortunate to have an item selling in auction that sees the bidding top $5,000 or more, you've got what is called a *big ticket item.* Big ticket items are listed—free of charge—on eBay's big ticket list. May you find yourself there one day.

How to Place a Bid

Before you can place a bid, you need to find the item you want to bid on. From there, you can start the bidding process.

ALERT

Bidders who wait until the closing minutes of an auction to place their bids, are called *snipers,* and they often take heat for their aggressive bidding practices. But there's nothing unscrupulous about it. The snipers play by the rules. Just know that they are out there and never take anything for granted.

Finding What You're Looking For

Start by going to the eBay main page *(www.ebay.com)*, and then look through the main categories. In a very general sense, this will cover just about every collectible item imaginable and then some. Once you've selected a main category, click on the link and you'll see a wide range of subcategories. Again, find the link that closely matches your particular interest, and click. Continue this process until you get to where you want to be. When you can't go any lower in dissecting your search, you've reached a page of listings in the most definitive collectible category possible. You'll notice that this page is more often than not multiple pages (sometimes hundreds of pages, depending on the particular collectible), meaning that there are multitudes of sellers of varying items peddling their wares in your area of interest. Now all you need to do is do a word search on exactly what you're looking for (7Up glasses), or you could—if you've got a few hours to burn and robust eyes—plod through every page and every auction one by one. This searching adventure sounds like a laborious process, but it took you longer to read this paragraph than it usually takes to find the precise page that you're looking for on eBay.

By the way, you can do a word search from the home page if you don't want to click on categories and subcategories. You just won't get as accurate a result.

Bidding on the Item

The beauty of eBay and other comparable online auction sites is that they employ a process known as *proxy bidding,* in which you don't have to be at your computer around the clock to raise your bids. Here's how proxy bidding works: You spot an item of interest to you. The minimum bid is $5 and no bids have been placed yet. You are willing to spend up to $50 for the item—but you obviously want to get it for the lowest possible price. So you set your *maximum bid* for $50, not $5—because when push comes to shove, you're willing to go up to $50. But here's the key: Your bid will show up not as $50, but as $5, the minimum bid. And if nobody comes along as a competing bidder, you've got what you wanted for $5, not the $50 you were willing to pay for it.

Now, let's say that Sam, a competing bidder, comes along and sees you as the top bidder at $5. Sam has no way of knowing what your maximum bid is. But he knows he's willing to pay $25 for the item, so he enters a maximum bid of $25. You are still the top bidder, because your maximum bid is $50. The eBay proxy bidding method raises your bids in what are called *bid increments,* up until your maximum bid is reached. In this instance, the price will rise to a small increment above $25, with you still on the top of the heap. Now let's say that Sam—or somebody else—enters $35 as the maximum bid. Well, your $50 is still the top bid, but it'll push your bid up to a small increment above $35 so as to keep you on top. And remember that all these raisings of your bids will be occurring by proxy, without you clicking away at your computer or even being aware that other bidders have joined in the hunt.

If, however, Alex enters the bidding fray and puts in a maximum bid of an amount *above* $50, then Alex becomes the highest bidder. If you still want the item, you would have to return to the auction page and enter a new and higher bid. And now you're in Sam's shoes. You have no way of knowing Alex's maximum bid.

Most eBay items are covered by the eBay Fraud Protection Program for up to $200 (less a $25 deductible). *Fraud* is plainly defined by eBay as a buyer making payment for an item and not receiving it, or receiving a winning item that was not what was described.

Here's another scenario that'll help you get a better handle on the way bidding increments work. Let's say you've placed a maximum bid of $150 on an item, with the bidding starting at $10. Your bid shows up at $10. Jill comes along and bids $20; your bid is still tops, but at $20.50 (because, remember, your maximum bid is $150 and you need to be higher than Jill's maximum bid). Jill puts in a new bid at $50. Your bid— still number one—now moves to $51. Another bidder, Sarah, joins in the fun and bids a maximum of $100. You're still the top dog, but now at

$102.50. What are these specific bid increments based on? Here are the price parameters eBay uses in raising bids:

Bid Increments

Current Price	Bid Increments
$0.01–$0.99	$0.05
$1.00–$4.99	$0.25
$5.00–$24.99	$0.50
$25.00–$99.99	$1.00
$100.00–$249.99	$2.50
$250.00–$499.99	$5.00
$500.00–$999.99	$10.00
$1,000.00–$2,499.99	$25.00
$2,500.00–$4,999.99	$50.00
$5,000.00 and up	$100.00

Retracting a Bid

What happens if you bid on an item and then, for some reason, you decide that you have to back out? You can retract your bid. Pulling out of an auction, however, will be part of your eBay dossier and in the public record for all fellow eBayers to see. Bidders who make a habit of retracting their bids are looked upon unfavorably.

There are some retraction guidelines relating to what are and aren't legitimate reasons to pull out of an auction. For instance, it's perfectly kosher for you to retract an accidental bid amount. If you meant to bid $10 and typed in $100 by mistake, you're on solid ground. If the seller changes the description of the item during the auction by adding some details that weren't disclosed when you placed your bid (which happens on occasion), you're within your rights to retract your bid. You can also retract your bid if you cannot make contact with a seller to have him or her answer a question or deal with a pressing concern relating to the item in auction.

Unacceptable reasons for bid retractions revolve around old-fashioned irresponsibility. You had a change of mind. You saw something that you liked better in another auction. You lost money on a horse and now can't afford to win the auction. The moral of the story? Before you place a bid, make sure you're prepared to pay up if you happen to win.

A small number of ignominious sellers have employed friends and family to bid in their auctions and help boost their final prices. This is called *shilling*, and it's forbidden by eBay. Don't do it! You are a prime candidate for suspension if you do.

How to Sell an Item

The first thing to consider before placing an item on the eBay auction block is how much you'd be willing to sell it for. What's the bare minimum you'd accept for it?

Setting the Price

Come up with a reasonable *minimum bid* for your item—the place where bidding will start. This number does not necessarily have to be what you think the item's worth, or even what you want to get for it. After all, eBay is an auction site, not a retail store. So, the minimum bid you set should be a compromise of sorts, reflecting the item's worth in your estimation, with the reality that low minimum bids have been proven effective in stimulating bidding. That is, starting the bidding at a few dollars versus starting it at a hundred will draw more bidders into the bidding pool on your item. Multiple bidders bidding against one another boosts the price. And that's what you want as a seller.

A way around this minimum bid conundrum is an available option called the *reserve price*. This is an amount that you can establish as the minimum that you would accept for your item. The reserve price is hidden from bidders, so you can start the bidding at any minimum price that suits your fancy, and not be contractually bound to sell the item unless your reserve price is matched or exceeded. Here's an example of how all this works. You place up for sale an autographed photograph of the legendary film star John Wayne, and you want at least $150 for it. But you'd rather not start the bidding at that high price. So you set your reserve price at $150 and set a minimum bid at, say, $2. If the bidding does not reach your $150 reserve price, you are under no obligation to sell the autograph. All bidders will be aware that you have a reserve price, but they won't know the amount of it until (and if) somebody meets or surpasses that price. When this occurs all the bidders and prospective bidders will be alerted on your auction page that your reserve price has been met.

If you have more than one of an identical item that you want to sell, but you don't want to run individual auctions one at a time or sell the bunch as one lot, you have another option. You can run what is called a *Dutch auction.* In a Dutch auction, multiple items can be sold individually. The only criterion is that the items be completely alike and number in quantity two or more.

How does a Dutch auction differ from a traditional auction? Let's say that you start a Dutch auction featuring ten Barbie dolls in their original packaging. They are all the same and need not be described individually. You begin the bidding at $5 per doll. Ten people come along and meet the $5 bid. Another five people come along and bid $7. The minimum bid is now upped to $7. The auction closes. There are five bidders at $7 who are guaranteed a doll. But what about the bidders at $5? There's only five dolls remaining with ten bidders at $5. The first five bidders at $5, in this instance, would get the dolls. So, in the end, all ten winning bidders would pay $5, because all the winners pay the same amount, which is always the lowest successful bid. Now, in this same example, had another five bidders come along and bid $7 or more, the ten winning bidders would be paying $7, because this number would be the lowest successful bid.

Most Dutch auction bidders get the items at the minimum bid. It's only when the bids surpass the quantity available that things sometimes get a little confusing. But it's a rather simple and very effective way to sell multiple items individually in one auction.

It shouldn't surprise you that there has been some abuse in Dutch auctions. It seems to be a mode of selling that scammers have found to their liking. The ability to make a quick killing with multiple items selling in one auction is something that attracts a fair share of sleaze balls. This lamentable reality is why eBay now requires that Dutch auction sellers have a minimum feedback of 50 or more and be a registered eBay member for sixty days or longer.

There is one exception to the Dutch auction's identical item rule. Miscellaneous trading cards, sold in lots, can be considered one item. That is, 100-card lots of baseball cards, for example, can be sold in Dutch auctions, even though the card lots are not absolutely identical. What is identical, in this example, is the 100-card total. Predictably, many negative buyer experiences occur in these particular Dutch auctions because of the arbitrary nature of the merchandise. The Barbie doll is the stated Barbie doll. A lot of assorted cards with some vague promises attached to them often disappoint customers. Look closely at the feedback of Dutch auction sellers, particularly those selling baseball card lots. See what experiences others have had before you place your bid.

If you are running a non-reserve price, traditional auction and you attract more than thirty bids, eBay automatically awards you a "lit match" icon, which signifies that you've got a "hot item" on your hands.

Describing Your Item

After selecting the proper collectible category in which to list your item, the next step in the "Sell Your Item" form is the "Title." This heading will be the link to your auction page in the eBay listings, so it's very important. You want people to click on that link. Don't call your auction "Rare Piece of Glassware" and stop there. Succinctly describe what you're selling. What kind of glassware is it? What is its condition? This one- or two-sentence heading has to make prospective bidders say, "I need to find out more about this thing." Another important consideration to keep in mind is that the various item searches—that eBayers are doing as you read these words—scan words in the titles. So keep exclamation points to a minimum (one will do) and avoid asterisks and the like, because they interfere with the search mechanism.

Now comes the time to describe your item. When you describe your item, you want the description to be as detailed as possible without it looking like the first chapter of that epic novel you've been writing. Spend a few minutes writing a paragraph made up of several sentences. Descriptions of condition, in particular, mean a lot. Don't give this aspect of your selling short shrift. Take the time to verbally describe the item you are putting on auction, carefully noting its condition from top to bottom, while citing any and all of its defects. If you fail to do this, you'll have problems down the road—guaranteed—with buyers claiming that they were misled by your description.

A thorough description alongside a good photograph will enhance your auction's status and uplift the item that you're trying to sell by making it more real—warts and all. Include in your description information about shipping charges. Buyers hate to be zinged after the auction is complete with an amount that surprises them and are much more comfortable knowing in advance what they are going to be required to pay for shipping. This sum can then be factored into their bidding.

Another advantage of a well-worded description is that the aforementioned searches done on a routine basis locate words within the descriptions. So, by adding a little extra background and history to your item, you'll get more and more people looking at it for sure. And more traffic at your auction page inevitably leads to more bidders and higher final prices.

Take the time to proofread your descriptive copy. Descriptions laden with errors and shoddy grammar reflect poorly on the seller.

Including a Photograph

If you are seriously planning on selling anything on eBay, it is crucial that you enclose a picture of your item along with a solid description. You're not required to have a picture. Technically speaking, just a description of what you have in auction will do. But a picture will make a big difference in the numbers of people who visit it and the numbers of people who actually bid on your item.

Potential bidders want to see what they are bidding on. Without an image, who's to say your item even exists? You know it does, but bidders can't be certain. And with all the scams out there, you can't be too careful. Yes, scams with pictures are plentiful, too. But still, you'd rather see a picture than no picture at all.

Most veteran sellers on eBay use scanners or digital cameras. The digital camera is the simplest way to get sharp photographs. No film is required. You take the pictures—and presto, they are ready to be shot into cyberspace for the entire world to see. Or you can take a picture with a traditional camera and scan it, saving it as a .jpg file. The increasingly popular copy centers (Kinko's, Mail Boxes Etc., and others) will scan pictures for you if you don't have a scanner at home.

Handling the Transaction

When you've successfully completed your first auction as a seller, what do you do next? The eBay guidelines say that sellers and buyers must contact one another within three business days of the auction's ending, or risk the transaction being declared null and void.

Generally speaking, the seller is the one responsible for contacting the winning bidder of his or her auction. It's the seller that has all the pertinent information that the winning bidder needs in order to complete the transaction. The seller is the one who provides the buyer with the total amount due with shipping added to the winning bid and lets the bidder know how to pay.

Increasing numbers of sellers who participate in eBay auctions use PayPal, Billpoint, and other online outfits, which process credit card sales. You, as a seller, can then offer your customers onsite instant payment. That is, clicking on a link and paying by credit card as soon as the auction is completed. And if an antsy buyer wants the winning item right away, he can pay immediately, before you as the seller even send out an e-missive.

Contact the winning bidder and let him or her know that you've received payment. Let the buyer know when the winning item will be shipped and via what mailing carrier (regular mail, UPS, and so on). In fact, keep your customers informed of the status of the transaction at all times. There's a wealth of mistrust online—and for good reason—that sometimes becomes irrational paranoia. Prevent a misunderstanding from turning into negative feedback. Negative feedback is, after all, the bane of every eBay seller's existence.

The two most popular mail options that sellers select are the U.S. Postal Service and UPS. Depending on what you are mailing and where it's going, a case could be made for either of these outfits. UPS does not deliver to post office boxes; they need a street address. Their rates are calculated by zip code. Visit the post office at *www.usps.org* and UPS at *www.ups.com* for answers to all your mailing questions.

Packing and Shipping the Item

Unless you want to personally deliver every item that you sell—in which case you could find yourself traversing the country coast to coast—you've got to pack boxes and envelopes and physically mail them. And this is not something to be taken lightly. It costs real money to ship things these days—more than ever before. And it's not getting any cheaper.

Throwing an item into a box and sealing it shut is not the route to take. Some new sellers have found this out in a hurry, when irate buyers complained to them about the poor packaging and hence, the poor condition that their winning merchandise was in when it arrived on their doorstep. Package anything fragile with ample bubble wrap and use Styrofoam pellets or copious amounts of newspapers. Make certain that what you're mailing cannot bounce around in its box.

Use a double box if you're shipping an especially fragile item. Put the item that you're mailing in one box wrapped as described and then place that box in another larger one. This usually does the trick, and you'll feel better about your item's journey from your hands to the waiting arms of the winner of your auction. The post office will also mark a fragile parcel as such if you ask them to, which is supposed to alert mail handlers not to treat these specially marked boxes like javelins in an Olympic field event.

Smaller mailed items can easily be shipped in padded envelopes or jiffy bags. But these items, too, should be bubble-wrapped or reinforced in some other way. A protective envelope is not commensurate with Superman's unitard. It doesn't make what you're shipping impervious to the slings and arrows of the postal expedition. Things can—and do all the time—get crushed while in a padded envelope.

Most sellers on eBay use the post office for mailing purposes. Convenience plays a big part. Plus, post office rates are also cheaper—in many instances—than are the alternatives, particularly on smaller items. Can you trust the post office to deliver for you? Yes and no. And that's why you should insure packages of any real value that you put in the mail. You decide what "value" means to you. You can insure a package for $50 at an added cost of $1.05; more expensive items can be insured for up to $5,000 via regular mail and $25,000 with registered mail. Then, if the unthinkable happens and your item gets damaged in transit, you can at least recoup your loss. Keep in mind to only insure packages for their monetary value. You'll need evidence of this to make any damage claim. The post office will not recompense you for sentimental value—it's not a sentimental body.

Another mailing option that you should consider making use of is called *delivery confirmation*. For an additional small fee, a bar code is attached to letters and packages and scanned at the point and time of delivery. Items with delivery confirmation can be tracked online, too. One of the more common occurrences on eBay revolves around winning bidders claiming that they never received their winning merchandise. And more times than not they are telling the truth. Without a delivery confirmation, however, you, as the seller, have got nothing to go on but your customer's word.

With lower-priced items—under $10—you might want to just affix stamps to the packages or envelopes and drop them in the mailbox using regular "no frills" first class mail. Many sellers go this route for expedience reasons. That is, they don't have to make a trip to the post office. This is a fine approach to take if you are willing to sustain a loss from time to time when a customer claims that his or her package never showed up.

A popular packaging source on the Internet is Brass Pack at *www.brasspack.com* or 888-525-3357. They've got it all: boxes, tape, labels, cushioning, stretch wrap, strapping, polybags, and mailers of all sorts. Another supplier of packing and mailing supplies can be found at *www.boxesonline.com.*

Why You Should Leave Feedback

eBay provides both its buyers and its sellers the opportunity to leave feedback after a transaction is complete. It allows participants in transactions on both sides of the aisle—buyers and sellers—to leave either positive, negative, or neutral feedback comments regarding the smoothness of their experiences (or lack thereof). This means that a winning bidder leaves positive feedback with a seller whom he or she believes accurately described the item in auction, packaged it properly, promptly mailed it, and so on. And a seller, conversely, leaves feedback on the punctuality of the buyer sending in payment, responding to e-mail, and so on.

Bidders, in particular, look upon a seller's feedback rating, which appears in a number next to his or her eBay User ID, as a main factor in whether or not to bid in a particular auction. The feedback rating is the aggregate accumulation of a buyer or seller's feedback (praise versus complaints). Each positive feedback counts as one point toward the final rating; every negative feedback deducts a point from it. So, if a buyer or seller has 663 positive feedback comments and 2 negative ones, his or her feedback rating would stand at 661.

But does a high feedback number tell the complete story? Many businesses, for example, have multiple auctions going on at any given moment in time and therefore sport very high feedback grades based on the sheer amount of their transactions. They may, of course, be highly deserving of their hefty feedback number, but bigger is not necessarily better. For instance, say an eBay seller flaunts a feedback rating of 2975. Quite impressive, you might think at first glance, considering that most buyers and sellers maintain considerably smaller totals. The key here is not the mega-high number; it's the breakdown of the seller's positives versus negatives. And if the 2975 were arrived at with 3225 positives offset by 250 negatives, this would ring those alarm bells.

What you've got to do next is check out the various negative feedback and the complaints that accompany them. It's all right there for you. You can even contact some of the people who have left the comments and query them about their experiences with the seller in question. A negative feedback now and then will happen, even if you are the most well intentioned buyer or seller in town. Misunderstandings and just plain pettiness will get you a negative feedback or two if you play the eBay game long enough. Accept this reality and don't let it get you down. But a string of the bad stuff is a bad sign.

eBay encourages both its buyers and sellers alike to get together, as it were, via a phone call or such, before placing any negative feedback. More times than not problems can be resolved amicably through a meeting of the minds.

Keep in mind that negative feedback is potentially libelous. Many businesses—big and small—and individuals, too, use eBay for serious income-generating purposes, and in some cases make their sole living selling in auctions. So any negative feedback could adversely affect their business—their income—by deterring bidders that otherwise would bid on their items. Gratuitous defamation is unacceptable and can significantly impact on people's livelihoods. So before you go down that road, be sure you have proper cause and have tried your utmost to resolve any dispute.

As your feedback rating grows in number, eBay awards you a star. The more you play the more positive feedback you'll get (optimistically speaking). The various colored stars next to eBay User IDs tell the numbers story. That is, at varying levels of accumulated feedback, a different color star is earned. Here are the colors and what they represent:

- Yellow star: Feedback rating of 10 to 99
- Turquoise star: Feedback rating of 100 to 499
- Purple star: Feedback rating of 500 to 999
- Red star: Feedback rating of 1,000 to 4,999

- Green star: Feedback rating of 5,000 to 9,999
- Yellow shooting star: Feedback rating of 10,000 to 24,999
- Turquoise shooting star: Feedback rating of 25,000 to 49,999
- Purple shooting star: Feedback rating of 50,000 to 99,999
- Red shooting star: Feedback rating of 100,000 or above

ESSENTIALS

If you have a problem on eBay, you can take your concern to their Safe Harbor. Safe Harbor will investigate various trading offenses and abuses in categories such as feedback, buying, selling, contact information/identity, and the miscellaneous (spam, threats, and profanity).

Tax Time

You thought you were going to get out of here scot-free. Sorry, not with the IRS looming nearby. Should you tell the tax collector about the things you sell on eBay? In a word, yes. You should tell the IRS about what you are doing on eBay, because sooner or later the federal government's money hound dogs will find out on their own. Your transactions on eBay are, after all, a matter of record. It's not a secret society that you are trading on. It's not a garage sale or a flea market.

The IRS is not about to let a good thing pass it by. It just has to figure the right course to take. It's supposed to be a kinder and gentler IRS these days. But, you can bet your tax refund that the IRS will worm its way into the online auction scene with a vengeance in the upcoming years. Regardless of what you may think of the IRS, if you make money on the Internet, it may be a taxable gain that you are legally required to declare as income.

If you are a casual seller who sells an item or two every couple of months and is making a few dollars, it's not something you need to worry about. If, however, you are selling items that are generating real money (hundreds or thousands of dollars), then you might consider filing a Schedule D attachment to your Form 1040, and treat your gains as you would a stock profit.

If you have reached a point where you consider yourself a business, then you can attach a Schedule C to your regular return. This is the form for profit and loss of a business entity, which the IRS defines as anything with a profit motive that is conducted on a regular basis. Otherwise, the IRS considers what you are doing a hobby. The differences between the two are felt when you declare losses from what you consider a business operation and what the IRS deems a hobby. You can write off losses from a business, but not from a hobby. A few years of declaring losses with no profits in your business enterprise and you'll be in a hobby before you know it, at least as far as the IRS is concerned.

Whatever route you take, it is always wise to keep detailed records and save any and all receipts. When running an eBay business, you can often deduct your computer-related expenses (from software to ISP to paper for your printer), car expenses, portions of your telephone and utilities bills (if you operate from your home), research materials—the list goes on.

Trying to comprehend the tax law in general is difficult enough. Trying to understand it as it relates to online businesses (and other home-based businesses) is like trying to keep the ocean from rushing to the shore—it's just impossible. Impossible because the IRS really doesn't know itself. You can download all IRS instructions and forms (including Schedule D and Schedule C) at *www.irs.ustreas.gov/forms_pubs* and read more—a lot more.

Another tax concern is collecting sales tax for your state. There are different laws in the states regarding the collection of their particular sales taxes. Generally speaking, you are legally responsible to pay sales tax on sales made to individuals in your state of residence or operation. That is, if you are from New York, then you collect sales tax from your customers who reside in New York only. If taxes are getting too complicated for you, find a trusty accountant who can lend you a helping hand—for a fee, of course.

CHAPTER 21

Start Collecting!

After reading about so many collectibles, you may find yourself on the proverbial fence—a potential collector who can't figure out what to collect. Collecting is a part of the human soul. But why do we collect the specific things that we do? In this chapter, I answer that question—and help you figure out which collectibles have your name on them.

How Collections Get Started

Not all collections are the byproducts of well-thought-out plans by collectors. Many collectors actually stumble onto their collectible hobby by chance, or by a peculiar twist of fate. A political button picked up at a campaign rally is put away in a dresser drawer; then another one from another year's campaign ends up in the same place, and—before you know it—a button collection is born.

On a whim, you buy a small angel figurine that you admired in a gift shop; then you buy another one a year or two later. A friend concludes that you have a thing for angels and buys you a third angel figurine for a Christmas present. Word soon gets out that you "collect angels." Another collection is in the making.

Whimsical purchases and things received as gifts, passed out at rallies, found by chance on the streets or in someone's garbage, are the beginnings of many collections—before even the presumptive collector realizes he or she is a collector.

FACTS

First-issue is the term applied to collectibles manufactured and marketed for the adult collector. More and more of these kinds of collectibles are being sold today—as opposed to the secondary market, where (usually older) items are bought, sold, and traded among fellow collectors.

Fads: The Root of Many Collections

How do "fad" collectibles fit into the overall critique of what makes collectors tick? A *fad* is something that creates an out-of-proportion zeal in the public. The exuberance for a fad is always followed by a fast fade back to reality, which in some cases means total oblivion for the now defunct fad.

Fad collecting touches the third rail of human nature. We've already noted humans' biological affinity with the pack rat. Likewise, we share much in common with the lemming. We follow the leader and often get swept up in fads, be they Madison Avenue–driven clothing fashions or the Pet Rock. But not all fads make great collectibles.

As a collector, you'll need to know about topics such as collection and care display, insurance, dispersal and estate planning, researching, and networking. The National Association of Collectors has amassed an abundance of information. Contact them at: The National Association of Collectors, P.O. Box 4389, Davidson, NC 28036 or *www.antiqueandcollectible.com.*

The Pet Rock

Remember the Pet Rock? Now there was a true fad! Created by advertising executive Gary Dahl, a man who considered dogs, cats, birds, and fish a real pain in neck, the Pet Rock sold over one million pieces in a several-month span. During that time, Dahl appeared twice on the *Tonight Show,* and as many as three-quarters of the country's daily newspapers featured articles on the Pet Rock. Christmas-time sales soared in 1975, as everyone who was anyone scooped up this box of nothing. Not too long after the holiday frenzy, however, the rock was stone dead and rarely heard from again. And Gary Dahl was a millionaire.

FACTS

Are you curious why so many collectible fields end in *-iana?* The suffix *-iana* (as in Breweriana and Railroadiana) refers to "collected items." The *-ia* tag, which is sometimes employed in collectible circles (for example, Automobilia and Orientalia) is attached to "things derived from or related to" a particular object.

Beanie Babies

The most recent fad collectible phenomenon was the Beanie Babies rage. Beanie Babies are like members of our own family. They were designed for and initially marketed to children. They were an attractive and unusual line of plush dolls that were destined to capture a child's imagination. And they did—albeit not immediately.

The original Beanie Babies debuted in 1993 and sold for $4.99. It's adults' imaginations, however, that got entangled in the collecting net—and it is adults, with the purchasing power, who fueled the buying and selling of Beanie Babies into a fever pitch. There were reports of collectors following UPS delivery trucks for miles, awaiting Beanie Babies deliveries.

Beanie Babies made for a fascinating fad because they make great collectibles (unlike the Pet Rock, of which there's only one). While the Beanie Babies fad delirium may have died, Beanies nevertheless remain one of the most sought-after collectibles ever introduced into the marketplace. Currently, there is a tenacious unpredictability in Beanie Babies values, with factors influencing prices ranging from the dolls' tags to rumors of retirement. Price volatility in the secondary market of collectibles is par for the course. And Beanie Babies are no exception to this rule.

Beanie Mania: The Complete Collector's Guide by Becky Phillips and Becky Estenssoro is a valuable and thorough book. A stopover at *www.beaniemom.com* will provide you with an abundance of information on Beanie Babies. The official Ty Beanie Babies site is another must for Beanie Babies aficionados. It's at *www.beaniebabies.com*.

Pokémon Cards

Another recent fad of monumental proportions was the Pokémon cards explosion. There's been nothing quite like it as a fad collectible. Pokémon cards and related merchandise spawned a $5 billion industry—seemingly overnight. And Pokémon remains incredibly popular, even though the overt mania has vanished.

Pokémon means "pocket monsters" in Japanese, the land of their origin. There are 150 monsters (cards) in fifteen different categories in the original Pokémon series. From Bulbasaur, card number one, to Mewtwo, card number 150, the objective of the Pokémon game is to find, capture, and train these distinct monsters to become the world's utmost Pokémon trainer. Each of the Pokémon monsters possesses special powers and abilities, so this is by no means an easy task.

Like all fads, the tumult subsided just as quickly as it had materialized. When all the Pokémon dust settled, who was left standing? You guessed it. The adult collector. As you might imagine, there are some very high-priced Pokémon cards out there. The cards' initial pricey costs, and their selective distribution, have made some cardholders very fortunate indeed. Pokémon cards with holograms on them are considered the most valuable.

Beware, too, of the Pokémon card counterfeiters. Thinner paper, which permits light to shine through, is a sure sign of a counterfeit card. And, if the card's been "Made in China," it's not the real thing.

The Investor: Collecting for Profit

There are people who invest in collectibles just as they do in the commodities market and mutual funds. They acquire items solely for the monetary gain—and the bigger the better—with no emotional bond to the collectibles themselves. These people are *investors*. The investor mindset is the exception to the collectible rule. Even though most collectors hope, anticipate, and pray that their collections' values will increase with time, they're in it primarily because they're passionate about what they collect. There are, however, many more people collecting things just for monetary reasons today than ever before. This is a reality that cannot be ignored in today's collectibles marketplace—it drives the market, and in some instances distorts it.

Most collectors, though, are emotionally attached to what they collect. Their collections are a part of who they are and what makes them get out of bed in the morning. A dollar yardstick cannot measure the pleasure they get out of their collectible crusade to locate items to add to their collections.

Video collectors are often perceived as loners who sit around watching old movies when they should be out enjoying the nightlife. But steer clear of making this stereotype. A 1962 Disney film called *Dr. Syn, Alias the Scarecrow* fetches over $250 in used condition!

Nostalgia: A Collector's Main Motivator

Outside of fads and strictly money-driven collecting, the majority of collectors trace the origins of their collections to key moments and times in their lives. If you're still a collector-in-waiting, you might want to ask yourself the following questions to uncover a collectible match that's right for you:

- Where is your home? Where are you from? Are you a country boy with fishing in your blood? A city gal who rides the subway to work? An immigrant with an attachment to your former homeland?
- What do you do for a living? Do you consider it a career? Is there a family business in the picture? What did your father do? Your mother? A close relative?
- What do you do in your spare time or for recreation? Are you a member of any organizations? Are you a sports zealot? A fan of anybody or anything? A history buff that can't get enough of books?
- Were you given a gift or did you inherit an item that piques your interest? Did you find something or pick up a souvenir someplace that you consider very special?
- What catches your eye? Things of beauty? Unusual oddities?
- Are you nostalgic, perhaps for your childhood games and toys? For a past vacation spot? For places that you once visited that are just pleasant memories now?

Ah, nostalgia. Nostalgia is omnipresent in the answers to just about all of these questions. Nostalgia rules in the collector's world. It is what drives most collections. It is what makes the collectible parameters so boundless. *Nostalgia* is a wistful and sometimes excessively sentimental yearning for the return of days past. It can veer into the abnormal arena on occasion, when the longing for the past paints a picture of a reality that never really was—so watch out. When channeled into the right places—like into collectibles—nostalgia is a positive force for keeping history and memories of the past alive.

Nearly forty years after her death, the name "Marilyn Monroe" still resonates with many people, even those who weren't alive when she was making movies and singing "Happy Birthday, Mr. President" to JFK. Check out *www.marilynmonroesales.com* to find videos, books, dolls, and even items personally owned by the curvaceous star.

The Things People Collect

So why do we collect what we do? It's always good to begin a journey—any journey—with a full tank of gas. And that's just what we're going to do. We're going to glimpse at an interesting cross-section of collectors and their choice of collectibles.

Collector's Universe at *www.collectors.com* lives up to its name with a bonanza of links and solid, up-to-date information on such favorite topics as stamps, coins, sports, records, and autographs. Collector's Universe is also the place to go to locate grading and authentication services for sports cards, stamps, coins, and autographs.

Gasoline Collectibles

Why would anybody be drawn into the collecting of gasoline-related collectibles? Glad you asked that question. Many people have. There are categories of gasoline collectibles devoted to the numerous companies that sell us gas and oil: Amoco, BP, Chevron/Standard Oil, Citgo, Esso, Exxon, Gulf, Pennzoil, Phillips 66, Quaker State, Shell, Sinclair, Sunoco, Texaco, Tydol, and Union '76.

A peek through the curtains into the lives of gasoline collectors reveals a host of pathways leading them down Gasoline Alley. Some of the collectors own or owned gas stations; others pumped gas as hired hands. (You'd be surprised at how many men have pulled a greasy rag from a boilersuit pocket at some point in their lives. It was a rite of passage.) For still others, the mere memories of those globe-topped gas pumps, free road maps, and friendly service from the fossil filling stations of the past jumpstarted their present collections.

Esso gasoline—now Exxon—was a favorite of so many kids, courtesy of its feline mascot and catchy advertising slogan, "Put a Tiger in Your Tank." And let's not forget their reassuring salutation, "Happy Motoring," extended to all the weary travelers who pulled up to their pumps. These kinds of memories die hard. For some people, the memories manifest themselves years later in a raging collectible fever—and a collection is born.

SSENTIALS

Gas and oil collectors should visit *www.oilcollectibles.com,* sellers of original gasoline pump globes and other related memorabilia. Also check out *www.openroadcollectibles.com,* where you can rest your weary eyes on the gas pumps themselves—a fine addition to anyone's living room.

World's Fair Collectibles

If you are old enough to remember a vintage World's Fair, you're very fortunate. World's Fair collectibles are highly sought after by those who recall with awe and excitement of having attended one. Ironically, twenty-first century World's Fairs do not engender the same sense of bigness and marvel that past World's Fairs did, even with the startling advances in today's technology. Britain's Millennium Dome was both a financial boondoggle and poorly attended. On the other hand, the Chicago World's Fair of 1933–1934 celebrated a "Century of Progress" with large, enthusiastic crowds. Collectibles from that momentous occasion range far and wide, from the pedestrian "I Was There" pin-back buttons to cookbooks, from spoons to thermometers, and from desk blotters to playing cards.

The New York World's Fair of 1939–1940, celebrating presumably five more years of progress, was another super-charged event. It was also a collectibles heaven. Fair attendees walked away with Heinz pickle-shaped pins, Mobil gas "Pegasus" charms, fraternity pins, scarves, Underwood Typewriter brass-finished metal mini-banks, perpetual calendars covering the years 1939 to 1960, and Scot Tissue packs of towels, with the familiar Trylon and Perisphere on its packaging, along with their original price: two paper towels for a penny. Collectors are coughing up a tad more for that pack of paper towels today!

ESSENTIALS

If you're looking for other people who collect what you do, check out the Seeking Collecting Clubs section of *www.collectors.org*. Some examples of these collectible inquiries include airline cutlery, Arizona tea bottles, black face sheep items, "Hear No Evil, See No Evil, Speak No Evil" figurines, and women's slips.

Again in 1964–1965, New York City took center stage, hosting another World's Fair in the same location as a quarter of a century before, in Flushing Meadows Park, Queens. This event showcased 140 pavilions on 646 acres of land with the bold mantra, "Man in a Shrinking Globe in an Expanding Universe." Among the varied items from this World's Fair, trading in today's collectible marketplace, are maps, wall plaques, ashtrays, Unisphere banks, flicker rings, even Schaefer "The One Beer to Have When You're Having More Than One" coasters. There are literally thousands of collectibles from the many World's Fairs (including fairs in Philadelphia, 1876; Chicago, 1893; Buffalo, 1901; St. Louis, 1904, and

Seattle, 1962). They were souvenir Shangri-las, with vendors of all sorts producing their own very unique "Souvenir of the World's Fair."

The pace of technological advancement is so swift now that World's Fairs—as they once existed—are extinct. The World's Fairs weren't carnivals just passing through town long enough to leave the scent of French fries wafting in the wind. They were monumental extravaganzas that have left their mark on many men and women who now collect and treasure World's Fair memorabilia.

War Memorabilia

Innumerable collections are merely the by-products of the collector's love and appreciation of history, both its gallant side and its more disturbing doppelgänger. *Militaria* is the name applied to the collecting genre devoted to war memorabilia. From the Revolutionary War to the Civil War, the Spanish American War, World War I, World War II, and Desert Storm, collectors in all walks of life keep history alive by amassing collections of uniforms, weaponry, field gear, medals, ribbons, posters, documents and maps, and other wartime ephemera.

SSENTIALS

The Web site *www.theonlinecollector.com* is dedicated to many of the most popular collecting classifications. If you collect in advertising, animation, autographs, antiques, books, cameras, coins, figurines, food and drink, glassware, guns, insulators, kitchenware, military, models, movies, music, orientalia, postcards, sci-fi, sports, stamps, and toys—you won't be disappointed.

Collectors' interests in war-related collectibles are often directly traced to their youth. Learning about historical events in school and from relatives, coupled with their own outside reading, captured the hearts of many collectors-to-be. They came to appreciate the magnitude of war and its impact in shaping all of our tomorrows. Many veterans, as well as active service men and women, collect militaria. Military service is more than just a job. Those that wear the uniform will tell you as much.

Even Hollywood can make a positive difference on a rare occasion. Steven Spielberg's *Saving Private Ryan* sparked a renewed interest in the D-Day landing on the shores of Normandy—and in World War II itself. Book sales on the subject skyrocketed, and so did collecting memorabilia from World War II, which is by far the most expansive war-related collectible field.

Bottles

What catches people's eyes often gives rise to a collection. Collecting bottles, for example, is a hobby that's more than half full. Putting down the bottle is not so easy for these particular collectors. All sorts of bottles make up collections, from attractive-looking, snappy ones to the most bland and utilitarian kinds.

You've probably seen those miniature whiskey bottles and other mini alcohol bottles around. People collect them. They collect the fruit jars that Grandma used to preserve her peaches and pickle her cucumbers. A stopover at Antique Bottle Collector's Haven at *www.antiquebottles.com,* the leading Internet site for locating, buying, selling, and educating collectors on antique bottles, reveals the scope of bottles collected. Its bottle classification categories run the gamut—from apothecary bottles to beer bottles, from seltzer bottles to poison bottles. Was that poison? Yep. Macabre tastes always make for interesting collections. The skull and crossbones on a bottle captures your attention when you need to exterminate roaches and water bugs, and it gets noticed in collections, too. An old bottle of "Petty's Lightning Fluid" with its sweeping claim that it "destroys all insect life" makes a nice addition to anybody's collection. Older bottles, in general, with their labels intact are considered the most valuable and desired by collectors. Unique, historical, and bottles with pleasing patterns are also prized.

A thriving subcategory among bottle collectibles is the fabled milk bottle. There's something about milk. It wasn't too long ago that all milk was sold in glass bottles. Even some New York City residents, remarkably, were having the milk truck deliver their milk and butter into the 1970s! The milk was placed in a galvanized steel milk box resting on their front stoops. Sometimes the milkman's money was left right there in the box. Guess you can see why the neighborhood milkman has fast become a relic of the past in the cities of America. His memory is alive and well—in many collections at least. And if you've got an old milk box around, hold onto it.

FACTS

In 1858, John Landis Mason designed a jar with a unique screw-on lid, something that we know today as the Mason jar (and that probably every home in America has at least one of). Nearly 150 years later, collectors seek out Mason jars with their unique factory monogram, trademark, and patent date. Mason jars that are decorated with animal designs and war heroes are real treasures.

Police and Firefighter Collectibles

It shouldn't surprise you to learn that there are collectors of police-related items, from badges to patches to nightsticks to license plates—even call boxes. The collectors in this field are very often police officers themselves, or their sons and daughters. There are families with long, proud traditions in law enforcement. And what better way to hold onto the memories of the past than to collect and preserve the hallowed instruments of crime-fighting?

SSENTIALS

Law Enforcement Memorabilia: Price and Identification Guide by Monty McCord is the first guide dedicated solely to police-related collectibles—proof of the growing popularity of this field. Although the pricing might be outdated, *Firefighting Collectibles* by Andrew Gurka is brimming with pictures of uniforms, tools, lanterns, fire extinguishers, and more.

Similarly, there's a flourishing collectible specialty devoted to firefighters. From the sprawling fire departments in cities to the all-volunteer units across rural America, collectors gather helmets, patches, extinguishers, and fireboxes, vintage and contemporary alike. As with their police brethren, there are numerous firefighters and firefighters' family members who want to preserve the tools of the trade of this chivalrous vocation.

Other civil service jobs are not generating the collector interest of the police and firefighters. There's not a great demand for IRS tax collection agent memorabilia, but there are people collecting IRS ephemera. Vintage IRS manuals, and old tax stamps and coupons for alcohol and tobacco are traded in today's collector's market. Nostalgia's bright light shines a little on the IRS. And that's an accomplishment!

Fishing Memorabilia

There are legions of collectors of fishing-related items who collect flies, lures, reels, and rods, all the accouterments of the fisherman. This is a prime collectible hobby born of location and recreational opportunities. A rural Minnesotan in the land of 10,000 lakes is more apt to be collecting fishing-related memorabilia than is an Upper West Side Manhattanite living in the land of one lake, who has caught nothing but a cab and a cold in his or her lifetime.

SSENTIALS

For both the fledgling collector and the pro, *www.collectors.org* is a Web site worth bookmarking. This comprehensive site unites the sundry worlds of collecting with a directory of over 2,500 collector clubs, a calendar of club conventions and collector shows, a flea-market directory, an auctioneers listing, and much more.

Forging Ahead into the World of Collectibles

The art of collecting and the very things that we collect take us many places. It is often both an interior and an exterior journey. From the flea markets to eBay to the great moral debates on discussion boards and in collector clubs, collecting is a very fascinating endeavor.

Your successes and failures as a collector essentially boil down to how willing you are to take the time to master the ins and outs and the ups and downs of the unpredictable collectible marketplace. It's entirely up to you to unearth everything you possibly can about your collectible passion—history, book values, fakes, and so on—and then make patient and wise decisions based on that acquired knowledge. It's up to you, too, to buy, sell, and barter as honestly and fairly as you know how. And you should expect and demand the very same treatment of you! Of course, even the best-intentioned of us will fall down and scrape a knee from time to time; so don't get discouraged if you blunder on occasion, or miss that buy of a lifetime. It's merely being human.

Common sense will never let you forget that rarity rules and condition is king on the collectible front. But common sense will also help you keep in mind that not everything is worth big money. Time and again, you've seen collectibles and memorabilia from a variety of fields that sell for big money. It makes for entertaining reading, and it's a considerable part of today's collector mindset. But it bears repeating that it's not what most collectors and collections are all about. Collecting is primarily about personal gratification. It's a part of people's lives that needn't be affected by other aspects of their lives in which they have no control. By and large, collectors are in control of their collecting—and this is the way it should be. The value of a collection is foremost its sentimental value, and many times a sentimental collection is simultaneously a very expensive collection. And that's the ultimate combination that so many of us want—and there's nothing wrong with that!

You've got a lot of collectible choices in this world. Choices on what to collect—sure. But also choices on how and where to locate your collectible finds, and how to care for them and display them. Make the choices that are right for you more times than the ones that will bring you grief, and you'll be a happy collector for years to come.

APPENDIX A
Further Reading

This book is just one of many collectibles resources you can turn to for information. In this appendix, you'll find numerous others that will serve as guides—no matter what you collect.

ADVERTISING

Anderton, Mark. *Encyclopedia of Petroliana: Identification and Price Guide.* (Iola, WI: Krause, 1999).

Benjamin, Scott and Wayne Henderson. *Gas Pump Collector's Guide.* (Osceola, WI: Motorbooks International, 1996).

Dotz, Warren. *Advertising Character Collectibles: An Identification & Value Guide.* (Paducah, KY: Collector Books, 1993).

Hake, Ted. *Hake's Guide to Advertising Collectibles.* (Radnor, PA: Wallace-Homestead, 1992).

Morrison, Tom. *More Root Beer Advertising and Collectibles.* (Atglen, PA: Schiffer, 2000).

Stephan, Elizabeth A. *Ultimate Price Guide to Fast Food Collectibles.* (Iola, WI: Krause, 1999).

Young, David and Micki Young. *Campbell's Soup Collectibles: A Price & Identification Guide.* (Iola, WI: Krause, 1998).

ANTIQUES

Rosson, Joe L. and Helaine W. Fendelman. *Treasures in Your Attic.* (New York: HarperResource, 2001).

AUCTIONS

Kovel, Ralph M. and Terry H. Kovel. *Kovels' Bid, Buy, and Sell Online: Basic Auction Information and Tricks of the Trade.* (New York: Three Rivers Press, 2001).

Prince, Dennis L. *Auction This!: Your Complete Guide to the World of Online Auctions,* 2nd edition. (Rocklin, CA: Prima Tech, 1999).

Sinclair, Joseph T. *eBay the Smart Way: Selling, Buying, and Profiting on the Web's #1 Auction Site.* (New York: AMACON, 2001).

AUTOGRAPHS

Ellis, Lee A. *The Celebrity Address Directory & Autograph Collector's Guide 2001.* (River Falls, WI: Americana Group, 2000).

Moore, David R. *The Address Directory of Celebrities in Entertainment, Sports, Business & Politics.* (River Falls, WI: Americana Group, 1999).

Smalling, Jack. *Baseball America's The Baseball Autograph Collector's Handbook.* (New York: Simon & Schuster, 1999).

BOOKS

Carter, John. *ABC for Book Collectors,* 7th edition. (New Castle, DE: Oak Knoll Press, 2000).

Ellis, Ian C. *Book Finds: How to Find, Buy, and Sell Used and Rare Books.* (New York: Perigee, 1996).

BOTTLES

Polak, Michael. *Bottles Identification and Price Guide,* 3rd edition. (New York: Avon Books, 2000).

COCA-COLA

Henrich, Bob and Debra Henrich. *Coca-Cola Commemorative Bottles: Identification & Value Guide,* 2nd edition. (Paducah, KY: Collector Books, 2000).

Schaeffer, Randy and Bill Bateman. *Coca-Cola: The Collector's Guide to New and Vintage Coca-Cola Memorabilia.* (Philadelphia, PA: Courage Books, 1995).

COINS

Otfinoski, Steve and Jack Graham (illustrator). *Coin Collecting for Kids.* (Norwalk, CT: Innovative KIDS, 2000).

COLLECTOR PLATES

Rinker, Harry L. *The Official Guide to Collector Plates,* 7th edition. (New York: House of Collectibles, 1999).

COUNTRY STORE PRODUCTS

Wilson, David L. *General Store Collectibles: An Identification and Value Guide.* (Paducah, KY: Collector Books, 1994).

DOLLS

Foulke, Jan and Howard Foulke. *Blue Book of Dolls & Values,* 14th edition. (Riverdale, MD: Hobby House, 1999).

Foulke, Jan and Howard Foulke. *Insider's Guide to Doll Buying & Selling: Antique to Modern.* (Riverdale, MD: Hobby House, 1995).

Peterson, Kathrine Palmer and Fannie Roach Palmer. *Dolls Aren't Just for Kids: The Ultimate Guide for Doll Lovers.* (South Berwick, ME: Garrison Oaks, 2000).

GLASSWARE

Florence, Gene. *Collectible Glassware from the 40s, 50s, 60s: An Illustrated Value Guide,* 5th edition. (Paducah, KY: Collector Books, 1999).

Florence, Gene. *Florence's Glassware Pattern Identification Guide: Easy Identification for Glassware from the 1920s through the 1960s.* (Paducah, KY: Collector Books, 1998).

Florence, Gene. *Kitchen Glassware of the Depression Years: Identification & Values,* 6th edition. (Paducah, KY: Collector Books, 2001).

JEWELRY

Bell, Jeanenne. *Answers to Questions About Old Jewelry, 1840–1950,* 5th edition. (Iola, WI: Krause, 1999).

Gilbert, Richard E. and James H. Wolf. *Complete Price Guide to Antique Jewelry.* (Sarasota, FL: Ashland Investments, 2000).

Miller, Anna M. *Illustrated Guide to Jewelry Appraising: Antique, Period, and Modern,* 2nd edition. (Woodstock, VT: GemStone Press, 1999).

KITCHEN

Franklin, Linda Campbell. *300 Years of Kitchen Collectibles,* 4th edition. (Iola, WI: Krause, 1998).

MILITARIA

Austin, Robert J. *The Official Price Guide to Military Collectibles.* (New York: House of Collectibles, 1998).

Foster, Frank. *U.S. Military Medals: 1939 to 1994,* 4th edition. (Fountain Inn, SC: Medals of America, 1998).

PHOTOGRAPHS

Mace, O. Henry. *Collector's Guide to Early Photographs,* 2nd edition. (Iola, WI: Krause, 1999).

PIN-BACK BUTTONS

Wisniewski, Debra J. *Antique & Collectible Buttons: Identification & Values.* (Paducah, KY: Collector Books, 1997).

POLITICAL AMERICANA

Warda, Mark. *100 Years of Political Campaign Collectibles.* (Clearwater, FL: Galt Press, 1996).

PORCELAIN/POTTERY

Battie, David. *Sotheby's Concise Encyclopedia of Porcelain.* (Boston: Little, Brown, 1990).

Forrest, Tim. *The Bulfinch Anatomy of Antique China & Silver: An Illustrated Guide to Tableware, Identifying Period, Detail, and Design.* (Boston: Bulfinch Press, 1998).

Harran, Jim and Susan Harran. *Collectible Cups & Saucers: Identification & Values.* (Paducah, KY: Collector Books, 1997).

Sasicki, Richard. *The Collector's Encyclopedia of Van Briggle Art Pottery: An Identification & Value Guide.* (Paducah, KY: Collector Books, 1992).

RECORDS/MUSIC

Augsburger, Jeff and Marty Eck and Rick Rann. *The Beatles Memorabilia Price Guide,* 3rd edition. (Dubuque, IA: Antique Trader, 1997).

Neely, Tim. *Goldmine Christmas Record Price Guide.* (Iola, WI: Krause, 1997).

Osborne, Jerry. *The Official Guide to the Money Records: The 1000 Most Valuable Records.* (New York: House of Collectibles, 1998).

SPORTS

Furjanic, Chuck. *Antique Golf Collectibles: A Price and Reference Guide,* 2nd edition. (Iola, WI: Krause, 2000).

Golenbock, Peter. *Barry Halper Collection of Baseball Memorabilia.* (New York: Harry N. Abrams, 2000).

Gracia, Oscar. *Collecting Michael Jordan: The Ultimate Identification & Value Guide.* (Iola, WI: Krause, 1998).

Larson, Mark K. *Complete Guide to Baseball Memorabilia,* 3rd edition. (Iola, WI: Krause, 1996).

Luckey, Carl F. *Old Fishing Lures & Tackle: Identification & Value Guide,* 5th edition. (Iola, WI: Krause, 1999).

STAMPS

Datz, Stephen R. *Top Dollar Paid!: The Complete Guide to Selling Your Stamps.* (Loveland, CO: General Trade, 1997).

Schmid, Paul W. *How to Detect Damaged, Altered and Repaired Stamps.* (Iola, WI: Krause, 1996).

The International Encyclopaedic Dictionary of Philately, 3rd edition. (Iola, WI: Krause, 1997).

TELEVISION

Caine, Dana. *Saturday Morning TV Collectibles '60s, '70s, '80s.* (Iola, WI: Krause, 2000).

Larue, William D. *Collecting Simpsons! An Unofficial Guide to Merchandise from* The Simpsons. (Liverpool, NY: KML Enterprises, 1999).

TELEVISION SETS

Durbal, Bryan and Glen Bubenheimer. *Collectors Guide to Vintage Televisions: Identification & Values.* (Paducah, KY: Collector Books, 1999).

TOYS

Johnson, Dana. *Matchbox Toys 1947 to 1998: Identification & Value Guide,* 3rd edition. (Paducah, KY: Collector Books, 1999).

Rich, Mark. *100 Greatest Baby Boomer Toys.* (Iola, WI: Krause, 2000).

Stephan, Elizabeth A. *O'Brien's Collecting Toy Cars and Trucks: Identification & Value Guide,* 3rd edition. (Iola, WI: Krause, 2000).

Stephan, Elizabeth A. *O'Brien's Collecting Toys: Identification & Value Guide,* 9th edition. (Iola, WI: Krause, 1999).

APPENDIX B

Web Resources

Throughout this book, I direct your attention to numerous Web sites that may be of use to you. But in this appendix, I gather them all together in one place, so you don't have to search for what you're looking for.

Alibris: Books You Thought You'd Never Find:
www.alibris.com

Amazon.com Auctions: www.auctions.amazon.com

American Museum of Photography:
www.photographymuseum.com

American Numismatic Association: www.money.org

American Philatelic Society: www.stamps.org

American Photographic Historical Society:
www.superexpo.com/aphs

American Political Items Collectors: www.apic.ws

Antique and Collectible Associations:
www.antiqueandcolletible.com

Antique Bottle Collector's Haven:
www.antiquebottles.com

Association of Game and Puzzle Collectors:
www.agca.com

AuctionJeweler.com: www.auctionjeweler.com

Autograph World: www.autographworld.com

AZillion SPARKLZ: www.sparkleplenty.com

The Bargain-Mall: www.bargain-mall.com

BCW Supplies.com: www.bcwsupplies.com

The Beanie Mom Beanie Lovers Web Site:
www.beaniemom.com

Beckett.com: www.beckett.com

Beer Can Collectors of America: www.bcca.com

BidBay Auctions: www2.bidbay.com

Black Baseball's Negro Baseball Leagues:
www.blackbaseball.com

BoxesOnline.com: www.boxesonline.com

BrassPack Packing Supply: www.brasspack.com

Brodart.com: www.brodart.com

Celebrity Locators!: www.celebritylocators.com

Coca-Cola Collectors Club: www.cocacolaclub.org

CoinClubs.com: www.coinclubs.com

CoinLink: www.coinlink.com

Collectibles Insurance Agency, Inc.:
www.collectinsure.com

collectiblestoday.com: www.collectiblestoday.com

Collectics: A Virtual Consignment Shop:
www.collectics.com

Collecto-Mania: www.collecto-mania.com

Collectors Gallery: www.collectorsgallery.com

Collectors Universe: www.collectors.com

Collectors.org: www.collectors.org

Cowan Pottery Associates: www.cowanpottery.org

Creative Sports Enterprises:
www.creativesportsent.com

Depression Glass Shopper: www.dgshopper.com

Deutsches Haus: www.deutscheshaus.cc

Doll Collecting: www.dollreader.com

Don and Pat's Marilyn Monroe and Hollywood Stars
Collectibles: www.marilynmonroesales.com

Dreamsicles: www.dreamsicles.com

eBay: www.ebay.com

Enesco Collectors' Club: www.enescoclubs.com

Federal Trade Commission: www.ftc.gov

FleaMarket.com: www.fleamarket.com

Funko! Home of the Wacky Wobbler:
www.funkotown.com

Garage Sales Across the Country:
www.garagesale.nearu.com

The Glass Encyclopedia:
www.encyclopedia.netnz.com

Hake's Americana and Collectibles: www.hakes.com

Hazel Atlas Glass Collectors Web Site:
www.hazelatlas.com

House of White Birches: www.whitebirches.com

Internal Revenue Service:
www.irs.ustreas.gov/forms_pubs

International Society of Appraisers: www.isa-
appraisers.org

Jewelry Mall: *www.jewelrymall.com*

Jim Mehrer's Postal History and Postcards: *www.deltiology.com*

Judy's Doll Shop: *www.judysdollshop.com*

Junior Philatelists of America: *www.jpastamps.org*

Krause Publications: *www.krause.com*

Light Impressions: The Leading Resource for Archival Supplies: *www.lightimpressionsdirect.com*

McDonald's Collectors Club: *www.mcdclub.com*

Mike's General Store: *www.mikesgeneralstore.com*

Mile High Comics: *www.milehighcomics.com*

Mostly McCoy: *www.mostlymccoy.com*

Movie-Memorabilia.net: *www.movie-memorabilia.net*

National Bobbin Head Club: *www.nationalbobbinheadclub.com*

Nostalgiaville: *www.nostalgiaville.com*

Off the Record Vinyl.com: *www.otrvinyl.com*

Official Beanie Babies Web Site: *www.beaniebabies.com*

Oil Company Collectibles, Inc.: *www.oilcollectibles.com*

Old Pete's: *www.old-pete.com*

Online Auction Users Association: *www.auctionusers.org*

The Online Collector: *www.theonlinecollector.com*

Open Road Collectibles.com: *www.openroadcollectibles.com*

Optix Document Management and Workflow Systems: *www.blueridge.com*

Our World of Dolls: *www.our-world-of-dolls.com*

Pez Collector's News: *www.pezcollectorsnews.com*

thePit.com: *www.thepit.com*

Playle's Auction Mall: *www.playle.com*

Postcard.org: *www.postcard.org*

Precious Moments Community: *www.preciousmomentscommunity.com*

Professional Sports Authenticator: *www.psacard.com*

QFlea.com: *www.qflea.com*

ScottOnline.com: *www.scottonline.com*

Software 4 Collectors: *www.software4collectors.com*

Someone Special: *www.someonespecial.com*

Sothebys: *www.sothebys.com*

Sportscard Guaranty Corporation: *www.sgccard.com*

Stamp Collecting for Stamp Collectors: *www.stamps.about.com*

The-Stamp-Collector.com: *www.the-stamp-collector.com*

The Star Archive: *www.stararchive.com*

Superior Archival Materials, Inc.: *www.superiorarchivalmats.com*

Toylectibles Toys: *www.toylectibles.com*

Trendco, Inc.: *www.trendco.com*

United Parcel Service (UPS): *www.ups.com*

United States Postal Service: *www.usps.org*

Universal Autograph Collectors Club: *www.uacc.org*

VintagePostcards.com: *www.vintagepostcards.com*

Weller Pottery: *www.wellerpottery.com*

WhatICollect.com: *www.whaticollect.com*

World Collectors Net: *www.worldcollectorsnet.com*

Yahoo! Auctions: *www.auctions.yahoo.com*

Index

Italicized page numbers refer to illustrations.

We Have EVERYTHING!

Everything® **After College Book**
$12.95, 1-55850-847-3

Everything® **American History Book**
$12.95, 1-58062-531-2

Everything® **Angels Book**
$12.95, 1-58062-398-0

Everything® **Anti-Aging Book**
$12.95, 1-58062-565-7

Everything® **Astrology Book**
$12.95, 1-58062-062-0

Everything® **Baby Names Book**
$12.95, 1-55850-655-1

Everything® **Baby Shower Book**
$12.95, 1-58062-305-0

Everything® **Baby's First Food Book**
$12.95, 1-58062-512-6

Everything® **Baby's First Year Book**
$12.95, 1-58062-581-9

Everything® **Barbeque Cookbook**
$12.95, 1-58062-316-6

Everything® **Bartender's Book**
$9.95, 1-55850-536-9

Everything® **Bedtime Story Book**
$12.95, 1-58062-147-3

Everything® **Bicycle Book**
$12.00, 1-55850-706-X

Everything® **Breastfeeding Book**
$12.95, 1-58062-582-7

Everything® **Build Your Own Home Page**
$12.95, 1-58062-339-5

Everything® **Business Planning Book**
$12.95, 1-58062-491-X

Everything® **Candlemaking Book**
$12.95, 1-58062-623-8

Everything® **Casino Gambling Book**
$12.95, 1-55850-762-0

Everything® **Cat Book**
$12.95, 1-55850-710-8

Everything® **Chocolate Cookbook**
$12.95, 1-58062-405-7

Everything® **Christmas Book**
$15.00, 1-55850-697-7

Everything® **Civil War Book**
$12.95, 1-58062-366-2

Everything® **Classical Mythology Book**
$12.95, 1-58062-653-X

Everything® **Collectibles Book**
$12.95, 1-58062-645-9

Everything® **College Survival Book**
$12.95, 1-55850-720-5

Everything® **Computer Book**
$12.95, 1-58062-401-4

Everything® **Cookbook**
$14.95, 1-58062-400-6

Everything® **Cover Letter Book**
$12.95, 1-58062-312-3

Everything® **Creative Writing Book**
$12.95, 1-58062-647-5

Everything® **Crossword and Puzzle Book**
$12.95, 1-55850-764-7

Everything® **Dating Book**
$12.95, 1-58062-185-6

Everything® **Dessert Book**
$12.95, 1-55850-717-5

Everything® **Digital Photography Book**
$12.95, 1-58062-574-6

Everything® **Dog Book**
$12.95, 1-58062-144-9

Everything® **Dreams Book**
$12.95, 1-55850-806-6

Everything® **Etiquette Book**
$12.95, 1-55850-807-4

Everything® **Fairy Tales Book**
$12.95, 1-58062-546-0

Everything® **Family Tree Book**
$12.95, 1-55850-763-9

Everything® **Feng Shui Book**
$12.95, 1-58062-587-8

Everything® **Fly-Fishing Book**
$12.95, 1-58062-148-1

Everything® **Games Book**
$12.95, 1-55850-643-8

Everything® **Get-A-Job Book**
$12.95, 1-58062-223-2

Everything® **Get Out of Debt Book**
$12.95, 1-58062-588-6

Everything® **Get Published Book**
$12.95, 1-58062-315-8

Everything® **Get Ready for Baby Book**
$12.95, 1-55850-844-9

Everything® **Get Rich Book**
$12.95, 1-58062-670-X

Everything® **Ghost Book**
$12.95, 1-58062-533-9

Everything® **Golf Book**
$12.95, 1-55850-814-7

Everything® **Grammar and Style Book**
$12.95, 1-58062-573-8

Everything® **Guide to Las Vegas**
$12.95, 1-58062-438-3

Everything® **Guide to New England**
$12.95, 1-58062-589-4

Everything® **Guide to New York City**
$12.95, 1-58062-314-X

Everything® **Guide to Walt Disney World®, Universal Studios®, and Greater Orlando, 2nd Edition**
$12.95, 1-58062-404-9

Everything® **Guide to Washington D.C.**
$12.95, 1-58062-313-1

Everything® **Guitar Book**
$12.95, 1-58062-555-X

Everything® **Herbal Remedies Book**
$12.95, 1-58062-331-X

Everything® **Home-Based Business Book**
$12.95, 1-58062-364-6

Everything® **Homebuying Book**
$12.95, 1-58062-074-4

Everything® **Homeselling Book**
$12.95, 1-58062-304-2

Everything® **Horse Book**
$12.95, 1-58062-564-9

Everything® **Hot Careers Book**
$12.95, 1-58062-486-3

Everything® **Internet Book**
$12.95, 1-58062-073-6

Everything® **Investing Book**
$12.95, 1-58062-149-X

Everything® **Jewish Wedding Book**
$12.95, 1-55850-801-5

Everything® **Job Interview Book**
$12.95, 1-58062-493-6

Everything® **Lawn Care Book**
$12.95, 1-58062-487-1

Everything® **Leadership Book**
$12.95, 1-58062-513-4

Everything® **Learning French Book**
$12.95, 1-58062-649-1

Everything® **Learning Spanish Book**
$12.95, 1-58062-575-4

Everything® **Low-Fat High-Flavor Cookbook**
$12.95, 1-55850-802-3

Everything® **Magic Book**
$12.95, 1-58062-418-9

Everything® **Managing People Book**
$12.95, 1-58062-577-0

Everything® **Microsoft® Word 2000 Book**
$12.95, 1-58062-306-9

Everything® **Money Book**
$12.95, 1-58062-145-7

Everything® **Mother Goose Book**
$12.95, 1-58062-490-1

Everything® **Motorcycle Book**
$12.95, 1-58062-554-1

Everything® **Mutual Funds Book**
$12.95, 1-58062-419-7

Everything® **One-Pot Cookbook**
$12.95, 1-58062-186-4

Everything® **Online Business Book**
$12.95, 1-58062-320-4

Everything® **Online Genealogy Book**
$12.95, 1-58062-402-2

Everything® **Online Investing Book**
$12.95, 1-58062-338-7

Everything® **Online Job Search Book**
$12.95, 1-58062-365-4

Everything® **Organize Your Home Book**
$12.95, 1-58062-617-3

Everything® **Pasta Book**
$12.95, 1-55850-719-1

Everything® **Philosophy Book**
$12.95, 1-58062-644-0

Everything® **Playing Piano and Keyboards Book**
$12.95, 1-58062-651-3

Everything® **Pregnancy Book**
$12.95, 1-58062-146-5

Everything® **Pregnancy Organizer**
$15.00, 1-58062-336-0

Everything® **Project Management Book**
$12.95, 1-58062-583-5

Everything® **Puppy Book**
$12.95, 1-58062-576-2

Everything® **Quick Meals Cookbook**
$12.95, 1-58062-488-X

Everything® **Resume Book**
$12.95, 1-58062-311-5

Everything® **Romance Book**
$12.95, 1-58062-566-5

Everything® **Running Book**
$12.95, 1-58062-618-1

Everything® **Sailing Book, 2nd Edition**
$12.95, 1-58062-671-8

Everything® **Saints Book**
$12.95, 1-58062-534-7

Everything® **Selling Book**
$12.95, 1-58062-319-0

Everything® **Shakespeare Book**
$12.95, 1-58062-591-6

Everything® **Spells and Charms Book**
$12.95, 1-58062-532-0

Everything® **Start Your Own Business Book**
$12.95, 1-58062-650-5

Everything® **Stress Management Book**
$12.95, 1-58062-578-9

Everything® **Study Book**
$12.95, 1-55850-615-2

Everything® **Tai Chi and QiGong Book**
$12.95, 1-58062-646-7

Everything® **Tall Tales, Legends, and Outrageous Lies Book**
$12.95, 1-58062-514-2

Everything® **Tarot Book**
$12.95, 1-58062-191-0

Everything® **Time Management Book**
$12.95, 1-58062-492-8

Everything® **Toasts Book**
$12.95, 1-58062-189-9

Everything® **Toddler Book**
$12.95, 1-58062-592-4

Everything® **Total Fitness Book**
$12.95, 1-58062-318-2

Everything® **Trivia Book**
$12.95, 1-58062-143-0

Everything® **Tropical Fish Book**
$12.95, 1-58062-343-3

Everything® **Vegetarian Cookbook**
$12.95, 1-58062-640-8

Everything® **Vitamins, Minerals, and Nutritional Supplements Book**
$12.95, 1-58062-496-0

Everything® **Wedding Book, 2nd Edition**
$12.95, 1-58062-190-2

Everything® **Wedding Checklist**
$7.95, 1-58062-456-1

Everything® **Wedding Etiquette Book**
$7.95, 1-58062-454-5

Everything® **Wedding Organizer**
$15.00, 1-55850-828-7

Everything® **Wedding Shower Book**
$7.95, 1-58062-188-0

Everything® **Wedding Vows Book**
$7.95, 1-58062-455-3

Everything® **Weight Training Book**
$12.95, 1-58062-593-2

Everything® **Wine Book**
$12.95, 1-55850-808-2

Everything® **World War II Book**
$12.95, 1-58062-572-X

Everything® **World's Religions Book**
$12.95, 1-58062-648-3

Everything® **Yoga Book**
$12.95, 1-58062-594-0

Visit us at everything.com

Everything® is a registered trademark of Adams Media Corporation.

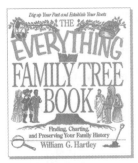